FLING OUT THE BANNER!

FLING OUT THE BANNER!

The National Church Ideal and the Foreign Mission
of the Episcopal Church

IAN T. DOUGLAS

THE CHURCH HYMNAL CORPORATION, NEW YORK

Library of Congress Card Catalog Number: 96-72141

THE CHURCH HYMNAL CORPORATION
445 Fifth Avenue
New York, NY 10016

5 4 3 2 1

CONTENTS

PREFACE   vii

INTRODUCTION   1

CHAPTER ONE   15
A CENTURY OF ENDEAVOR
Origins of Episcopal Foreign Mission, 1821 to 1900

CHAPTER TWO   73
THE NATIONAL CHURCH IDEAL
The Growth of Episcopal Foreign Mission, 1900 to 1919

CHAPTER THREE   138
OUR EXPANDING CHURCH
The Ideal and the National Council, 1919 to 1946

CHAPTER FOUR   209
AMERICAN SUPREMACY
The Ideal and the Emerging Anglican Communion,
1946 to 1963

CHAPTER FIVE   268
CRISIS AND REDEFINITION
The Ideal in a New World, 1963 to 1985

Fling out the banner! let it float
Skyward and seaward, high and wide;
The sun that lights its shining folds,
The cross, on which the Saviour died.

Fling out the banner! heathen lands
Shall see from far the glorious sight,
And nations, crowding to be born,
Baptize their spirits in its light.

Fling out the banner! sin-sick souls
That sink and perish in the strife,
Shall touch in faith its radiant hem,
And spring immortal into life.

Fling out the banner! let it float
Skyward and seaward, high and wide,
Our glory, only in the cross;
Our only hope, the Crucified!

Fling out the banner! wide and high,
Seaward and skyward, let it shine:
Nor skill, nor might, nor merit ours;
We conquer only in that sign.

GEORGE WASHINGTON DOANE

from
The Hymnal of the Protestant Episcopal Church
1892, 1916, 1940

PREFACE

From 1984-1996 I had the good fortune to serve as the Associate for Overseas Leadership Development on the staff of the Presiding Bishop and Executive Council at the Episcopal Church Center in New York City. Working in what was then the World Mission Unit at the Church Center, it became clear to me that the Episcopal Church lacked a comprehensive history of its foreign mission work. I decided to leave my position in New York and undertake doctoral studies at Boston University as a means to write the institutional history of the Domestic and Foreign Missionary Society of the Protestant Episcopal Church. With the generous support of the Episcopal Church Foundation as one of its Graduate Fellows, I completed my studies in the fall of 1992.

This book was originally written as a dissertation in partial fulfillment for the degree of Doctor of Philosophy in the Division of Religious and Theological Studies at the Graduate School of Boston University. I thus want to thank my dissertation advisors, Professor Dana L. Robert of Boston University and Professor William Hutchison of Harvard University, for their assistance in the preparation of the original version of this study.

I want to acknowledge my colleagues at the Episcopal Divinity School, especially Fredrica Harris Thompsett. Their many comments in classrooms, in the dining hall, and around the campus have contributed greatly to this study. I want to single out my fellow "mission activist," Titus Presler. His critiques have inspired me to better scholarship and a deeper commitment to God's mission. Thanks go to my associates at the Episcopal Church Center, especially Avis Harvey and Pat Mauney, for providing invaluable materials for this investigation. In addition, I want to acknolwedge my many friends and co-workers on the Standing Commission for World Mission and in the Episcopal Council for Global Mission. Their commitment to the many and diverse missionary activities in the Episcopal Church is inspirational.

And finally, I want to thank my family. My parents, Gladys and Duncan Douglas, nurtured me in the Gospel and helped me to appreciate the breadth of the Episcopal Church. My brother Craig taught me to live life in the moment without fear and anxiety about the future. My children, Luke, Timothy and Johanna, continuously remind me of what is truly important in life. I want to thank them for their smiles and hugs that sustained me during the writing of my "chapters." Most of all, I want to thank my wife, my friend, and my partner: Kristin Harris. I could not have completed this book without her never-failing love, support and patience. Her generous encouragement and insightful comments contributed greatly to this study. This work is dedicated to Kristin.

Ian T. Douglas
Cambridge, Massachusetts
August 1996

INTRODUCTION

In February 1994, the national Executive Council of the Episcopal Church proposed that the Domestic and Foreign Missionary Society "no longer fund appointments of Missionaries and Volunteers for Mission on a regular basis."[1] Ostensibly the reasons for ending the Society's direct support of missionaries were the combination of declining financial resources at the national level and the relinquishing of missionary programs to local networks and independent voluntary societies. Such a move would signal the end of the Episcopal Church's 173-year commitment to the sending of missionaries as a unified national organization. The Domestic and Foreign Missionary Society would be reduced to the incorporated appellation of the Episcopal Church in the United States. As such it would be a missionary society in name only.[2]

Before such a policy decision could be fully realized, the General Convention of the Episcopal Church, the church's highest legislative and canonical body, had to ratify the program and budget proposed by the Executive Council. The decision to end the regular support of missionaries by the Domestic and Foreign Missionary Society was far from final.

Mission activists, both within the power structures of the Episcopal Church and those on the margin, decried the proposal of the Executive Council. The Standing Commission on World Mission, the interim body of the General Convention responsible for evaluation and review of world mission policy for the General Convention, put the convention on notice. Their report to the 71st meeting of the General Convention in Indianapolis in August 1994 warned of "the crisis in the missionary structures of the Episcopal Church."[3] At the same time, the Episcopal Council for Global Mission swung into action to save the missionary programs of the Domestic and Foreign Missionary Society.

The Episcopal Council for Global Mission (ECGM) was organized in 1990 as a network of over thirty mission education, mission funding, and missionary sending organizations in the Episcopal Church. Its aim is to promote the unity and effectiveness of the various world mission initiatives in the Episcopal Church through open communication, dialogue, and the sharing of information. Arguably one of the most diverse and eclectic networks in the Episcopal Church, the ECGM embraces a wide variety of mission theologies and organizations. Voluntary missionary societies, parishes, dioceses, seminaries, funding agents such as the United Thank Offering and the Presiding Bishop's Fund for World Relief, as well as canonical bodies of the church like the Standing Commission on World Mission, participate in the ECGM.

At its annual meeting in April 1994, the Episcopal Council for Global Mission crafted two resolutions for the Indianapolis General Convention. The first resolution sought to save the missionary programs of the Domestic and Foreign Missionary Society by reversing the proposed cutback in missionary appointments, specifically maintaining funding for the Volunteers for Mission program. The second resolution asked the Standing Commission on World Mission and the Episcopal Council for Global Mission to draft a plan by which the sending and receiving of missionaries by the Domestic and Foreign Missionary Society would continue into the future.

Arriving in Indianapolis in August 1994, many bishops and deputies attending the General Convention were upset by the Executive Council's proposal to cease the sending of missionaries on a "regular basis." They saw the proposal as a symbolic statement that the Domestic and Foreign Missionary Society was getting out of the missionary business. These bishops and deputies combined energies with the mission activists of the ECGM to rebuff the Executive Council's plans. For three days the World

Mission Legislative Committee of the General Convention, the committee through which all resolutions pertaining to world mission are brought before the Convention, planned an appropriate response. By Friday of the first week of the convention, the Committee had formulated a slate of resolutions that called for: an increase in funding for missionary support by the Domestic and Foreign Missionary Society, new forms of mission engagement and education in parishes, dioceses and seminaries, and a plan for developing new missionary structures.

In a series of inspiring and grace-filled testimonies before the House of Deputies, the House of Bishops, and the committee responsible for the national budget of the Episcopal Church, members of the World Mission Legislative Committee put their case before the convention. By the end of the tenth legislative day three resolutions restoring funding for missionary programs and overseas dioceses under the purview of the Domestic and Foreign Missionary Society had passed both the House of Deputies and the powerful Program, Budget, and Finance Committee.[4] Two additional resolutions were passed by the Convention challenging parishes, dioceses and seminaries to a new level of commitment to world mission.[5] The 71st General Convention had gone on record that cuts in missionary programming of the national Episcopal Church were unacceptable. World mission had triumphed in Indianapolis.

Perhaps the greatest symbol of the hope for world mission present in Indianapolis was the birth of the newest autonomous church in the Anglican Communion, the Mexican Episcopal Church. On the final day of Convention, the House of Bishops approved the organization of the church from the five previously Province IX dioceses in Mexico. It was with a real mixture of joy for the new Mexican Episcopal Church and sadness at their leave-taking from the Episcopal Church, U.S.A., that the bishops from all theological and ideological persuasions applauded the new sister church. Expressed commitments to mutual responsibility and interdependence between Mexican and American Episcopalians gave new meaning to the old familiar line, "In Christ there is no East or West, in him no South or North."

In addition to the reinstatement of existing missionary pro-
grams and the granting of autonomy to the church in Mexico, a
plan to develop new structures for missionary support in the
Episcopal Church was also initiated in Indianapolis. Resolution
D016a, "Developing New Missionary Structures," directed the
Standing Commission on World Mission, in partnership with the
Episcopal Council for Global Mission, to develop a theological
basis for mission as well as new strategies and structures through
which the Domestic and Foreign Missionary Society of the
Episcopal Church would continue the church's work of sending
and receiving missionaries in cooperation with parishes, dioceses,
and existing voluntary agencies. Originally drafted at the April
1994 meeting of the Episcopal Council for Global Mission and
affirmed by the national Executive Council in February 1995,
Resolution D016a linked mission and missionary support to discussions of structural change in the Episcopal Church.[6]

Questions related to mission and the structures of the
Episcopal Church at the national level are increasingly on the lips
of Episcopalians today. At its annual convention in 1991, the
Diocese of East Tennessee called for the development of a plan of
structural change that would prepare the church for mission in
the twenty-first century. In a few short years what had become
known as the East Tennessee Initiative emerged into a major force
in the Episcopal Church. More than 1,000 people from 93 dioceses and five nations traveled to St. Louis in the summer of 1993 to
attend the "Shaping Our Future" symposium sponsored by the
East Tennessee Initiative. Whether driven by negative feelings
toward the national church or a desire to envision new models for
church organization, those who traveled to the flooded midwest
in 1993 found that healthy and exciting discussions of mission
awaited them.[7] The "Shaping Our Future" symposium resulted in
some venturesome resolutions to the 1994 General Convention,
calling for a profound reworking of the structures of the
Episcopal Church. By the time the dust had settled in
Indianapolis, however, few changes had been made to existing
structures in the Episcopal Church, save for a shortening of the
term of office of the Presiding Bishop from twelve to nine years.[8]

Initiative for structural change in the Episcopal Church did not die in Indianapolis; quite the contrary. The pace and importance given to discussions concerning the mission and corresponding national structures of the Episcopal Church have increased since the summer of 1994. Following Indianapolis, Presiding Bishop Edmond L. Browning and House of Deputies President Pamela P. Chinnis charged the Standing Commission on the Structure of the Church to go beyond their canonical mandate to study and make recommendations as to the structure of the General Convention and the church. Bishop Browning and President Chinnis challenged the Structure Commission to consider how the Episcopal Church would organize itself if it were starting a new institution. At the initiation of the Standing Commission on the Structure of the Church, the Presiding Bishop and the President of the House of Deputies invited all the interim bodies of the General Convention to a joint meeting in Minneapolis in October 1995. The goal of the meeting was to discuss with the Standing Commission on Structure how the church could best be organized to purse its mission in the world today. What resulted from that meeting and subsequent meetings of the Standing Commission on the Structure of the Church was a draft report suggesting substantive changes to the current national structures of the Episcopal Church.[9] The future of the suggestions made by the Standing Commission on Structure is unknown at this time and will be left up to the 72nd General Convention, meeting in Philadelphia in 1997. Time will tell what the outcome will be. What is clear, however, is that change is ripe in the Episcopal Church and questions concerning mission and structure are vitally important to those Episcopalians concerned about what God would have us do in the world today.

Why this Book?

Institutions and individuals that lack an historical memory have difficulty mining the blessings of the past, while often repeating previous failings. In current discussions over the mission and structure of the Episcopal Church, precious little attention is being paid to our common history. For too long the story of the Domestic and Foreign Missionary Society, especially in the twentieth century, has been beyond the reach of both the person in the pew as well as the leadership and policy makers of the Episcopal Church.[10] This study is thus a first step in the telling of that story. As such it is an institutional history of the Protestant Episcopal Church in the United States of America.

The point of departure for this institutional history of the Episcopal Church is the church's work *outside* of the United States. It seeks to answer the question: What were the theological assumptions and formulations that motivated the Episcopal Church's commitment to, and involvement in, foreign mission? In other words: Why did we do what we did, when we did it? By answering these questions, we in the Episcopal Church today will be given new insights into our discussions about mission and the appropriate structures of the church. Our foreign mission history can serve as a mirror to reflect the values and theological presuppositions that have brought us to this point in time. In addition, discovering the contributions and failings of the Episcopal Church in the development of the modern Anglican Communion, Episcopalians can become better partners in mission with sisters and brothers in Christ around the world.

This book makes the assumption that the foreign mission work of the Episcopal Church has changed radically within the last three decades. During the first half of the twentieth century the Episcopal Church supported a large number of missionaries in the church's overseas districts. In the post-colonial era, however, the number of Episcopalian foreign missionaries declined dramatically, while financial grants to newly autonomous Anglican churches around the world increased. Partnership and international development replaced "good schools, good hospitals, and right-ordered worship" as the new watchwords for the Episcopal Church's foreign mission initiatives.

The changes in the Episcopal Church's foreign mission were precipitated by dramatic geopolitical, ecclesiastical, and theological developments in the twentieth century. The growth of Christianity in Africa, Asia and Latin America, the advent of independent indigenous Anglican churches in the historic mission fields of the West, the decline of mainline Protestantism in American society, and the entrance of the United States government into international humanistic endeavors after World War II—all have contributed to the changes in foreign mission work of the Episcopal Church. At the same time, Episcopal foreign missions were affected by the theological debates over mission raised by international ecumenical assemblies such as the International Missionary Council and the World Council of Churches. Such debates undermined both the confidence and historic missionary methods of Episcopalians engaged in foreign mission.

Unfortunately the radical changes in both world Christianity and mission thought during the twentieth century have not been given proper attention by the leadership of mainline Protestant churches. For the majority of liberal American Protestants, mission connotes nineteenth-century imperialism and culturally insensitive proselytism. Emerging patterns of church-to-church partnership, however, demand a radically different understanding of mission. We in the West are being asked to re-examine our mission theology and foreign mission history in light of the contemporary reality of global Christianity. We are challenged by churches in Africa, Asia, Latin America, and the Middle East to move from our historic paternalistic patterns of interaction to a mutual and interdependent sharing of God's mission throughout the world.

In his annual statistical analysis of global mission, Anglican missiologist David B. Barrett documents the changes in world Christianity during the twentieth century.[11] In 1900, 76% of the 558 million Christians in the world lived in Europe or North America. Today less that 50% of the world's two billion Christians live in the industrialized West. By the year 2000, Barrett predicts that 68% of the world's 2.1 billion Christians will live outside of Western Europe and North America. The changing nature of global Christianity in the twentieth century, from a predominantly Western, Euro-American community to a church of the Southern Hemisphere, is a little known and seldom acknowledged fact in American conciliar Protestant churches.

Changes in Anglicanism are characteristic of the transformation in world Christianity over the last few decades. At the beginning of the twentieth century, the Anglican Communion was comprised of the Church of England, the Episcopal Church in the United States, and the Anglican churches in Canada and Australia. Each of these four autonomous Anglican "provinces" supported and controlled their own missions around the world.[12] Today, however, there are 36 independent churches in the Anglican Communion and the few remaining missionary dioceses are well on their way to becoming autonomous churches. In his address to the 1985 General Convention of the Episcopal Church, the Most Rev. Robert Runcie, Archbishop of Canterbury, emphasized that the Anglican Communion is no longer limited to England and the United States.

> We have developed into a worldwide family of Churches. Today there are 70 million members of what is arguably the second most widely distributed body of Christians. No longer are we identified by having some kind of English heritage. English today is now the second language of the Communion. There are more black members than white. Our local diversities span the spectrum of the world's races, needs, and aspirations. We have only to think of Bishop Tutu's courageous witness in South Africa to be reminded that we are no longer a Church of the white middle classes allied only to the prosperous western world.[13]

Unfortunately, very few American Episcopalians comprehend the radically different face of the modern Anglican Communion. Because the history of foreign mission work of the Episcopal Church has not been adequately documented, it is extremely difficult for American Episcopalians to appreciate and understand how the Anglican Communion has changed from an Anglo-American church to a church where English is a second language.

For too long, mainline American Protestant churches, and the Episcopal Church in particular, have neglected mission as a primary focus of the work of the church. Too often liberals are handicapped with a sense of guilt and shame over the indiscretions and mistakes of past foreign mission policies. As a result our churches suffer from a lack of vision and action in response to God's call. We can no longer hide from the wider world. Today Christian brothers and sisters in Africa, Asia, Latin America and the Middle East challenge us to new forms of partnership and mutuality in God's mission throughout the world. We are asked to re-evaluate our histories of foreign mission work in order to reclaim our roots as churches dedicated to mission. We must not be afraid to give mission its proper place. We must move into a new era which truly recognizes the universal call of all Christians to work for God's reign throughout the world.

This study will assist in the building of bridges between Episcopalians in the United States and Anglican partners in Christ around the world, while at the same time informing discussions about mission and structure in the Episcopal Church today. The history of foreign mission work of the Episcopal Church will inform current relationships between the church in the United States and the newly independent and autonomous Anglican churches around the world. Reviewing the theological presuppositions behind Episcopal foreign mission initiatives will help the church to better understand itself as it wrestles with new forms of mission in the Anglican Communion, world Christianity, and beyond.

As primarily an institutional history of the Episcopal Church's involvement in foreign mission, in-depth investigation into the activities of any particular Episcopal foreign mission district, such as Liberia, China, or the Philippines, is beyond the scope of this book. The histories of Episcopal missionary work in specific overseas locations belong to the local indigenous Christians as their own church history. Overseas missionary jurisdictions are referred to, however, in order to illustrate the policies and strategies of Episcopal foreign mission work.

The primary methodology of this study is chronological historical documentation and analysis. Chapter divisions are based upon different time periods within the foreign mission work of the Episcopal Church. Significant changes in mission strategy or missionary support mark the transition from one period of history to the next. The first chapter is a review of the origins of Episcopal foreign mission in the nineteenth century and augments Julia Emery's earlier work. The second chapter concentrates on the development of a "national church ideal" at the opening of the twentieth century. Chapter three examines the foreign mission of the Episcopal Church from the founding of the church's National Council in 1919 until 1946. The fourth chapter describes the emergence of the Episcopal Church as the preeminent church in the Anglican Communion following World War Two. Chapter five concludes the book with an investigation of the redefinition of mission and the national structures of the Episcopal Church in the post-colonial era.

These discussions about the foreign mission work of the Episcopal Church, however, cannot be divorced from cross-currents in conciliar Protestant mission theology.[14] Each chapter thus begins with an overview of developments in conciliar Protestant foreign missions and mission theology during the period under investigation. Major missionary conferences as well as influential mission theorists are presented to characterize the missiological climate of each era. The historical reviews of the theology of conciliar Protestant foreign missions are intended to set the context for Episcopal foreign mission work throughout the twentieth century. Parallels and discontinuities between conciliar Protestant foreign mission thought and Episcopal foreign mission initiatives are noted. These extended discussions of conciliar mission thought, taken as a whole, could serve as a missiological primer for the average Episcopalian.

A note about the title of this book is in order. Those familiar with *The Hymnal 1940* will recognize the familiar words of "Fling Out the Banner!" as one of the most popular of missionary hymns in the old book. Penned in 1848 by the Right Rev. George Washington Doane, Bishop of New Jersey, the hymn was originally written at the request of the girls at St. Mary's School, Burlington, New Jersey, of which Doane was the founder, to accompany their flag-raising ceremony.[15] Doane, who had been a key player in the organization of the Domestic and Foreign Missionary Society in the first part of the nineteenth century, struck a high missionary tone in the new hymn for the St. Mary's girls. The close connection between American imperialism and Episcopal foreign mission at the turn of the century resulted in a new view of the hymn whereby the banner increasingly was taken for the stars and stripes. "Fling Out the Banner!" thus came to embody the missiological tenets of the national church ideal, to spread the richness of Anglican tradition and the riches of American democracy to the ends of the world. It is no surprise that in the post-colonial era, imperialist associations of "Fling Out the Banner!" forced it to be dropped from the *The Hymnal 1982*.[16]

The current effort to re-engineer the Domestic and Foreign Missionary Society is important and exciting work, the results of which will affect all Episcopalians as we participate in God's worldwide mission. It is hoped that this study will assist in those efforts both by reviewing our own history and helping Episcopalians to be better partners in mission with sisters and brothers in Christ around the world. Guided by prayer and empowered by the Holy Spirit, God will do a new thing as we seek to be faithful to God's call "to restore all people to unity with God and each other in Christ."[17]

NOTES

[1]Letter by the Rev. Canon J. Patrick Mauney, Executive for Partnerships, The Episcopal Church Center, to Appointed Missionaries and Volunteers for Mission, January 20, 1994.

[2]Report of the Standing Commission on World Mission, *The Blue Book: Reports of the Committees, Commissions, Boards, and Agencies of the General Convention of the Episcopal Church to the 71st General Convention* (New York: The General Convention of the Episcopal Church, 1994), 529.

[3]Ibid., 528.

[4]Resolutions #D-107a, "Continuing the Volunteers for Mission Program", #D-032s, "The National Church and World Mission," and #D-108, "Reinstatement of 5% Reduction of Funding for Overseas Dioceses," turned back the cutbacks proposed by the Executive Council. Since each of these resolutions had significant budget ramifications, all three had to receive funding approval by the Program, Budget, and Finance Committee (PB&F). Ultimately these three resolutions were part of close to twenty resolutions

that passed the House of Deputies and received funding by PB&F but were inadvertently omitted from the legislative calendar of the House of Bishops for concurrence. This mistake left the three resolutions in legislative limbo, although the overwhelming support by the House of Deputies and the guarantee of funding from PB&F assured that these actions of General Convention were efficacious in the 1994-1997 triennium.

[5]Taking off from the sexuality studies of the 1991-1994 triennium, Resolution #A-137a, "Diocesan and Congregational Study and Action on World Mission," called each parish and diocese in the church to recommit itself to the global mission of Christ through both study and the sending and receiving of missionaries. A related resolution #A-139 established a task force to develop "World Mission/Cross Cultural" internships for seminarians.

[6]As with resolutions #D-107a, #D-032s, #D-108, resolution #D-016a, "Developing New Missionary Structures," was also mistakenly left off the concurrence calendar by the House of Bishops although it had passed resoundingly in the House of Deputies and was funded by the Program Budget, and Finance Committee. Ratification of #D-016a by the Executive Council corrected this oversight.

The Standing Commission on World Mission and the Episcopal Council for Global Mission identified a seven-person "working group" to begin the envisioning of a new Domestic and Foreign Missionary Society. The working group's suggestions with related resolutions will be presented in the report of the Standing Commission on World Mission to the 72nd General Convention in 1997.

[7]For a report on the symposium with transcripts of the presentations see: J. Stephen Freeman, ed., *Shaping Our Future: Challenges for the Church in the Twenty-First Century* (Boston: Cowley Publications, 1994).

[8]The Legislative Committee on Structure dealt at length with the question of what constitutes the church's mission and what are the most effective structures to enable that mission to go forward.

Listening to the "grass-roots," the Committee combined a host of resolutions into one omnibus resolution (#C-032). The Resolution called for two new committees in the 1994-1997 triennium, one to organize forums around the church to engage structural questions and the other to draft a plan for structural change. Although the resolution passed handily in the House of Deputies, the Bishops, concerned over stewardship and the duplication of existing interim bodies, failed to concur with the "upper House."

[9]See: Standing Commission on the Structure of the Church, *Comment Draft Report on the Structure of the Church* (New York: The General Convention of the Episcopal Church, 1996), p. 1 of abstract.

[10]The only substantive history of the Domestic and Foreign Missionary Society is Julia Emery's book *A Century of Endeavor,* written in 1921 to celebrate the centennial of the society. See: Julia C. Emery, *A Century of Endeavor, 1821-1921: A Record of the First Hundred Years of the Domestic and Foreign Missionary Society of the Protestant Episcopal Church in the United States of America* (New York: The Department of Missions, Protestant Episcopal Church in the United States of America, 1921).

[11]David B. Barrett, "Annual Statistical Table on Global Mission: 1996," *International Bulletin of Missionary Research* 20 (January 1996): 24-25.

[12]John Howe, *Highways and Hedges: Anglicanism and the Universal Church* (Toronto: Anglican Book Centre, 1985), 14-17.

[13]"Pastoral Letter from the House of Bishops to the People of the Episcopal Church" in General Convention of the Episcopal Church, *Journal of the General Convention of the Episcopal Church: 1985* (New York: The General Convention, 1985), 12.

[14]The study of mission theology is often divided along the ecclesiastical lines of ecumenical (or conciliar), evangelical and Roman Catholic. Rodger Bassham, in his comprehensive review of twentieth-century mission theology, emphasizes the different historical

and theological backgrounds in ecumenical, evangelical, and Roman Catholic missions. See: Rodger C. Bassham, *Mission Theology, 1948-1975: Years of Worldwide Creative Tensions; Ecumenical, Evangelical, and Roman Catholic* (Pasadena, Calif.: William Carey Library, 1979).

[15]Joint Commission on the Revision of the Hymnal, *The Hymnal 1940 Companion* Third Revised Edition, (New York: The Church Pension Fund, 1951), 172.

[16]I am indebted to the Rev. Zane W. Gordy, a priest and organist from New Jersey, for pointing me in the direction of Doane's hymn.

[17]Answer to the question: "What is the mission of the Church?" in "An Outline of the Faith commonly called the Catechism," The Book of Common Prayer (The Church Hymnal Corporation, New York, 1979), 855.

CHAPTER ONE

A CENTURY OF ENDEAVOR
Origins of Episcopal Foreign Mission
1821 to 1900

Kenneth Scott Latourette called the nineteenth century "The Great Century" of Protestant missions.[1] In the early 1800s American Protestants began to organize themselves for foreign missions. By the end of the century, Protestant foreign missions had become a significant player in the expansion of American political, economic and cultural interests around the world.

Protestant missionaries were motivated by their sense of America's Manifest Destiny. Beginning in the 1840s the United States saw itself as having a national mission, assigned by Providence, for extending the blessings of America to other people.[2] As ambassadors of the "new Israel," a chosen people, American Protestant missionaries felt called to spread the glory of their "Christian civilization." The increase in the number of missionaries in the last half of the nineteenth century and the rising commitment to schools and hospitals in foreign missions resulted from American Protestantism's "errand to the world."[3]

The Episcopal Church in the United States, however, did not share in the growth of American Protestant foreign missions in the nineteenth century. It is true that the official Episcopal missionary society, The Domestic and Foreign Missionary Society of the Protestant Episcopal Church, was founded in the early 1800s.

It is also true that Episcopalian foreign missionaries participated in the spread of American Christian civilization through mission schools and hospitals. The golden years, however, of Episcopal foreign mission work had to wait until the twentieth century. The disparity between the forward progress of most American Protestant foreign missions and the struggling efforts of Episcopal missionaries in the nineteenth century is related to the unique theology and organization of Episcopal mission work.

AMERICAN PROTESTANT MISSION IN THE NINETEENTH CENTURY

The roots of American foreign missions lie in the Great Awakenings of the 1740s and early 1800s. David Brainerd, Jonathan Edwards, and Samuel Hopkins provided the intellectual foundation for American missionary endeavors[4] As a missionary to the Indians of New England, David Brainerd exemplified fortitude in the face of difficult and dangerous circumstances. His self-sacrificing work on behalf of the Indians personified the belief that all mission work was for the greater glory of God. Whereas Brainerd was the practitioner, Jonathan Edwards was the thinker. Edwards's millennial eschatology led him to the conclusion that all nonbelievers needed to be evangelized. He was certain that the millennium would begin when all the nations were converted. For Edwards, the Great Awakening was evidence that the end time was beginning.[5] As a student of Edwards, Samuel Hopkins brought together the millennialism of Edwards and the self-sacrificing missionary motives of Brainerd in his theory of "universal disinterested benevolence." Universal disinterested benevolence meant that all Christians should work to do God's will in the world with no thought of reward or gain in this life or the next.[6] For Hopkins the highest service was to work and suffer for God and for all of humanity. And the greatest way to show love and service to God was to give oneself in mission.[7]

No doubt, the thoughts of Brainerd, Edwards and Hopkins were well known by the individuals who are credited with the birth of American foreign missions. In 1806 a group of students at Williams College, led by Samuel J Mills, were the first to organize themselves for "missions to the heathen."[8] The story goes that Mills and like-minded students from Williams found themselves sheltered from a rainstorm in a common haystack. There, after praying together, the students were moved by the spirit of God and dedicated themselves to the cause of foreign missions. The students then organized themselves into a secret society, called the Brethren, to promote missionary concerns.[9] After graduating from Williams, Mills and others members of the Society of the Brethren carried their missionary zeal into formal theological studies at Andover Seminary.

At Andover, Mills met another young student who shared his missionary convictions and zeal, Adoniram Judson. Together Mills and Judson pushed the cause of foreign missions in the seminary and in local churches. In 1810 Mills, Judson and others brought their hopes to become foreign missionaries before the Congregationalist General Association of Massachusetts. The Association thereupon founded what was to become the first and most important missionary society in the United States, the American Board of Commissioners for Foreign Missions (ABCFM).[10]

Following the lead of the English missionaries, Adoniram Judson and his wife, Ann Hasseltine Judson, along with other young missionaries including Samuel and Harriet Newell, were sent to India by the ABCFM in 1812. En route to India the Judsons read the writings of the Baptist William Carey. They became convinced of the efficacy of adult baptism and were converted to the Baptist understanding of the faith. Now Baptists, the Judsons had to leave the predominantly Congregationalist ABCFM. They returned to the United States and were instrumental in the founding of the Baptist Board of Foreign Missions in 1814. As Baptist missionaries, Adoniram and Ann Judson were then sent out to pursue a mission to Burma.

Meanwhile Samuel Mills remained in the United States to promote and organize missions in foreign lands and on the Western frontier. He played a significant role in the founding of two important missionary societies in 1817, the American Bible Society, and the United Christian Missionary Society. Because of his concern for blacks freed from slavery, Mills took an active role in the American Colonization Society and was one of its first two agents.[11]

With the advent of well organized missionary societies and the beginning of new mission work on the Western frontier and in foreign lands, enthusiasm for missions grew. America's sense of election as the new Israel was increasingly affirmed. The United States, as the chosen nation, felt called to follow Christ's lead of selfless love and service to all the world. Conversion of the "heathen" was God's plan; American missionaries saw themselves as Christ's servants to the world. The national and religious impulses to redeem the world were inseparable.[12] By 1850, however, the idealism of the first generation of American missionaries had begun to wane. The perception of success in selected foreign fields, such as the Sandwich Islands (Hawaii), was tempered by the failure of missionary efforts with Indians at home. Other foreign missions to lands such as India and Burma had shown mixed results.[13] American missions left their enthusiastic childhood and entered their turbulent adolescence.

As the vanguard for the new Israel, American missionaries were commissioned to bring Western Christian civilization to the "heathen" peoples of the world. Most American Protestant missionaries thus were preoccupied with the establishment and administration of schools, hospitals and other "civilizing" institutions. American missionaries believed that it was their responsibility as a "chosen people" to share their light with the rest of the world. Significant dissenting voices, however, were raised against this "civilizing" priority in American Protestant foreign missions. The most important critic of the emphasis of civilization was Rufus Anderson, the preeminent secretary of the American Board of Commissioners for Foreign Missions from 1826 until 1866.

After careful study and review of the educational ventures of American missions, Anderson concluded that missionary activities focusing on societal and institutional change were misguided.

He believed that the time, energy and resources used to build mission schools and hospitals would be better spent in the strictly defined task of preaching the Gospel. Anderson cautioned against civilizing activities in missionary methods.

> Unless this [civilizing] influence is guarded against by their directors, the result is that the missions have a two-fold object of pursuit; the one, that simple and sublime spiritual object of the ambassador for Christ mentioned in the text, "persuading men to be reconciled to God;" the other, the reorganizing, by various direct means, of the structure of that social system, of which the converts form a part. Thus the object of missions becomes more or less complicated, leading to a complicated, burdensome, and perhaps expensive course of measures for its attainment.[14]

Anderson maintained that the true object of missions was to plant selfsupporting, self-governing and self-propagating indigenous churches. Anderson and his counterpart in the Anglican Church Missionary Society, Henry Venn, were the first to articulate systematically what has come to be known as three-self mission theory.[15]

For Anderson, the vocation of the missionary was a unique, spiritual calling. Relying on the power of the Holy Spirit, the missionary was to foster new groups of believers through the preaching of God's word. Once this was accomplished, the missionary should either return home or move on, allowing the young church to develop on its own. In other words, "the Kingdom of God is a seed. The missionary is a planter. The missionary plants the seed. The missionary leaves. Yankee go home."[16]

Few missionaries heeded Anderson's admonitions to return home and even fewer agreed that civilizing activities should be de-emphasized in foreign missions. The debate between evangelization or civilization seemed to fade away as American foreign missions entered the imperialist era of the late nineteenth century. Although theological differences existed between the liberal Social Gospelers and the more conservative premillennialists, all agreed that the American "Christian" civilization was superior to the heathen nations around the world.

Premillennial theology found a sympathetic ear in the more conservative quarters of American foreign missions during the last few decades of the 1800s. Premillennialists believed that the second coming of Jesus Christ was imminent. The responsibility of Christian believers was to spread the gospel in order to expedite the second coming and to "gather in the church."[17] The forward advance of the American Christian civilization as the nineteenth century drew to a close, augmented by the United States victory in the Spanish-American War, was seen as a sign of Christ's imminent return. The need to preach the Gospel to the ends of the earth was punctuated with an eschatological urgency for the premillennialist.

The foremost premillennialist in American foreign missions was the Presbyterian preacher and popularizer of missions, Arthur Tappan Pierson. As the editor of the interdenominational *Missionary Review of the World* from 1887 to 1911, Pierson stirred the hearts and minds of many for the cause of foreign missions. His classic, *The Crisis of Missions; or, The Voice Out of the Cloud* published in 1886, summarized his premillennial motives for mission. The crisis of missions for Pierson was that although the world had never been more ripe for the harvest, too few laborers were available to accomplish God's work. He believed that the end times were close at hand and that all humanity should be brought into the fold. Pierson thus stressed that each and every Christian had the responsibility to participate in the spreading of the Gospel to all who had not yet heard the good news. Because of his premillennial views, Pierson maintained that preaching the word was paramount in foreign missions. Preaching, however, was not limited to simple evangelistic witness but included church planting and institutional development.

> Dr. Gordon and myself firmly believe that "preaching the Gospel as a witness among all nations" means setting up churches, schools, a sanctified press, medical missions, and in fact, all the institutions which are a fruit of Christianity and constitute part of its witness;... Missions begin in evangelization, but have everything to do with Christian education, and the printing press, and the organization of churches, and the training of a native pastorate.[18]

Although liberal mission advocates did not agree with Pierson's premillennialism they did share his assumptions that Christ and Western culture were coterminous and that civilizing activities were an appropriate goal for missions.

Premillennialists and liberals shared an enthusiasm for Western culture as the Christian hope for the world; but liberals in particular made a larger contribution to the civilizing emphasis in foreign missions than their more conservative counterparts.[19] Unlike the premillennialists, the liberals lacked a strict doctrine of evangelization, were skeptical of quick and easy conversions and took a more sympathetic view of other religions.[20] As a result, liberal missiologists did not have the urgency for conversion that was central to the premillennialists.

American liberals in missions carried forward an idea given currency by the mid-century theologian Horace Bushnell: salvation is a gradual process in which environmental influences play a major role. Liberals neither expected an imminent end of the world nor believed all those untouched by the Gospel would go straight to Hell. As a result, their conception of the core of Christianity, of the simple message to which everything else can be reduced, was substantially different from that of conservative evangelicals. For the latter, the central message had to be expressed in the language of radical conversion — "believe and be saved" — while for liberal theologians the key was that "the Kingdom of God is within you."[21]

The priority of Kingdom over conversion led the liberals to emphasize civilizing rather than evangelizing activities in foreign missions.

The foremost spokesperson for liberal missions at the end of the nineteenth century was James Dennis. Dennis's three-volume study *Christian Missions and Social Progress*, published between 1897 and 1906, celebrated the social accomplishments of American Protestant missions. This review of the cultural achievements of missionaries appealed greatly to the general public and helped to make Dennis a popular apologist for the cause of foreign missions.[22] Dennis embraced the Social Gospel and saw missions as a way to internationalize the advances of this liberal theology. He maintained that mission activities that sought to change the social order of the heathen were significantly more important than evangelistic enterprises. Dennis argued that although "the evangelistic aim is still first...a new significance has been given to missions as a factor in the social regeneration of the world."[23] This priority on social mission was based upon the implicit assumption that

American Christian civilization was far superior to any "heathen" culture.

Although the "civilizing" ideology of American missions was shaped primarily by liberalism and the Social Gospel, liberals and premillennialists all agreed that the West had a divine right to conquer the peoples of the world and define reality for them.[24] The idea that Western Christian culture was superior and should be exported throughout the world was normative to liberal and conservative mission theory. Both liberals and premillennialists had

> a common inability to take seriously any norms or testimonies not originating in Western Christendom, an unwillingness to grant exotic cultures the kind of hearing automatically expected for Christian and Western values. In such matters James Dennis and Arthur T. Pierson were twins, not opposites.[25]

A review of American foreign missions in the nineteenth century is incomplete without acknowledging the significant role of women in foreign missions. American women provided a foundation for the missionary movement through prayer, promotion, financial support, and the sending of women missionaries. Because women were not given equal status in the general missionary boards of the established Protestant churches, they organized themselves into separate, independent women's missionary societies.

In the women's missionary societies, American women discovered opportunities for ministry not available in the United States. "Women's work for women," the rallying cry of many of the women's societies, expressed the activism and solidarity of women's involvement in foreign missions.[26] By the end of the nineteenth century women's missionary societies were central to the foreign mission thrust of United States churches. In fact, the majority of American missionaries at the turn of the century were women.

> By 1890 there were 34 American women's societies supporting 926 missionaries in various fields, and together with the married women of the general missionary boards, they composed 60 percent of the total American missionary force. By 1900 there were 41 women's agencies supporting over 1,200 single women missionaries. In 1910 the women's foreign missionary movement claimed a total supporting membership of 2,000,000.[27]

The growth in the number of women missionaries in the last decade of the 1800s paralleled the forward thrust of American Protestant missions at the turn of the nineteenth century.

EPISCOPAL FOREIGN MISSIONS IN THE NINETEENTH CENTURY

The 1800s were not a "great century" for Episcopal missions. Although the basic tenets of Episcopal mission theology were developed in the nineteenth century, the golden years of Episcopal foreign mission work had to wait until the mid-twentieth century. Julia C. Emery, the distinguished secretary of the Woman's Auxiliary to the Board of Missions of the Domestic and Foreign Missionary Society of the Protestant Episcopal Church from 1876-1916, called the first hundred years of Episcopal mission work "a century of endeavor."[28] Her history of the Domestic and Foreign Missionary Society of the Protestant Episcopal Church, published in 1921, acknowledges that Episcopal missionary endeavors struggled throughout the 1800s. The title of Emery's book, *A Century of Endeavor*, recognizes the limits of Episcopal mission undertakings in the nineteenth century while looking forward to a hopeful future in the twentieth. Why was the Episcopal record in missions less dramatic than that of other American Protestant churches in the nineteenth century?

A review of the Episcopal missionary outreach from 1821 to 1900 will reveal that the church suffered from a schizophrenic understanding of mission. As Anglicans, Episcopalians attempted to implement a catholic theology of mission in an American Protestant missionary context. The inability to reconcile successfully a catholic missiology with an American Protestant missionary strategy significantly hindered the missionary outreach of the Episcopal Church in the nineteenth century.

Unlike most American Protestant churches, the Episcopal Church embraced a more catholic missiology that saw the church itself as mission. Beginning in the early nineteenth century, mission endeavors were considered the work of the whole church

and each Episcopalian was to be involved in the missionary outreach of the church. Rather than relying upon special interest
groups and voluntary societies to support missionaries in the
United States and overseas, the Episcopal Church organized one
unified domestic and foreign missionary society of which each
baptized Episcopalian was a member. The missionary work of the
Episcopal Church in the nineteenth century suffered, however,
because the connection between Episcopalians in the pew and
the missionary work of the church was weak.

Although theological differences existed between the missiology of the Episcopal Church and other American Protestants,
Episcopalians could not divorce themselves from the wider context of American Protestantism. Episcopalians shared wholeheartedly in the view that American civilization was the Christian hope
for the world. The important place of the Episcopal Church in the
Social Gospel movement intensified Episcopalian commitment to
"civilizing activities" in foreign missions. Episcopal missionary
endeavors thus resembled closely those of other Protestant missionary societies.

Roots of Episcopal Foreign Mission

In the few decades following the Revolutionary War
Episcopalians in the United States were preoccupied with the con-
textualization of an independent Anglican church in post-revolu-
tionary America. A great deal of energy was spent trying to rescue
the church from its earlier associations with the British crown. In
the late eighteenth century Episcopalians had four primary concerns: the organization of dioceses, the forming of a national constitution, the adaptation of the Prayer Book to the post-revolu-
tionary political reality, and the need to secure an indigenous episcopate.[29] Although the first General Convention of the Protestant
Episcopal Church in the United States of America was held in
1785, a unified church was not achieved until 1789. At the General
Convention of 1789, held in Philadelphia, twenty-two clergymen
(including two bishops) and sixteen laymen hammered out a constitution and set of canons and adopted a Book of Common

Prayer.[30] The General Convention of 1789 accomplished a union of independent churches in the several states. It ensured continuity in the ordained ministry, a uniform liturgy, and a means of determining common membership in the newly autonomous Anglican church.[31] But for nearly half a century the young Episcopal Church would struggle to define its identity and its place in the United States.

In the late 1700s and early 1800s, fledgling attempts were made in the Episcopal Church to support missionary outreach. The focus of these missionary activities was to build up the church where it was already established in the Eastern states and to push forward into the American West. The General Convention of 1792 adopted a plan "for supporting missionaries to preach the Gospel on the frontiers." This plan provided for a Joint Committee to direct missionary work and requested clergy to take collections on the second Sunday in Advent to support missionaries. Unfortunately most Episcopal churches were having such a difficult time supporting their own local congregations that funds contributed to work beyond their own parishes were pitifully small.[32] Recognizing that the national plan to provide for missionaries was receiving little or no endorsement, the General Convention of 1795 referred the question of missionary support back to the dioceses.[33]

For the next twenty-five years missionary work on the American frontier was undertaken by various diocesan bodies. By the second decade of the nineteenth century, missionary, Prayer Book, and tract societies had been established in New Jersey, Pennsylvania, Delaware, Maryland, Virginia and South Carolina.[34] Although the outreach of these diocesan societies was modest and loosely organized, their existence was a sign of the increasing expansion of the missionary work of the Episcopal Church. Subsequent General Conventions would point to the Committee of the Convention of New York for Propagating the Gospel, the New York Missionary and Education Society, the Society for the Advancement of Christianity in South Carolina, and similar societies in Pennsylvania and Georgia as contributing to the establishment of a general missionary society of the Episcopal Church.[35]

Whereas the impetus for domestic missions came from diocesan missionary societies within the church, the push for foreign missions in the Episcopal Church came from outside the church. At least three groups held up the foreign mission agenda before Episcopalians. First, American Protestant churches were beginning to organize missionary societies specifically dedicated to missions beyond the United States. The founding of the American Board of Commissioners for Foreign Missions in 1810 and the Baptist Board of Foreign Missions in 1814 was a source of inspiration for Episcopalians looking beyond the Western frontier.

Second, and perhaps more important, the British Church Missionary Society (CMS), founded in 1799, challenged the Episcopal Church to play its part in "bringing the Faith to the heathen in Africa and the East." In 1815 the Rev. Josiah Pratt, secretary of the CMS, wrote to several leaders of the Episcopal Church in the United States asking for cooperation in foreign missions. The Right Rev. Alexander Viets Griswold, bishop of the Eastern Diocese (which included all of New England outside of Connecticut) was receptive to the CMS invitation. Griswold was an old-fashioned evangelical who had been born again in a revival in his own parish at Bristol, Rhode Island.[36] As bishop he had challenged his clergy in 1814 to take seriously the missionary duty of the church. In 1816 Griswold responded to Pratt, suggesting the appointment of one of his clergymen, the Rev. Joseph R. Andrus, as a missionary to Ceylon. The CMS expressed its willingness to make the appointment but also suggested that the American church form its own missionary society dedicated to foreign missions and offered financial assistance to that end.[37] Andrus, however, was never appointed a CMS missionary although in 1821 he was sent to Liberia as an agent of the American Colonization Society. He died in West Africa the following year.[38] The eagerness of the Church Missionary Society to assist in the founding of an American Episcopal missionary society was reiterated in the society's 1817 annual report that emphasized "the expediency of forming in the Episcopal

Church of the United States a Missionary Society for the advancement of the Kingdom of Christ among the heathen."[39] These conversations would be picked up again, three years later, when Episcopalians began to organize a general missionary society for the whole church.

Finally, the formation of the American Colonization Society in 1816 played a significant role in turning the attention of American Episcopalians to Africa. The Rev. Joseph Andrus (the same individual who had offered himself for service in Ceylon) and three other clergymen, as well as laymen John Bankson and Ephraim Bacon, were among the first agents of the American Colonization Society. These six Episcopalians, and others, helped the Episcopal Church to learn about Africa and the necessity to locate a mission in the colony founded by the Colonization Society.[40]

The Domestic and Foreign Missionary Society

In 1816 the involvement of the Episcopal Church in domestic mission and the push for missionary outreach beyond the United States came together. In that year, Episcopalians in Pennsylvania organized the Protestant Episcopal Missionary Society of Pennsylvania. At the time most diocesan missionary societies were preoccupied with local outreach and only secondarily interested in mission to the frontier. The Pennsylvania Society, however, was founded to support both domestic and foreign mission ventures.[41] Four years later, three members of the Pennsylvania Society, the Rev. Jackson Kemper, later the first missionary bishop of the Episcopal Church; the Rev. George Boyd, later the first secretary of the Board of Missions; and the Rev. William A. Muhlenberg, drafted a report to be presented to the next General Convention. The report proposed that the General Convention consider establishing a General Missionary Society for Foreign and Domestic Missions as an organization for the whole Episcopal Church.[42]

The next General Convention of the Episcopal Church met in Philadelphia on May 16, 1820. On the third day of the meeting, George Boyd, one of the deputies to the convention from

Pennsylvania, offered a resolution on the subject of a general missionary society and presented the report of the Pennsylvania Society. The matter was referred to a committee consisting of Boyd, the Rev. John P. K. Henshaw of Rhode Island, and laymen Duncan Cameron of North Carolina and Francis Scott Key of Maryland (author of "The Star Spangled Banner"). Because of the press of business related to the founding of a seminary for the Episcopal Church, the committee did not report back to the convention until its last day of meeting. In the last few hours of the meeting, and with considerable haste, the convention adopted a constitution for a general missionary society: "The Protestant Episcopal Missionary Society in the United States for Foreign and Domestic Missions."[43]

Although the Missionary Society was an official organ of the church, constitutionally it was organized as a voluntary society. Following the model of existing British and American missionary societies, membership in the Episcopal Church's Missionary Society was voluntary and based on one's monetary contributions. Dues for individuals were $3.00 a year and any person giving $50 or more was considered a lifetime patron. The constitution encouraged the establishment of auxiliary societies in each diocese in order to secure patronage and to enlarge the funds of the organization.[44] Unlike voluntary societies, however, bishops were to play a primary role in the organization and work of the association. Each diocesan bishop was to be the president of the local auxiliary and the Presiding Bishop (the senior bishop in the church) was to be the president of the whole society. As such, the Presiding Bishop was seen as the focal point for the missionary endeavors of the Episcopal Church.

> Assuming that the society was functioning at times other than the meetings of the General Convention, its president, the Presiding Bishop, was so to speak, the permanent "Chief Missionary" of the Church, and the "key man" in the missionary activity of the Church by virtue of his being the head of a society concerned for the advancement of foreign and domestic missions.[45]

Unfortunately, this first attempt to organize a general missionary society had significant flaws. The constitution provided for a Board of Managers to govern the affairs of the Missionary Society. The bishops, however, had no official voice or vote in the decisions of the organization. This was considered an unworkable situation and resulted in a stillbirth of the general missionary society.

Although the flaws in the constitution prohibited the undertaking of missionary activities, the founding of the society was communicated to the missionary societies of the Church of England. Josiah Pratt, the secretary of the Church Missionary Society and the one who earlier communicated with Bishop Griswold, welcomed the founding of the general missionary society for the Episcopal Church. In his letter to George Boyd, who had left Pennsylvania to become the first secretary of the Missionary Society, Pratt applauded the organizational advantages of the society as an organ of the Episcopal Church. He wrote:

> It is with peculiar feelings of satisfaction that we witness the Protestant Episcopal Church in the United States embodying itself into a Society, for the purpose of concentrating its strength and rendering its exertions more efficient in this Holy Cause[46]

Remembering Pratt's promise of financial assistance, Griswold also wrote to the CMS about the founding of the Episcopal Missionary Society. In response Pratt made available £200 to the Missionary Society of the Episcopal Church.[47] This sum was equal to the annual salary for one CMS missionary and was intended as support for the first missionary of the Episcopal Church.

Fortunately, the flawed constitution had to remain in effect for only one year. The Episcopal Church planned to have a special General Convention in 1821 to work on the question of a general seminary for the whole church. As a result, the corrections in the organization of the Missionary Society did not have to wait the normal three years between General Conventions.

The first Special General Convention of the Episcopal Church met in Philadelphia in the summer of 1821. The majority of the convention was dedicated to the establishment of a general theological seminary for the training of ordained ministers in the Episcopal Church. A significant amount of time and effort, however, was spent on correcting the flaws in the constitution of the Missionary Society. A new constitution and new name were adopted for the society: the Domestic and Foreign Missionary Society of the Protestant Episcopal Church in the United States of America. (D&FMS) A new board of directors was constituted that included, in voice and vote, the bishops of the church. Membership in the Missionary Society, however, remained voluntary and based upon financial contributions. With the addition of a general seminary and the newly constituted Missionary Society, the Episcopal Church in 1821 was in a position to take significant steps forward in its outreach at home and abroad.[48]

A Slow Start

The Episcopal Church now had a structure in place to begin domestic and foreign missionary ventures; however, support from the church for missionary work was modest at best. The Episcopal Church suffered from a parochialism that saw the work and needs of the local diocese as more important than that of the Missionary Society. Bishop Hobart of New York spoke for many of the bishops when he reported to Bishop Griswold in 1822:

> Any systematic attempt to collect funds for the general purposes of the Missionary Society, in this diocese, would in my judgment, on many accounts be inexpedient. Some specific object of missionary exertion however, may occur, to which the Episcopalians of this diocese, might be directed, without any material interference with the plans in operation for diocesan purposes, and in such case I shall be happy to aid the operation of the Society.[49]

Because of this parochialism membership in the society reported at the next General Convention in 1823 was dismally small with only twenty-one patrons (individuals contributing $50 or more), eleven life members (individuals contributing $30) and seventy-four annual subscribers at $3.00 per year. Lacking financial support, the society was unable to employ a single domestic or foreign missionary. In the next triennium, 1823-1826, the situation had improved little with the number of patrons and life members doubling but the number of annual paid members increasing by only eight.[50] It was becoming increasingly clear that the idea of voluntary membership in a general church missionary society did not have much support.

By the General Convention of 1829, support for the Missionary Society had reached a crisis. With only four domestic missionaries employed and membership of eighty-three patrons, forty-four life members, and thirty-six annual subscribers, the Domestic and Foreign Missionary Society was greatly in debt. The treasurer reported that there existed outstanding debts of $800 and the society had borrowed $316.64 from its endowed funds.[51] A pamphlet published in 1829, entitled "The Crisis in the Affairs of the Domestic and Foreign Missionary Society of the Protestant Episcopal Church in the United States of America: and an Appeal to Episcopalians on Its Behalf," emphasized the problems of the Missionary Society. It pointed out that the average annual income of the society since its founding had not exceeded $1500, and that the organization lacked a general agent to promote its activities.[52] The General Convention lamented the difficulties of the Missionary Society but did little to address the problem of its support.

Despite the difficulties of the Missionary Society, bold attempts were made to advance the missionary work of the Episcopal Church. On the domestic front the House of Bishops in 1829 and 1832 called for "a plan for extending to new States and Territories in which the Church is not organized under Episcopal supervision."[53] In the same period the Episcopal Church saw the appointment of its first foreign missionaries, who sailed for Greece on October 2, 1829.

The first Episcopal foreign mission, the mission to Greece, was to be characteristic of most of nineteenth-century Episcopalian foreign mission work in two ways. First, it concentrated on civilizing rather than evangelizing activities. Second, it was an individually initiated rather than a well-planned venture instituted by the Missionary Society.

On the last day of 1828, the Rev. John J. Robertson sailed for Greece on his own initiative. He had convinced the Domestic and Foreign Missionary Society, however, to appoint him an agent in order to "inquire into the state of religion in that country and to ascertain the disposition of the people for receiving Protestant Episcopal Missionaries."[54] Upon his return in 1829 Robertson made his case for a mission to Greece before the Foreign Committee of the Missionary Society. The goal of his mission was not "to convert the Greeks for they were already Christian, but to provide them with the opportunities for education which their long subjugation [under the Turks] and present condition of poverty had prevented."[55] Anxious to begin some kind of foreign mission activity, the society appointed Robertson and his wife, the Rev. John H. Hill and his wife Frances Maria, and a printer, Solomon Bingham as missionaries to Greece.[56] The leadership of the Missionary Society recognized that the Greeks were Christians and so the point of the mission was not conversion but rather social uplift through education and the printed word.

> The official position of the Protestant Episcopal Church with respect to the missionaries was made explicit in the instructions Bishop Griswold hand-ed to Messrs. Robertson and Hill when they left Boston for Greece. "...you are by no means to say or write or do anything which may justly give rise to the impression that you have visited the Greeks for the purpose of intro-ducing another form of Christianity or establishing another church than that in which they have been nurtured."[57]

Within five years this first band of Episcopal foreign mission-aries had founded three educational institutions in Athens. An infant school, a school for young boys and girls, and a teacher training school had a total enrollment of over 600 students. By 1835, a printing press established to assist with the educational endeavors had produced over 30,000 copies of secular and reli-gious books.[58] In 1832, Mrs. Hill's sister, Elizabeth Milligan, joined the other five Episcopal missionaries as a teacher in the schools at Athens. Milligan was the first appointment of an unmarried woman to the foreign field made by the Domestic and Foreign Missionary Society.[59]

Although the educational and printing accomplishments in Greece were laudable, this first foreign mission of the Episcopal Church was poorly planned. The initiative for the Greek mission came from Robertson alone. The Domestic and Foreign Missionary Society was more of a passive bystander in the mission than an active participant. The lack of strategic planning by the Missionary Society in the founding of the Greek mission would be characteristic of much of the foreign mission work of the D&FMS throughout the nineteenth century.

> It may seem strange that with a non-Christian population throughout the world numbering many hundreds of millions the Church should have chosen Greece for its first venture abroad. It might be counted an early example of the Church's tendency to be sporadic and impulsive in selecting its foreign fields. It has too often happened, we must confess, that a small group has been seized by the conviction that a mission here or a mission there would be a glorious idea; and after a little pressure the Church has adopted the proposal with no regard to broader plans or general strategy.[60]

The Church is Mission

By the General Convention of 1832, the Episcopal Church was poised for forward steps in mission. Domestic missionary stations had been opened in Wisconsin and in Florida. Missionary aid had been extended to Tennessee, Kentucky, Mississippi, Missouri, Illinois, and Alabama. The educational mission in Greece was growing, and significant efforts were underway to begin work in West Africa (Liberia). Although these advances were duly noted, the Missionary Society still had only 108 patrons, eighty-five lifetime members and fifty-eight annual subscribers.[61] What was needed was a plan to motivate all Episcopalians to participate in the missionary outreach of the church. The Standing Committee of the Domestic and Foreign Missionary Society reported that a bold new venture could significantly increase the missionary outreach of the Episcopal Church. The committee emphasized

> it is abundantly manifest, from a review of the triennial report, that nothing is wanting under God, to an adequate supply of resources for all missionary exigencies of the Church, but *a general and uniform plan for cooperation among her members*. (Italics in original)[62]

On the last day of the 1832 General Convention, the Rev. George Washington Doane was consecrated bishop of New Jersey and appointed to the Board of Directors of the Domestic and Foreign Missionary Society. Bishop Doane would soon play the most important role in the reshaping of the strategy and theology of the Missionary Society.[63] As a militant high-churchman, Doane would bring a more catholic understanding of the church as mission to Episcopal missionary activities. It was Doane who wrote the hymn "Fling Out the Banner," one of the most popular mission hymns of the Episcopal Church in the late nineteenth and early twentieth centuries.

Early in 1835 the Board of Directors of the Missionary Society appointed a committee of seven individuals to prepare a report for the upcoming General Convention. Primary issues to be addressed were the organizational and membership problems of the D&FMS as well as the need for a plan to effect more financial giving to missions. Before the committee met, the members found that they were of one mind in their vision for mission and the Episcopal Church. Bishop Doane, the chair of the committee, credited this unanimity to nothing less than the work of God. Bishop Doane later reported:

> "What would you think," said Dr. Milnor, who had moved the resolution for the appointment of a committee, "what should you think of reporting that the Church is the Missionary Society, and should carry on the work of missions by a board appointed by the General Convention?" "Why," replied Bishop Doane, "it is the very plan which I have long thought ought to have been adopted, and for the adoption of which I should thank God with my whole heart." "How very strange is this," said Bishop McIlvaine. "I surely knew nothing of the mind of either of you, and yet this is the very plan which I have introduced into the sermon which I am to preach before the society!" When the committee met, the three members above named stated their views as above, and found them cordially reciprocated by all their associates. Thus, as to the principle of their report the committee were, from the first, unanimous. To whom shall the praise be given, but to the God that maketh men to be of one mind in a house?[64]

And so the directors of the Missionary Society prepared for the next General Convention of the Episcopal Church.

The General Convention of 1835 is considered by many to be the most important event in the history of the missionary work of the Episcopal Church.[65] By the end of the meeting, the bishops, clergy and lay delegates to the Convention had endorsed a radically new understanding of mission and had adopted new structures to promote and carry forward the Good News of Jesus Christ into the world. These developments were reflected in the significant changes in the constitution of the Domestic and Foreign Missionary Society.

Bishop Doane opened up the issue of membership in the Missionary Society at the General Convention. He argued:

> that by the original constitution of Christ, the Church as the Church, was the one great Missionary Society; and the Apostles, and the Bishops, their successors, his perpetual trustees; and that this great trust could not, and should never be divided or deputed. The duty...to support the Church in preaching the Gospel to every creature, was one which passed on every Christian by terms of his baptismal vow, and from which he could never be absolved[66]

Following the report of the Board of Directors of the Missionary Society and Bishop Doane's stirring address, the Convention adopted the idea that the church and the Missionary Society should be one and the same. No longer was the Missionary Society seen as a voluntary organization to which individuals subscribed. Instead the Episcopal Church stated that the church itself is the Missionary Society. In a brief but powerful statement the second article of the new constitution of the Domestic and Foreign Missionary Society stated: "The Society shall be considered as comprehending all persons who are members of this Church." In other words every Episcopalian, by virtue of his/her baptism, is a member of the Domestic and Foreign Missionary Society. Mission and missionary support were no longer the sole responsibility of a peripheral voluntary association in the church. Instead, beginning in 1835 and continuing for the next century and a half, the Episcopal Church would say that mission and the church are inseparable. To be an Episcopalian is to be involved in mission. The church is mission.[67]

The new constitution of the Domestic and Foreign Missionary Society, adopted in 1835, emphasized the unity of the missionary calling of the Episcopal Church. Since 1820 the missionary ventures of the society had been overseen by two separate committees, domestic and foreign. Unfortunately the differentiation between committees, with separate funding sources for each, resulted in a competitive relationship between missionary work in the United States and overseas. The new constitution of 1835 did not do away with the domestic and foreign committees but took steps to emphasize that there was only one mission field — the world. Article X of the 1835 constitution states explicitly for the first time the unified mission of the Church.

> For the guidance of the Committees it is declared that the missionary field is always to be regarded as one, THE WORLD — the terms domestic and foreign being understood as terms of locality adopted for convenience. *Domestic* missions are those which are established *within*, and *foreign* missions are those that are established *without*, the territory of the United States. (Capitals and italics in original)[68]

Constitutional changes, however, do not a reality make. The separation of domestic and foreign missions continued after 1835. Increasingly there developed a tacit understanding that the domestic field was the domain of high-church catholics while low-church evangelicals looked beyond the shores of the United States. This division between high-church and low-church mission fields would exacerbate the separation between domestic and foreign missions and led to the development of a separate independent missionary society in the 1850s.

The constitutional changes in the Missionary Society are often overlooked in the face of the other significant action of the 1835 General Convention — the creation of the missionary episcopate. For over a decade the Episcopal Church had wrestled with episcopal oversight of the missionary work on the frontier of the United States. Struggling congregations in the West often had to wait years before a bishop would visit to perform episcopal functions such as confirmations and ordinations. Recalling the difficulty that the young American church had had in securing its own episcopate following the Revolution, the Episcopal Church took steps to establish episcopal sees in its mission fields. And so the General Convention of 1835 elected the first two missionary bishops, Jackson Kemper for the Northwest and Francis Lister Hawks for the Southwest. Kemper soon would move forward boldly into the northwestern frontier setting up churches and laying the foundations for the dioceses of Missouri, Indiana, Iowa, Minnesota, and Wisconsin. Hawks, however, did not accept the election and the southwest had to wait until the election and consecration of Leonidas Polk in 1838.[69] It was Bishop Doane, once again, who clearly articulated the missiological significance of missionary bishops. He said a missionary bishop is

a bishop sent forth by the Church, not sought for of the Church; going before to organize the Church, not waiting till the Church has partially been organized; a leader not a follower, in the march of the Redeemer's conquering and triumphant Gospel . . . sent by the Church, even as the Church is sent by Christ.[70]

Episcopalians believed that maintaining the worship and discipline of the catholic church was the unique missionary calling of the Episcopal Church.[71] Missionary bishops would provide both episcopal oversight of the emerging church in the mission field as well as be a catalyst for new missionary activities. Up until this time neither the Episcopal Church nor the Church of England had elevated men to the episcopate specifically for missionary purposes. The English church had quietly posted a few bishops as chaplains to overseas English colonies. Unlike the American missionary bishops, these English bishops did not have a mandate to advance the church beyond the confines of the expatriate community. It was the American Episcopal Church that first put the office of the bishop and the missionary outreach of the church together in one office. The institution of missionary bishops, begun in 1835, would become the greatest contribution of the Episcopal Church to Anglican missions.[72]

To promote the missionary work of the whole Episcopal Church, the General Convention of 1835 founded the official missionary publication: *The Spirit of Missions*. Beginning in January 1836 and continuing for over a century, this missionary magazine would inform and excite Episcopalians about their corporate involvement in the domestic and foreign missionary outreach of the church.[73] In general the Episcopal missionaries were portrayed as upholding the true catholic church in the mission field while bringing the light of the best of Western civilization to the heathen of the world.

The depiction of missionary figures as cosmopolitan, learned and dignified in contrast to missionaries of other denominations became almost a cliché portrait which conveniently served to vindicate the church's conviction about the importance and necessity of its unique missionary endeavor.[74]

The General Convention of 1835 thus set the stage for the domestic and foreign missionary outreach of the Episcopal Church for the rest of the nineteenth century. Following the leadership of Bishop George Washington Doane, the Episcopal Church had endorsed a catholic theology of mission. It affirmed that mission belonged to the whole church and every person by virtue of his or her baptism is called to participate in it. As the historic symbol of the catholic church, the bishop became the chief missionary. With the bishop went the church, as he was called to both plant and oversee the fledgling Christian community. The question that lay before the Episcopal Church was: Would each and every Episcopalian take seriously his/her baptismal responsibility to spread the Good News of Jesus Christ near and far?

The Big Three: Liberia, China and Japan

This study focuses on the theological underpinnings of the foreign mission work of the Episcopal Church. As such, it cannot examine in detail the specific missionary activities in each of the Episcopal foreign mission fields. It is helpful, however, to review a bit of the history of the primary foreign mission fields of the Episcopal Church in the nineteenth century. By examining the missions in Liberia, China and Japan, we can see a few of the particularities of Episcopal foreign missions in the 1800s. In all three fields we find the priority of the missionary bishop as the chief missionary and guardian of the catholic faith, combined with an emphasis on the establishment of schools and hospitals in Episcopal foreign missions.

Because of the influence of the American Colonization Society on the founding of the Domestic and Foreign Missionary Society, Liberia had been a prospective foreign mission of the Episcopal Church since 1820. In 1822, Ephraim Bacon, who had previously visited Liberia as an agent of the Colonization Society, offered himself as a missionary to the fledgling Domestic and Foreign Missionary Society. Bacon and his wife were then appointed the first missionaries of the Missionary Society, six years before the Robertsons and Hills sailed for Greece. Upon their appointment, the Bacons traveled around the Episcopal Church raising funds for the founding of a school in Liberia. Bacon's departure as one of the agents of the American Colonization Society, however, resulted in poor relations between the church and the Colonization Society. As a result the Bacons lost favor with the Colonization Society and were prohibited from working in West Africa. The establishment of a mission in Liberia was delayed for twelve years.[75]

The Foreign Committee of the Missionary Society never lost interest in Liberia. A school to train African missionaries, established by the Episcopal Church, existed briefly in Hartford, Connecticut. In 1827 a graduate of the school, Jacob Olsen of New Haven, was appointed a missionary to Liberia but died before he could depart.[76] The first Episcopal missionary to work in West Africa waited until 1835 when the Domestic and Foreign Missionary Society appointed James S. Thompson. Thompson was an African-American who had moved to Liberia as a colonist. Originally born in Demarara, South America, he took up residence in Monrovia. In Monrovia Thompson was active as a lay leader and teacher in a fledgling Episcopal church and its school. In 1835 the D&FMS appointed Thompson as a missionary to oversee the work of the school and assist with the pastoral needs of the congregation.[77] Thus the first Episcopal missionary in Africa was an African-American lay teacher — not a white cleric from the United States.

The year after the sweeping changes of the General Convention of 1835, four more Episcopalian missionaries were sent to join Thompson — the Rev. Thomas Savage, a priest and physician, the Rev. and Mrs. Thomas Payne, and the Rev. Lancelot B. Minor.[78] Black and white, lay and ordained, male and female, these early church workers sought to forge one Episcopal Church out of the diverse group of American missionaries, Americo-Liberians and indigenous Africans.

By the middle of the nineteenth century, Episcopal mission work in West Africa centered on Cape Palmas on the southern shore of Liberia. As the work around Cape Palmas grew in the early 1840s, the Foreign Committee of the Missionary Society took steps to elevate the mission to the level of missionary district with its own bishop. At the General Convention of 1844 the missionary district of Cape Palmas and Parts Adjacent was established and the Rev. Alexander Glennie of South Carolina was elected bishop. Glennie declined the election and the new missionary district was left without episcopal direction for the next seven years[79]

With the establishment of the independent republic of Liberia in 1847, interest in the West African mission grew and increased attention was given to the mission in *The Spirit of Missions*. The General Convention of 1850 again tried to appoint a missionary bishop for Liberia and elected John Payne as "Bishop of Cape Palmas and Parts Adjacent."[80] Having served as a missionary in Liberia for fifteen years prior to his election as bishop, Payne seemed better qualified to serve as bishop in West Africa than the earlier elected Glennie. Consecrated in the United States, Payne returned to Liberia in 1851 as the first bishop of the missionary district of Cape Palmas and Parts Adjacent. In 1852 Payne's jurisdiction was extended to Monrovia, and the following year the General Convention further broadened the missionary district of Cape Palmas and Parts Adjacent to include "the whole territory on the Coast of Western Africa not at present occupied by any colonial Bishop of the Church of England."[81] At that time the missionary district was comprised of fourteen stations, 240 communicants and at least fifteen schools.[82]

Payne's episcopate was hindered by serious administrative problems and the bishop's own ill health. There were some advances, however, and upon his retirement in 1871 the missionary district had grown to twenty-two mission stations, nine organized churches and two schools for training boys and young men.[83] For the next two decades the mission in Liberia would suffer from lack of episcopal oversight. John G. Auer, a fellow missionary, followed Payne as bishop but his episcopate lasted only ten months. No other bishop was appointed until 1877 when Bishop Charles C. Penwick was sent from the United States. Upon his arrival in Liberia he lamented the loss of significant advances in education and mission stations since Payne's retirement.

"The work here," he explained, "has been so long without any head that the disorder is very great . . . no educational system, not the first move toward self-support."[84]

Penwick served for five years as bishop of Cape Palmas and Parts Adjacent until ill-heath forced him to retire in 1883. The missionary district was left without a bishop for a period of two years.

In 1884, the House of Bishops of the Episcopal Church elected the African-American missionary to Liberia, the Rev. Samuel D. Ferguson, bishop of Cape Palmas and Parts Adjacent. Bishop Ferguson was the second bishop of African heritage to be elevated to the episcopate by the House of Bishops of the Episcopal Church but the first to serve in one of the church's jurisdictions.[85] At the time of his consecration he had been a missionary in West Africa for almost two decades. Ferguson would serve as missionary bishop for thirty-one years from 1885 until 1916. During his episcopate the number of clergy in Liberia would increase from six to twenty-three and the number of communicants from 435 to 2,400. He was responsible also for the founding of one of the foremost educational institutions in Liberia — Cuttington College.[86] As bishop for thirty-one years, Ferguson provided the continuity of episcopal leadership Liberia needed so desperately. Years later Ferguson would be considered the true father of the Episcopal Church in Liberia.

The jewel in the crown of Episcopal foreign missions in the nineteenth century was China. More missionaries and more money would be sent to China than to any other foreign missionary jurisdiction of the Episcopal Church. By the year 1900, the estimated value of the mission property held by the Episcopal Church in China was over $275,000, as compared to $230,000 in Japan and only $62,000 in Liberia.[87] The fact that China was the foremost foreign mission of the Episcopal Church in the 1800s is consistent with other American Protestant churches that looked to the ancient empire as a fertile field for advancing the church.

Like the Episcopal mission to West Africa, the China mission of the Episcopal Church began in 1835. Seven weeks before the General Convention met to consider anew the missionary call of the Episcopal Church, the Rev. Henry Lockwood and the Rev. Francis Hanson sailed from New York to Canton.[88] Lockwood had just graduated from the General Seminary, and all of the students of General accompanied the two men to the pier in New York when they sailed for China.[89] The vision for the General Seminary as a training school for missionaries, first articulated in 1822, was beginning to be realized. Hanson, however, was a recent graduate of the Protestant Episcopal Theological Seminary in Virginia. It was the Virginia Theological Seminary, and not General, that would provide the majority of missionaries for China and other foreign fields for the Episcopal Church in the nineteenth century.

Hanson and Lockwood set out for China with high hopes. Arriving in Canton they found China closed to foreigners and so sailed to Batavia (Jakarta) for language study among the many Chinese living in Java. The tropical climate proved to be too much for the two young missionaries. Illness forced Hanson to return to the United States in 1838 and Lockwood followed his companion a year later.[90]

Before leaving Java, Hanson and Lockwood were joined by the Rev. William J. Boone and his wife in 1837. Boone was a graduate of the Virginia Seminary and was also trained as a medical doctor. After five years of patient waiting and language study, the Boones entered the district of Amoy in 1842. They were the first American Episcopalian missionaries on Chinese soil.[91] Two years later Mrs. Boone died and William Boone returned to the United States to place his children in school[92] Boone, however, never lost his commitment to the China Mission. In the United States he worked tirelessly to promote the work in China.

At this time Episcopalians committed to foreign missions began to raise the idea of a missionary episcopate for foreign parts. The success of Kemper and Polk as missionary bishops to the American West was noted. Editorials in *The Spirit of Missions* argued:

Why practically do we work as Presbyterians abroad and as Episcopalians at home? Is it more consistent that the very first missionary to any [foreign] country should be himself a Bishop.[93]

At the General Convention of 1844 the Episcopal Church endorsed the idea of foreign missionary bishops and elected William J. Boone, bishop of Amoy and Other Parts of China. As the first foreign missionary bishop of the Episcopal Church, Boone was charged with planting the church in China under the direction of the historic episcopate.[94] And so the unique vision of Episcopal foreign missions as both catholic and protestant was galvanized. The belief that Episcopal foreign missions embodied the best of reformed theology and catholic tradition was summed up in the sermon preached at Boone's consecration by Bishop Elliott of Georgia.

> As the Lord opens the world before us...let us strive and pray that we may be permitted to guard with jealousy His Holy Ark, and present her ever to the world, under an unchangeable aspect — Catholic for every truth of God — Protestant against every error of man.[95]

In 1842 China was forced open by the British victory over the Chinese, and the Treaty of Nanking allowed for missionary work. In 1844 Boone returned to China accompanied by eight new missionary colleagues. This band was charged by the House of Bishops to build up the church through education and an indigenous priesthood.

> So vast is the population of the empire, so great the difficulty of the language, so small the number of missionaries and teachers that we can send out from this country, and so heavy the expense of mantainment that there is an imperative necessity for taking immediate steps for rearing a band of Christian teachers; a body of able translators, and above all, an efficient ministry.[96]

The priority on education and training of Chinese clergy would be the backbone of the Episcopal mission throughout the nineteenth century. For two decades Boone struggled to build up schools and plant churches in China.

When Boone died in 1864, the mission to China was entering a low point. The American Civil War had cut the flow of funds from the United States. Schools closed and all but two missionaries returned to the United States.[97] For the next twelve years episcopal oversight of the mission would be provided by Bishop Channing Moore Williams who split his time between the mission in Japan and China. The China mission would not have its own bishop again until 1877 when Samuel I. J. Schereschewsky, one of the two missionaries left in China after Boone's death, was consecrated bishop of Shanghai.

Samuel Isaac Joseph Schereschewsky is perhaps the best known and most celebrated Episcopal foreign missionary. Schereschewsky was born in Lithuania and raised as an Orthodox Jew. As a young Jewish scholar Schereschewsky read a Hebrew translation of the New Testament and came to the conclusion that Jesus was the Messiah spoken of by the prophets. Schereschewsky immigrated to the United States in 1854 and was baptized in a Baptist church in New York the same year.[98] While attending General Theological Seminary to study scripture, Schereschewsky became an Episcopalian and graduated in 1858. The following year he sailed for China as a missionary of the Episcopal Church.

Previous to his consecration to the episcopate, Schereschewsky dedicated his life to the translation of the Bible into Chinese. In 1872 he helped to publish a Mandarin translation of the New Testament and two years later he completed the Old Testament in the same language.[99] The American Bible Society paid for the majority of Schereschewsky's translation work although technically he was a missionary of the Episcopal Church.[100] Schereschewsky's dedication to scholarship and translation continued to play an important role in his life as a bishop. As a bishop he founded St. John's University in Shanghai. Dedicated to both secular and sacred learning, St. John's was to become one of the premier educational institutions in China.

> One of China's first Western-style schools of higher learning, St. John's was directed not only to educate a native priesthood ("the true Apostles of China must be natives," Schereschewsky wrote) but also to teach modern science ("religion and true science go hand in hand.")[101]

In addition to St. John's, Schereschewsky founded St. Mary's School and St. Luke's Hospital in Shanghai, the Boone Memorial School in Wuchang, and expanded the school and hospital in Hankow.[102] After only four years as bishop, Schereschewsky was paralyzed by a stroke in 1881. He remained bishop until 1883 and continued his translation work until his death in 1906. For the last twenty-five years of his life Schereschewsky's ministry was made possible only because of the unfailing support and assistance of his wife Susan.[103]

Schereschewsky's successor was the Right Rev. William J. Boone, son of the first Bishop Boone. William Boone served as bishop from 1884-1891. During his episcopate Episcopal mission work was firmly established in four mission centers, Shanghai, Hankow, Wuchang and Ichang. Following Boone, the Rev. Frederick Rogers Graves was elected missionary bishop of Shanghai in 1893. Bishop Graves would serve as bishop for the next forty five years. Under his leadership the Episcopal mission to China would grow significantly and the missionary district would eventually be divided into three dioceses. His insistence that American Episcopalians and British Anglicans should work together in China resulted in the first conference of Anglican Bishops in China in 1897. This collaboration sought to redress decades of competition between the English and American missions and was the first step toward a union of missionary efforts in the early twentieth century.[104]

As in China, the Episcopal Mission to Japan concentrated on the "civilizing" activities of schools and hospitals rather than direct evangelistic outreach. This occurred for two reasons. First, the earliest Episcopal missionaries to Japan had been missionaries in China and so were well versed in the establishment of health and educational institutions. Second, the Japanese government prohibited any evangelistic attempts to convert the Japanese people until the early 1870s. The first Episcopal missionaries to Japan thus concentrated on education and medical service.

The Episcopal Mission to Japan started much later than those to Liberia and China. The reason for this was that Japan was a country closed to outsiders until Commodore Perry of the United States Navy sailed into Tokyo Bay in 1853 and demanded a trading agreement with the Japanese government. Part of the agreement provided for an American agent to be in residence in Japan. The first agent was Townshend Harris, a devout Episcopalian.[105]

Encouraged by Harris, Episcopalian missionaries stood poised to enter Japan. In July 1859 the United States and Japan entered into a formal trading treaty that allowed foreigners to practice their own religion in Japan. A few weeks after the treaty went into effect, three Episcopal missionaries, a physician by the name of Schmidt and two priests, Channing Moore Williams and John Liggins, were transferred to Japan from China. These three Episcopalian missionaries were the first Protestant missionaries ever to step foot on Japanese soil. This fact is stated proudly by Episcopalians who remember Williams and Liggins.

> *The Christianity in Japan today goes back to these two men,* the first Protestant missionaries ever to land in Japan, the first founders of all modern Japanese Christianity of any sort. Their immediate followers were Presbyterians and Dutch Reformed. (Italics in original)[106]

It must be emphasized, however, that Episcopalians were the first Protestant missionaries to Japan because the church was closely aligned with the mercantile class and trading interests of the United States.

Because of the prohibition on evangelistic activities, Williams, Liggins and Schmidt concentrated on the study of Japanese language and culture and the offering of medical and educational services. By 1862 Williams was the only person left in the Japanese mission. Liggins returned home because of illness and Schmidt was forced back to the United States when his funding diminished during the American Civil War.[107] Since the edict prohibiting direct evangelization remained in effect, Williams concentrated his efforts on the publication of Christian literature. He worked unfailingly as the only Episcopal missionary in Japan. In 1866 Williams was elected bishop of both China and Japan by the House of Bishops of the General Convention. Once again the Episcopal Church emphasized the primacy of the missionary episcopate by elevating the first, and in this case the only, missionary in the field to the office of bishop. For the next twelve years Williams served as bishop of both China and Japan, spending one quarter of his time in China. When Schereschewsky was elected bishop of Shanghai in 1874, Williams was free to concentrate all of his efforts on Japan. At that time the name of Williams's see was changed to the Missionary District of Yedo (Tokyo).[108]

In 1871 the Japanese rulers began to relax the edict that had restricted missionary activities for over two decades. In Tokyo Williams was joined by other Episcopalian missionaries. Believing that the Episcopal Church should concentrate its missionary efforts on the educated class of the samurai, Williams set about establishing mission schools for the samurai. The Japanese people seemed open to Western civilization as it was promulgated through the mission schools.

> Education, therefore, was heavily stressed as a missionary method, and most of the converts were above the average in intelligence and ability. Under these circumstances, early in the 'eighties the attitude of the Japanese toward Western civilization, and toward Christianity as part of that culture, became so favorable that for six or eight years the growth of all the Churches was surprisingly rapid, and there was even talk that Christianity would soon become the state religion.[109]

A divinity school that Williams founded in Tokyo was later to become St. Paul's University, one of the foremost Western-style schools in Japan. In addition to schools for the middle class, Williams, who was concerned about the medical needs of the Japanese, also established St. Luke's Hospital in Tokyo.[110]

The optimism of American Episcopalians about the Japanese mission spilled over into the English Anglican missions in Japan. In their earlier years, the work of the English missionary societies paled in comparison to the American efforts at establishing schools and hospitals. Following the American lead, an English bishop was sent to oversee the British missions in 1887. In the same year, at Williams's urging, the American and British missions came together in a synod. What resulted from this meeting was the first steps toward an autonomous Anglican church in Japan, the *Nippon Sei Ko Kai* or the Holy Catholic Church of Japan.[111] Using the recently adopted Chicago-Lambeth Quadrilateral and the Thirty-nine Articles of Religion, in addition to the Anglican Prayer Book, the *Nippon Sei Ko Kai* sought to be a fully independent Anglican Church in Japan.[112] The independence, however, was illusory since the dioceses of the *Nippon Sei Ko Kai* were still missionary districts of the Episcopal Church and the Church of England. Thus Episcopal oversight and financial support for the new church remained in Western hands.

Two years after the founding of the *Nippon Sei Ko Kai*, Bishop Williams resigned from the episcopacy and returned to parish work in Kyoto. Williams believed that a younger man was needed to fulfill adequately the responsibilities of a bishop.[113] In 1893 John McKim was elected missionary bishop. At the same time the name of the missionary district was changed from Yedo to Tokyo.[114] The following year the synod of the *Nippon Sei Ko Kai* divided the church into six dioceses. For the remainder of the nineteenth century, the American Episcopal Church, under the episcopal oversight of Bishop McKim, controlled the two largest dioceses of the Japanese Church, Tokyo and Kyoto.

The American Church Missionary Society and Beyond

As described above, the most significant foreign mission fields of the Episcopal Church in the nineteenth century were Liberia, China and Japan. Other fields, such as the early mission to Greece and its stepchild in Constantinople, held sporadic interest for Episcopalians. Not all overseas mission work of the Episcopal Church was under the auspices of the Domestic and Foreign Missionary Society. In the last half of the nineteenth century, the American Church Missionary Society played an important role in developing new Episcopal missions outside of the United States.

Like the Episcopalian mission to Greece, the Constantinople mission of the Episcopal Church was initiated by and dependent upon the efforts of one individual, Horatio Southgate. Raised a New England Congregationalist, Southgate entered Andover Seminary in 1832.[115] At Andover, Southgate was exposed to the foreign mission work of the Congregationalists and the ABCFM. Two years into his seminary studies Southgate became an Episcopalian and was confirmed by Bishop Griswold in 1834. Griswold's enthusiasm for mission work combined with Southgate's experiences at Andover motivated the new Episcopalian to become a foreign missionary.

Following the lead of the ABCFM and its work in the Middle East, Southgate set off for Turkey and Persia in 1836. For the next two and a half years Southgate traveled throughout Turkey and Persia surveying the missionary opportunities among both the Muslims and the ancient Christian churches such as the Nestorians and Jacobites. Southgate was impressed by the mission activities of the ABCFM among Armenian Christians. As a convert to Anglicanism, however, Southgate mourned the fact that American missions to the ancient Christians lacked the historic episcopate. Returning to the United States in 1838, Southgate argued for a mission to Turkey and Persia before the Foreign Committee of the Domestic and Foreign Missionary Society.

> As yet in these Missions no use has been made of the Episcopal principle. By this neglect the Episcopal Church has failed to employ the chief advantage which Providence has put into our hands. It is the only plan upon which Missions from the Church of England or of America to the Churches of the East can be formed.[116]

It is clear that Southgate believed that the Western churches, and in particular the Episcopal Church, were the true repository of authentic catholic Christianity. His mission was to bring the historic episcopate, realized in the Anglican tradition, to the Eastern churches.

In 1840, the Domestic and Foreign Missionary Society of the Episcopal Church appointed Southgate missionary to Turkey, and he was sent to join the Rev. John J. Robertson in Constantinople. Crowded by the growth of British missionary work in Greece, Robertson had left his original mission in Greece the year before. For three years Robertson and Southgate labored side by side to build an Episcopal Church among the Muslims and ancient Christians. Their efforts were met with little success and both returned to the United States in 1843.

Southgate, however, would not give up his dream of a Western Episcopate for Eastern Christians. His timing could not have been better, for the Episcopal Church was moving forward with the idea of foreign missionary bishops. Just after Boone was raised to the episcopate in China, the General Convention of 1844 elected

Southgate bishop of the Dominions and Dependencies of the Sultan of Turkey. For the next five years Bishop Southgate worked to establish the Episcopal Church in Constantinople. Unfortunately Southgate's mission was misunderstood both in Turkey and in the United States.[117] In his churchmanship, Southgate was a high-church anglo-catholic. As the foreign mission work of the Episcopal Church increasingly became the domain of low-church evangelicals, the support for Southgate's mission declined.[118] Having met with little success in Constantinople, Southgate resigned in 1850 and returned to the United States to become rector of the Church of the Advent in Boston, a bastion of the anglo-catholic movement in the Episcopal Church.[119] Since the Constantinople mission had always been dependent on the efforts of one man and not the Episcopal Church at large, the mission was closed permanently when Southgate returned to the United States.

The pro-catholic Oxford Movement that swept through England in the 1830s and 1840s had a significant effect on the Episcopal Church in the United States. The tracts published by the Oxford theologians, Keble, Newman, Pusey, and Froude, struck a favorable chord among high-church American Episcopalians. Increasingly a gulf opened between the high-church catholics and the low-church evangelicals in the Episcopal Church.

The Domestic and Foreign Missionary Society was not immune to the tensions between catholic and evangelical Episcopalians. Increasingly a *de facto* separation between the domestic and foreign mission fields occurred. The high-church party controlled the Domestic Committee while low-church Episcopalians controlled the Foreign Committee. In an attempt to curtail the high-church monopoly on domestic mission activities, a group of evangelicals meeting in Philadelphia in 1851 organized the Missionary Society for the West. The Missionary Society for the West tried to work within the existing structures of the larger Missionary Society and was originally conceived of as an auxiliary to the Domestic Committee of the Domestic and Foreign Missionary Society. The goal of the Missionary Society for the West was to raise funds for the support of domestic missionaries who were representative of the low-church evangelical position. When tensions between high- and low-church Episcopalians intensified, the role of the Missionary Society for the West as an auxiliary to the Domestic Committee became increasingly unworkable. By the end of the 1850s it had become clear that a more radical measure was needed to increase the evangelical position in domestic missions.[120]

Under the leadership of Herman Dyer, evangelicals in the Episcopal Church founded the American Church Missionary Society in 1859. Dyer was a committed low-church evangelical who had been a professor at Kenyan College in Gambier, Ohio, in the 1830s and 1840s. Living in Philadelphia in the 1850s, Dyer became corresponding secretary and general agent of the Protestant Episcopal Society for the Promotion of Evangelical Knowledge and served on the Foreign Committee of the Domestic and Foreign Missionary Society.[121] As the name implies, the Society for the Promotion of Evangelical Knowledge "had been formed to 'counteract through its publications, the evil tendencies' of the Oxford Movement, and 'to maintain the principles of the Protestant Episcopal Church.'"[122] In 1859 Dyer and his associates founded the American Church Missionary Society (ACMS) as a voluntary missionary society similar to the evangelical Church Missionary Society in the Church of England. Dyer was appointed its first secretary and the ACMS began to send out domestic and foreign missionaries who would champion the low-church position of evangelical Episcopalians.

For the next two decades the American Church Missionary Society worked as an independent Episcopal missionary society, often in conflict with the official program and policies of the Domestic and Foreign Missionary Society.

> The American Church Missionary Society was a rival, rather than a helper, to both [the Domestic and Foreign] Committees, and its aggressive methods were not altogether pleasing, as it would press work it had assumed upon the one Committee, or intrude, not altogether considerately, upon the field of the other.[123]

As the tensions between high-church and low-church Episcopalians began to subside in the 1870s, so also did the animosities between the ACMS and the Domestic and Foreign

Missionary Society. In 1871 the American Church Missionary Society accepted an offer to work more closely with the D&FMS. At first, the ACMS insisted on retaining its own organization, charter and appropriation of funds. It promised to work only in those missions that were mutually agreed upon with the Domestic and Foreign Missionary Society.[124] As time went on, the constituency of the American Church Missionary Society dwindled. The ACMS finally relinquished its independent status and became an auxiliary of the Domestic and Foreign Missionary Society in 1877. [125]

The major foreign missions of the American Church Missionary Society, both as an independent organization and as an auxiliary of the Domestic and Foreign Missionary Society, were in Latin America and the Caribbean. The ACMS briefly supported Episcopal mission work in Mexico and Haiti, but the two largest foreign fields of the American Church Missionary Society were Brazil and Cuba.

The first, and preeminent, foreign field of the American Church Missionary Society was Brazil. The mission to Brazil was opened in 1859 shortly after the founding of the ACMS. At first, the Brazilian mission suffered from inadequate funding and the mission was temporarily closed in 1864. In the late 1880s, a committed group of evangelical seminarians from the Virginia Seminary turned their attention, once again, to Brazil. Two students in particular, James Morris and Lucien L. Kinsolving, offered themselves for the Brazilian Mission. When they learned that the Domestic and Foreign Missionary Society would not support them and their plans for Brazil, they turned to the American Church Missionary Society.[126] In 1889 Kinsolving, Morris and their wives landed in southern Brazil and began their work at Porto Alegre. This second wave of Episcopal missionaries was responsible for planting the Episcopal Church in Brazil. With the assistance of the ACMS, other earnest evangelicals, mainly from the Virginia Seminary, followed Kinsolving and Morris to Brazil.

The mission strategy of these evangelical Episcopalians did not differ greatly from their brothers and sisters working in Liberia, China and Japan. The raising up of indigenous educated church leaders through church-sponsored schools was the primary method of outreach.

From the outset [Kinsolving and colleagues] have had three main points in their policy: (1) To build up a native-controlled and self-supporting Church; (2) to convert and train a native ministry; (3) to provide, and try to excite others to provide, Christian schools.[127]

It is important to note, however, that as low-church evangelicals, the Brazilian ACMS missionaries did not give a high priority to the missionary episcopate. If anything, their goal was to counter the "popish" tendencies of the Roman Catholic Church already well established in Brazil. It was not until 1899, when the primary responsibility for the Brazilian mission moved from the hands of the ACMS to the Domestic and Foreign Missionary Society, that Lucien Kinsolving was elected bishop of Southern Brazil.

The work of the American Church Missionary Society in Cuba was not as extensive as that in Brazil. The first Episcopal missionary in Cuba was the Rev. Edward Kenny, who in 1871 held services primarily for English and American residents. Working in conjunction with the Domestic and Foreign Missionary Society in the 1880s, the ACMS supported three mission stations and held services in a storehouse in Havana. The ACMS was assisted in Cuba by the Female Bible Society and the Ladies Cuban Guild, both of Philadelphia. The women of these independent missionary organizations worked closely with the American Church Missionary Society in the distribution of Bibles and the support of an ACMS agent in Cuba.[128] The mission work in Cuba was hampered, however, by the opposition of the Roman Catholic Church. It was not until after the Spanish-American War, when Cuba became a territory of the United States, that Episcopal mission work on the island became firmly established. As was the case with Brazil, the work of the ACMS in Cuba would be assumed by the D&FMS in the twentieth century.

The Woman's Auxiliary

Episcopal women played a primary role in the missionary outreach of the Episcopal Church. Because of the male bias of most historiography, the unique contribution of Episcopal women to foreign and domestic missions is often overlooked.[129] Throughout the nineteenth century Episcopal women organized, promoted and funded much of the missionary outreach of the Episcopal Church. The voluntary affiliation of Episcopal women in the work of the Domestic and Foreign Missionary Society was often the single most important source of support for the official missionary society of the church. The energetic and voluntary association of women with Episcopal missionary activities often stood in contrast to the lackluster contribution of the church at large. Without the organizing efforts of Episcopal women the catholic ideal of grass-roots participation in the church's missionary work would never have been realized.

Women Episcopalians were involved in the missionary outreach of the Episcopal Church from the very beginning. When the Domestic and Foreign Missionary Society called for local auxiliaries to support its work, women were quick to respond. In 1822 eight of the eleven auxiliaries initially instituted to augment the work of the missionary society were organized by women. These eight "female" auxiliaries were the predecessors to the Woman's Auxiliary to the Board of Missions.[130] In addition to providing support through the auxiliaries, women were well represented in the domestic and foreign missions. At first most Episcopal women missionaries were supported as the spouses of male missionaries. Too often though, the crucial role of the missionary wife is forgotten or considered "auxiliary" to that of her husband. History books overlook the fact that women's contributions to the missionary endeavors of the church were every bit as important as those of their husbands'. The names of these women missionaries are thus forgotten and they are relegated to the faceless position of the "missionary wife." For example, two of the first foreign missionaries of the Episcopal Church sent to Greece were women. Most history books, however, list them simply as the "wives" of the Revs. John J. Robertson and John J. Hill. Research has shown that these two women played a central role in the development of the Greek mission of the Episcopal Church. Frances Maria Hill was a leader in the church's educational work. She taught the young women of Greece for over half a century from 1830 until her death in 1884. In addition, Hill's commitment to women's education caught the attention of Emma Willard, founder of the Troy Female Seminary, one of the first schools in the United States with a scholarly curriculum for women. Willard supported Hill in her work by founding at Troy the Society for the Advancement of Female Education in Greece, one of the first independent missionary societies associated with Episcopal foreign missions.[131]

Frances Maria Hill exemplifies the role of the "missionary wife" in the nineteenth century. As a woman, she was excluded from the clerically centered evangelism of the Episcopal Church. Turning to education, Hill pursued a more secular, or civilizing, approach to missionary outreach. Like many of the female Episcopalian teachers and nurses who followed her, Hill maintained close communication with her friends and acquaintances in the United States. The strong connection between the female missionary and her "sisters back home" resulted in Episcopal women becoming significant promoters of missionary activities in the Episcopal Church.

By the middle of the nineteenth century, the Episcopal Church increasingly looked to the women of the church to support its missionary endeavors. In 1850 Bishop Horatio Potter of New York, realizing that the parishes had failed to stimulate the missionary giving anticipated in 1835, suggested that the women of the church be organized to effect support of missionaries. By 1868 the Board of the Domestic and Foreign Missionary Society acknowledged that women's support for domestic missions was critical and so helped to organize the Ladies Domestic Missionary Relief Association.[132] The association was founded to systematize and promote the sending of supply boxes to individual missionaries and their families in the domestic missions.[133] Eventually the supply box program would grow to become one of the most significant and important mission support activities in both the domestic and foreign fields. These supply boxes provided needed resources to the missionaries and linked individual parishes and women's associations to flesh and blood missionaries in the field.

The connection between missionaries and the women back home, through the supply boxes and written communications, provided a tangible link in the sometimes faceless program of the Missionary Society.

The General Convention of 1871 took two important steps in the hope of strengthening the work of the Domestic and Foreign Missionary Society. The first was the invitation to the American Church Missionary Society to become an auxiliary to the Board of Missions of the D&FMS. Since the animosities between high- and low-church factions in the church had waned, this move was intended to heal the division between Episcopalians as well as to provide increased resources for the official Missionary Society. The second step was the authorization of a second auxiliary, the Woman's Auxiliary to the Board of Missions. Originally conceived, the Woman's Auxiliary was to be an outgrowth of the Ladies Domestic Missionary Relief Association. But when the association declined to enlarge its scope, the secretaries of the Missionary Society independently undertook to establish the Woman's Auxiliary. In 1872 officials of the Missionary Society rented an additional room at headquarters for the new Auxiliary, added a "women's work" section in *The Spirit of Missions*, and called Mary Abbot Emery of Dorchester, Massachusetts, to be its first secretary.[134]

Mary Abbot Emery served as the national secretary of the new Woman's Auxiliary from 1872 until 1876. Although she served only four years, her great administrative skill helped to establish the Woman's Auxiliary as one of the most important national organizations in the Episcopal Church. Because Mary Emery took office at the request of the General Convention, and not in response to a grass-roots movement of women in the Episcopal Church, her first task was to gain the confidence of the women of the church. She immediately set about gathering the existing women's groups in the Episcopal Church under the umbrella of the Woman's Auxiliary. The genius of Emery's administrative skills was that she could combine an effective national organization with locally administered and independently controlled associations. Emery asked the rector of every Episcopal church to appoint a secretary who would correspond with the national secretary about the work of the women in each parish. Women in parishes were free to organize in any way they chose as long as they maintained a common association with the larger Woman's Auxiliary. Emery was very successful with this plan and eventually the majority of missionary associations of Episcopal women chose to affiliate with the Woman's Auxiliary. Perhaps the crowning achievement of Emery's organizational efforts was the decision in 1874 of the Ladies Domestic Missionary Relief Association to discontinue its independent organization and to work through the auxiliary. During Emery's short administration more than 350 local secretaries were appointed and diocesan groups formed in nine dioceses.[135] Mary Abbot Emery had managed to organize the women of the Episcopal Church under a national organization that was associated with the church's official Missionary Society rather than independent from it.

Under Mary Emery's leadership the Woman's Auxiliary became an important source of support for the missionary activities of the Episcopal Church. In 1875 Emery centralized and enlarged the distribution of missionary supply boxes. She established in the Auxiliary's offices a central clearinghouse to which missionaries could send their list of needed articles. These lists would then be sent to local parish women's associations who would pack and send the supply boxes to the missionary. In this way Emery maintained oversight of the supply box program, yet did not undermine the connection of the local parish with the missionary. The supply box program continued to grow throughout the nineteenth century from $61,000 in 1875, to $127,000 in 1885 and $191,000 in 1900.[136] In addition to the supply box program, the Woman's Auxiliary paid for fringe benefits for mission clergy. These fringe benefits included a life insurance fund for foreign missionaries, scholarships for missionary children attending boarding schools and colleges, and benefits for missionary widows. On the domestic front, the Woman's Auxiliary helped to fund secondary schools for women established by the Episcopal Church in every major city in the western United States.[137]

In 1876 Mary Abbot Emery resigned as national secretary of the Woman's Auxiliary to marry the Rev. A. T. Twing, who was domestic secretary of the Missionary Society. Six years later Twing died leaving Mary Twing a young widow. Because she wanted to return to the missionary work of the women of the Episcopal Church, the position of honorary secretary of the Woman's Auxiliary was created for her in 1882. For the next two decades Twing traveled widely, promoting women's involvement in the missionary work of the Episcopal Church. While attending the General Convention in San Francisco in 1901, she died suddenly. The whole representative body of the Episcopal Church then assembled to pay tribute to Mary Emery Twing's life and ministry.[138]

It would seem that the position of the honorary secretary would be in competition with the previously established national secretary of the Woman's Auxiliary. Under ordinary circumstances this might have been true, except that the successor to Mary Emery in the position of national secretary was her younger sister, Julia Chester Emery. These two sisters worked side by side to build up the involvement of women in the missionary outreach of the Episcopal Church. Eventually Mary and Julia were joined in work by two other sisters, Susan Lavinia Emery and Margaret Theresa Emery. No other family contributed so much to the Woman's Auxiliary and the missionary work of the Episcopal Church as the Emerys.[139]

Julia Chester Emery proved to be a perfect complement to the highly organized, more assertive Mary. Less charismatic than her sister, Julia appeared to be quiet, soft-spoken and gentle in her manner. Julia, however, had a determined spirit and was completely dedicated to the women of the Episcopal Church.[140] She was just the person to carry forward the work begun by Mary Emery Twing. Julia Chester Emery was only twenty-four years old when she became the national secretary of the Woman's Auxiliary. Her youthful energy would sustain her in this position for over forty years.

"Miss Emery," as Julia Chester Emery came to be known, nurtured a connectedness between the women of the Episcopal

Church. She helped Episcopal women to feel included in, and a part of, the wider mission activities of the Episcopal Church. By earnest prayer and laborious efforts Julia Chester Emery was successful

> in awakening an interest among women who knew no work beyond their homes, and who were timid and cautious, and could only spread the knowledge of the Church's missionary work by telling their personal friends. It was through this same "personal touch" that Miss Emery herself persuaded others to enter into the ranks of the Auxiliary. When asked once how she trained the workers, she replied, "I do not try to train them, I love them."... She loved first of all her Saviour, she loved His Church and His Children, and wanted all to know Him and be members of His Kingdom. No one was ever too small and insignificant nor too great and conspicuous but could find a place in her loving heart.[141]

Under the steady and gentle hand of Julia Chester Emery, in consultation with her sister Mary Emery Twing, the role of the Woman's Auxiliary in the funding of Episcopal mission work continued to grow. By 1882 the Episcopal Church was supporting twenty-nine missionary bishops — seven foreign and twenty-two domestic. Often strapped for funds to pay for the many mission institutions, missionary bishops increasingly looked to the Woman's Auxiliary for financial support. In addition it was significantly easier for the bishops to appeal directly to the women than to go through the Domestic and Foreign Committees of the Missionary Society.[142] And the women of the Episcopal Church responded generously. Through direct contributions called "specials," the Woman's Auxiliary became a primary funder for the work of the missionary bishops. The secretaries of the Missionary Society were threatened by the lack of control over the women's financial matters and the "specials" became a source of contention. In 1886, the Rev. William S. Langford, General Secretary of the D&FMS, attempted to rein in the Woman's Auxiliary by placing its finances directly under the control of the Board of Missions. Julia Emery and Mary Twing countered this scheme with a detailed plan to increase the giving of the women to both the Missionary Society as well as to the "specials." Pleased with the new proposal, the Board of Missions enthusiastically endorsed this plan of the Woman's Auxiliary that allowed the women of the church to conduct their own affairs.[143]

Beginning in 1874, diocesan representatives of the Woman's Auxiliary came together for General Annual Meetings. These gatherings were both educational and consultative. The meetings included time for prayer for missions as well as presentations by missionaries and secretaries of the D&FMS. In 1877, the General Convention reorganized the Board of Missions of the Missionary Society and made its meetings triennial, to coincide with the convention's own schedule. The Woman's Auxiliary followed suit.[144] When the women assembled at the General Convention, in what would come to be known as the Triennial Meeting, offerings were collected to support missionary activities.

At the 1889 Triennial Meeting in New York, the Woman's Auxiliary expanded this donation and instituted the United Offering for support of specific mission projects and individual missionaries. The myth of the founding of the United Offering gives credit to Mrs. Ida Soule of Pittsburgh as its originator. According to the popular story, Soule challenged the hearts, minds and purses of the women to contribute directly to building a mission church in Anvik, Alaska, and to support a woman missionary teacher in Japan. The women responded generously, and the first United Offering amounted to $2,188.64. Mary Donovan has shown, however, that the plan to develop a United Offering was much more than a spirt-filled challenge by a devout and committed laywoman. Soule had been a long-time acquaintance of the Emerys and had grown up in Boston. Julia Emery had arranged for Soule's hotel accommodations at the meeting to be next door to her and her sister Mary. In all probability, Julia Emery was the genius behind the first United Offering. She knew that the Woman's Auxiliary, which had recently been endorsed by the Board of Missions in 1886, had to show growth and new vitality. And so working behind the scenes in conjunction with Soule and Twing, Emery struck upon the idea of a United Offering for support of specific missionary projects.[145] The United Offering became known eventually as the United Thank Offering (UTO) to be given by the women of the Episcopal Church in thanksgiving for the many blessings of this life. In time the UTO became the single most important extra-budgetary source for funding of specific missionary projects, growing from just over $2,000 in 1889 to $107,027.83 by the end of the century.[146]

The other significant event of the General Convention of 1889 was the acceptance of a canon allowing for the order of deaconesses in the Episcopal Church. Mary Twing was the primary promoter of deaconesses. She believed strongly that a professional ministerial order was needed to validate and advance women's vocations in the church.[147] The canon approving deaconesses in the Episcopal Church was a significant step in recognizing the important ministries of Episcopal churchwomen.

With the increasing financial support of the United Offering and the institution of a professional ministerial order in the deaconesses, the Woman's Auxiliary began to focus specifically on the support of missionary women. At the Triennial Meeting of 1892, Julia Emery called for specific gifts "devoted to distinctive woman's work; to training and support of women as missionaries, to support of girls at school, to the building of schools for girls, hospitals for women, homes for orphans."[148] Within three years the Woman's Auxiliary had received over 100 applications from women who wanted to serve as missionaries. From these applications the Auxiliary recommended twenty-four women for appointment by the Board of Missions, twelve for general mission work and twelve for nursing. The Board, however, sent out only six women.

Disturbed by the poor response of the officials of the Missionary Society, Emery and the Woman's Auxiliary decided in 1895 to devote the whole United Offering of the next Triennial to the salaries of women missionaries. The women of the Episcopal Church realized that the responsibility for paying for women missionaries rested on them alone. The women responded generously, increasing the United Offering by 47% to $82,743.[149] This United Offering placed forty women workers in training for missions or in the domestic and foreign missions directly, including three in China, two in Japan, one in Cuba and one in Brazil.[150] The women missionaries sponsored by the United Offering were clearly designated United Offering

Missionary Workers. No longer were Episcopal women shut out of the missionary work because of insufficient funds provided by the Board of the official Missionary Society.

As the nineteenth century drew to a close, the Woman's Auxiliary was auxiliary to the Board of Missions in name only. In its direct financial grants to the Domestic and Foreign Missionary Society, missionary supply boxes, "specials" and the United Offering, the Woman's Auxiliary had become a primary source of support for Episcopal missionaries in both the domestic and foreign missions. More important, the Woman's Auxiliary had managed to go beyond the shortcomings of the church's official Missionary Society by involving women at the grass-roots parish level in Episcopal mission work. By the turn of the century Episcopalian women were a potent force in the missionary outreach of the Episcopal Church.[151]

NOTES

[1]Kenneth Scott Latourette, *A History of the Expansion of Christianity* (New York: Harper & Brothers, 1938-1946), vol. iv, *The Great Century 1800-1914*.

[2]Gerald Anderson, "American Protestants in Pursuit of Mission: 1886-1986," *International Bulletin of Missionary Research* 12 (July 1988): 98.

[3]The expression is borrowed from William R. Hutchison's study of American Protestant thought and foreign missions. See: William R. Hutchison, *Errand to the World: American Protestant Thought and Foreign Missions* (Chicago: The University of Chicago Press, 1987).

[4]Charles W. Forman, "A History of Foreign Mission Theory in America," in *American Missions in Bicentennial Perspective*, ed. R. Pierce Beaver (South Pasadena, Calif.: William Carey Library, 1976), 71.

[5]Hutchison, 41.

[6]Forman, 71.

[7]For a full discussion of early missions to Native Americans and universal disinterested benevolence see: Charles Chaney, *The Birth of Missions in America* (South Pasadena, Calif.: William Carey Library, 1976).

[8]Kenneth Scott Latourette, *A History of the Expansion of Christianity* (New York: Harper & Brothers, 1941), vol. iv, *The Great Century 1800-1914*, 80.

[9]Ibid.

[10]Ibid., 81.

[11]Ibid., 84-85.

[12]Hutchison, 45.

[13]Ibid., 65.

[14]Rufus Anderson, "The Theory of Missions to the Heathen," in *To Advance the Gospel: Rufus Anderson*, ed. R. Pierce Beaver (Grand Rapids, Mich.: William B. Eerdmans Publishing Co., 1967), 74-75.

[15]It is interesting to note that Anderson stressed self-propagating churches while Venn argued for self-extending churches. Although subtle, there is an important ecclesiastical difference between these two positions. Venn, the Anglican, had a more catholic vision of one church extending itself to the ends of the earth, whereas the reformed theology of Anderson considered each new church to be wholly separate and independent.
    Today most people associate three-self church movements with the official post-denominational Christian church in China and have all but forgotten Rufus Anderson and Henry Venn.

[16]Hutchison, *Errand*, 89.

[17]Dana L. Robert, "The Legacy of Arthur Tappan Pierson," *International Bulletin of Missionary Research* 8 (July 1984): 122.

[18]Arthur T. Pierson, "The Improvement of the *Review,*" *The Missionary Review of the World* (November 1882): 864. In Robert, 122.

[19]William R. Hutchison, "A Moral Equivalent for Imperialism: Americans and the Promotion of 'Christian' Civilization, 1880-1910," in *Missionary Ideologies in the Imperialist Era: 1880-1920,* ed. Torben Christensen and William R. Hutchison (Struer, Denmark: Aros, 1982), 169.

[20]Ibid., 169-171.

[21]Hutchison, *Errand*, 104.

[22]Forman, 83.

[23]James S. Dennis, *Christian Missions and Social Progress*, vol. 1 (New York: Fleming H. Revell, 1897), 23. In Hutchison, *Errand*, 108.

[24]Hutchison, "Moral Equivalent," 112-113.

[25]Hutchison, *Errand*, 113.

[26]R. Pierce Beaver, *All Loves Excelling: American Protestant Women in World Mission* (Grand Rapids, Mich.: William B. Eerdmans Publishing Co., 1968), 115-143.

[27]Anderson, 102.

[28]Julia C. Emery, *A Century of Endeavor, 1821-1921: A Record of the First Hundred Years of the Domestic and Foreign Missionary Society of the Protestant Episcopal Church in the United States of America* (New York: The Department of Missions, Protestant Episcopal Church in the United States of America, 1921), x.

[29]E. Clowes Chorley, "The Missionary March of the American Episcopal Church, 1789-1935," *Historical Magazine of the Protestant Episcopal Church* 15 (September 1946): 170.

[30]James Thayer Addison, *The Episcopal Church in the United States: 1789-1931* (New York: Scribner, 1951), 65.

[31]Lawrence L. Brown, "Beginnings of Missionary Work in the Episcopal Church," *Historical Magazine of the Protestant Episcopal Church* 40 (September 1971): 337.

[32]Ibid., 338.

[33]The term diocese is used loosely here. The Episcopal Church in the late 1700s saw itself as an organization of states, not dioceses. The word diocese is not used in the General Convention until 1838 when the Episcopal Church in the State of New York was divided into two dioceses. See: Chorley, 183.

[34]Emery, 26.

[35]*Journal of the Proceedings of the Bishops, Clergy and Laity of the Protestant Episcopal Church in the United States of America in a General Convention 1835* (New York: Swords, Stanford and Company, 1835), 122.

[36]Chorley, 180.

[37]Ibid., 183-184.

[38]Ibid.

[39]Emery, 28.

[40]Ibid., 29.

[41]Robert Ernest Holzhammer, "The Formation of the Domestic and Foreign Missionary Society," *Historical Magazine of the Protestant Episcopal Church* 40 (September 1971): 257.

[42]Chorley, 184.

[43]Ibid., 185.

[44]*Journal of the Proceedings of the Bishops, Clergy and Laity of the Protestant Episcopal Church in the United States of America in a General Convention, 1820* (Philadelphia: S. Potter and Co., 1820), 85-86.

[45]William Joseph Barnds, "A Study in the Development of the Office of Presiding Bishop of the American Episcopal Church, 1794-1944," *Historical Magazine of the Protestant Episcopal Church* 27 (December 1958): 257.

[46]*Journal of the General Convention, 1820*, 46.

[47]Ibid., 48.

[48]It was argued at the Convention of 1821 that a general theological seminary would assist greatly with the recruitment and training of prospective missionaries for the Domestic and Foreign Missionary Society. In the Pastoral Letter of 1823, the bishops of the Episcopal Church emphasized this connection between the theological seminary and the Missionary Society.

[49]Holzhammer, 268.

[50]Chorley, 190.

[51]*Journal of the Proceedings of the Bishops, Clergy and Laity of the Protestant Episcopal Church in the United States of America in a General Convention 1829* (New York: T. and J. Swords 1829), 106-107.

[52]Chorley, 192.

[53]Emery, 56.

[54]Robert Ernest Holzhammer, "The Domestic and Foreign Missionary Society: The Period of Expansion and Development," *Historical Magazine of the Protestant Episcopal Church* 40 (December 1971): 383.

[55]Ibid.

[56]As is often the case, Mrs. Robertson's name is not available because of the historiographical bias that stresses the work of the male missionary and overlooks the contributions of the female spouse. See: Mary Sudman Donovan, "Women and Mission: Towards a More Inclusive Historiography," *Historical Magazine of the Protestant Episcopal Church* 53 (December 1984): 297-305.

[57]Theodore Saloutos, "American Missionaries in Greece: 1820-1869," *Church History* 24 (June 1955): 164.

[58]Addison, 131.

[59]Emery, 57.

[60]Addison, 130-131.

[61]"Report of the Standing Committee on the Domestic and Foreign Missionary Society" in *Journal of the Proceedings of the Bishops, Clergy, and Laity of the Protestant Episcopal Church in the United States of America in a General Convention, 1832* (New York: Protestant Episcopal Press, 1832), 60-62.

[62]Ibid.

[63]Holzhammer, (December 1971), 391.

[64] George Washington Doane, No Title, *The Missionary*, periodical of the Diocese of New Jersey, 1 (September 19, 1835, 44): 175. Reported in Chorley, 203.

[65]Chorley, 202.

[66]Walter Herbert Stowe, "A Turning Point — General Convention of 1835," *Historical Magazine of the Protestant Episcopal Church* 4 (September 1935): 176.

[67]The major opponent of this change in the membership of the Missionary Society was Bishop Griswold. Because of his close association with the Church Missionary Society, Bishop Griswold wanted to maintain the principle of a voluntary association like the British societies. See: Chorley, 205.

[68]*Journal of the General Convention 1835*, 131.

[69]DuBose Murphy, "From 'Churches' to Church," *Historical Magazine of the Protestant Episcopal Church* 15 (June 1956): 195.

[70]Stowe, 171.

[71]Frank Sugeno, "The Establishmentarian Ideal and the Mission of the Episcopal Church," *Historical Magazine of the Protestant Episcopal Church* 53 (December 1984): 289.

[72]Robert S. Bosher argues that the early development of the Anglican Communion owes much to the American Episcopal Church and the institution of missionary bishops. See: Robert S. Bosher, "The American Church and the Formation of the Anglican Communion, 1823-1853," The M. Dwight Johnson Memorial Lecture in Church History, 1962 (Evanston, Ill.: Seabury-Western Theological Seminary, 1962).

[73]G. Warfield Hobbs, "The Centennial of the Spirit of Missions," *Historical Magazine of the Protestant Episcopal Church* 4 (December 1935): 300.

[74]Sugeno, 289.

[75]Holzhammer, (September 1971), 269-272.

[76]Nelson R. Burr, *Mission: 1821-1971, An Essay to Commemorate the Sesquicentennial of the Domestic and Foreign Missionary Society of the Episcopal Church in the United States* (Hartford, Conn.: The Church Missions Publishing Company, 1971), 22.

[77]Ibid.

[78]Addison, 148.

[79]Emery, 95-98.

[80]There is some confusion as to the race of John Payne. Burr and Raymond W. Albright in his *History of the Protestant Episcopal Church*, both identify Payne as being a "negro." This is improbable since Payne was a graduate of the Episcopal Seminary in Virginia which did not accept African-Americans in the middle nineteenth century. Also it is a commonly accepted fact that the first African-American bishop in the Episcopal Church was the Right Rev. Samuel D. Ferguson, Bishop of Liberia from 1885-1916.

[81]Emery, 132.

[82]Addison, 149.

[83]Ibid., 239.

[84]Ibid.

[85]James Theodore Holly, an Episcopal priest who had immigrated to Haiti, was the first African-American to be elevated to the episcopate by the American church. He was elected bishop of the Orthodox Apostolic Church of Haiti by the Episcopal House of Bishops and consecrated at Grace Church in New York City on November 8, 1874. At the time, however, the Orthodox Apostolic Church of Haiti was not a jurisdiction of the American Episcopal Church but an autonomous Anglican church started by Holly.

[86]Burr, 23.

[87]Domestic and Foreign Missionary Society of the Protestant Episcopal Church in the United States of America, *Annual Report of the Domestic and Foreign Missionary Society of the Protestant Episcopal Church in the United States of America, 1900* (New York: Church Missions House, 1900), 209-223.

[88]Addison, 134.

[89]Emery, 62.

[90]Burr, 24.

[91]There is some inconsistency in the actual date the Boones arrived in China. A few sources cite 1842 while others 1840. Addison maintains they landed in China in 1842. Addison, 150.

[92]A. C. Zabriskie, "The Seminary's Contribution to Foreign Missions," *The Bulletin of The Protestant Episcopal Theological Seminary in Virginia* 3 (January 1930): 18.

[93] Emery, 92.

[94]At the same convention the Rev. Alexander Glennie of South Carolina was elected missionary bishop of Cape Palmas and Parts Adjacent but declined the election.

[95]Emery, 98.

[96]Addison, 150.

[97]Zabriskie, 19.

[98]Anne E. Allen, "Samuel Isaac Joseph Schereschewsky: Evangelist to the Chinese People," *The Living Church*, 8 October 1989, 12.

[99]Ibid.

[100]Emery, 180.

[101]Allen, 13

[102]Addison, 241.

[103]Mary Sudman Donovan, "Women and Mission: Towards a More Inclusive Historiography," *Historical Magazine of the Protestant Episcopal Church* 53 (December 1984): 299-300.

[104]Addison, 241.

[105]Stephen Neill, *A History of Christian Missions* (New York: Penguin Books, 1964), 324-325.

[106]Zabriskie, 23.

[107]Ibid.

[108]Emery, 438.

[109]Addison, 240.

[110]Burr, 27.

[111]Zabriskie, 24.

[112]Addison, 242.

[113]Zabriskie, 24.

[114]Emery, 438.

[115]Ibid., 89.

[116]Ibid., 90.

[117]Addison, 148.

[118]Emery, 127-130.

[119]Burr, 21.

[120]William W. Manross, *A History of the American Episcopal Church* (New York: Morehouse-Gorham Co., 1950), 262.

[121]Emery, 143-144.

[122]Ibid., 144.

[123]Ibid., 183.

[124]Ibid., 190.

[125]The same General Convention also replaced the Board of Missions of the Domestic and Foreign Missionary Society with a more streamlined and workable Board of Managers.

[126]Zabriskie, 26.

[127]Ibid., 27.

[128]Burr, 35.

[129]In recent years important steps have been taken to address the lack of historical research documenting women's experience in the Episcopal Church. The Episcopal Women's Historical Project and the scholarship of Mary Sudman Donovan are two examples of current efforts to tell the story of Episcopal women.

[130]Emery, 36.

[131]Donovan, "Women and Mission: Towards a More Inclusive Historiography," 297-298.

[132]Margaret M. Sherman, *True to Their Heritage: A Brief History of the Woman's Auxiliary, 1871-1958* (New York: National Council of the Protestant Episcopal Church, 1958), 4.

[133]Emery, 176.

[134]Ibid., 185.

[135]Mary Sudman Donovan, *A Different Call: Women's Ministries in the Episcopal Church, 1850-1920* (Wilton, Conn.: Morehouse-Barlow, 1986), 68-72.

[136]Ibid.

[137]Ibid., 71.

[138]Emery, 245.

[139]Donovan, *A Different Call*, 67.

[140] Ibid., 73.

[141]Margaret A. Tomes, *Julia Chester Emery* (New York: The Woman's Auxiliary to the National Council of the Protestant Episcopal Church, 1924), 27.

[142]Donovan, *A Different Call*, 71.

[143]Emery, 209-212.

[144]Sherman, 8-9.

[145]Donovan, *A Different Call*, 76.

[146]Frances M. Young, *Thankfulness Unites: The History of the United Thank* Offering (Cincinnati: Foward Movement, 1979), 85.

[147]Donovan, *A Different Call*, 76-77.

[148]Julia Emery, "Twenty-first Annual Report of the Woman's Auxiliary to the Board of Missions," Board of Missions, *Proceedings of the Board of Missions of the Domestic and Foreign Missionary Society of the Protestant Episcopal Church in the United States of America*, 1892, 201-202. From Donovan, *A Different Call*, 78.

[149]Donovan, *A Different Call*, 78-80.

[150]Young, 16.

[151]The most comprehensive review of this growth in women's participation in the foreign mission of the Episcopal Church and the development of the United Offering Worker is Mary Donovan, "Women as Foreign Missionaries in the Episcopal Church, 1830-1920," *Anglican and Episcopal History* 62 (March 1992): 16-39.

CHAPTER TWO

THE NATIONAL CHURCH IDEAL

The Growth of Episcopal Foreign Mission 1900 to 1919

The rise of American imperialism and nationalism at the turn of the nineteenth century had a profound effect on American Protestant foreign missions. Evangelization and individual conversions increasingly gave way to humanitarian activities and social regeneration as their primary motives. American popular opinion saw foreign missionaries as ambassadors of Christian democratic ideals. The role of the missionary was to help both the emerging churches and the young nation-states around the world to develop along the lines of Western "Christian" civilization. With the closing of the Western frontier and the addition of the Philippines and Puerto Rico to the territory of the United States following the Spanish-American War, American Protestants turned their full attention to foreign missions. The late 1890s marked the high point of imperialist and nationalist feelings in American missions.[1]

> Not only was the Christian mission linked with national purpose, but the mission to America became subservient to the mission of America, and the nation replaced the church as the new Israel. Clearly the mood at the turn of the century in both church and state was forward-looking in terms of progress and expansion, with a triumphant expectation that this would be "the Christian century."[2]

As American nationalism grew so also did nationalistic tendencies in foreign missions.[3] Conservatives and liberals alike shared an activism that sought to bring the best of the democratic Christian civilization of the United States to the "unenlightened" nations of the world.

Episcopalians found new kinship with their Protestant brothers and sisters in the growing humanitarian and nationalistic direction of American foreign missions. Throughout the nineteenth century Episcopalians had emphasized schools and hospitals in foreign missions. The leading role of the Episcopal Church in the Social Gospel movement of the late 1800s confirmed the church's belief that social service and humanitarian activities were primary to the Episcopal Church's outreach at home and abroad. At the same time the Episcopal Church increasingly saw itself as the purveyor of a "national church" for the United States. Individuals such as William Reed Huntington saw the catholic yet reformed theology of the Episcopal Church as the future for both frontier Protestants and immigrant Roman Catholics.

In the first two decades of the twentieth century the American emphasis on social progress and the Anglican idea of a national church came together in a new and dynamic way in Episcopal mission activities. The merging of the Social Gospel with Anglican establishmentarian tradition gave birth to a national church ideal in the Episcopal Church. In Episcopal foreign mission fields the national church ideal sought to build up national churches that would minister to the social and spiritual needs of the local people while maintaining communion in a universal (catholic) church. The dramatic advance of Episcopal foreign missions from 1900 to 1919 resulted from the Episcopal Church's self-perceived calling to bestow the goodness of American society and the richness of Anglican tradition to the ends of the earth.

AMERICAN PROTESTANT FOREIGN MISSIONS AT THE TURN OF THE CENTURY

The organization that embodied the progress in American Protestant missions at the turn of the century was the Student

Volunteer Movement for Foreign Missions (SVM). The SVM was a student organization that promoted foreign missions and challenged American college students to give themselves to the cause. The SVM was not a missionary-sending agency but instead encouraged young people to volunteer for overseas service through their own denominational boards. The SVM is credited with raising up close to 13,000 volunteers for overseas service between the years 1886 and 1936.[4] In the Student Volunteer Movement the premillennial urge to preach the gospel to the ends of the world, advocated by individuals such as A. T. Pierson, and the liberal emphasis on social missions, celebrated by James S. Dennis, converged.

The origins of the Student Volunteer Movement are found in a conference for leaders of the Young Men's Christian Association, sponsored by Dwight L. Moody, at Northfield, Massachusetts, in 1886. Prominent missionaries and mission advocates such as Arthur T. Pierson addressed the gathering encouraging the young men to consider becoming foreign missionaries.[5] In one of his addresses Pierson presented the cause of foreign missions to the young YMCA leaders and outlined a plan for "the evangelization of the world in this generation." By the end of the conference 100 college men had dedicated their lives to foreign missions and had adopted "the evangelization of the world in this generation" as their watchword. The excitement and interest in foreign missions of the "Mt. Hermon 100" was carried back to college campuses throughout the United States and within two years the Student Volunteer Movement was born.

Among the founders of the Student Volunteer Movement that emerged from the Mt. Hermon 100 were two of the greatest American mission thinkers, John R. Mott and Robert E. Speer. It was Mott and Speer who took the premillennial spirit of the watchword and adapted it to the civilizing emphasis of the more liberal missiology. Mott and Speer were the standard-bearers in foreign missions as American Protestantism marched triumphantly into the twentieth century.

As the first chairman of the Student Volunteer Movement, it was John R. Mott's job to harness the vision of the Mt. Hermon 100 and to organize effectively college students for foreign missions. Because of his superior organizational skills and ability to survey the totality of missionary work, Mott made plausible earlier plans for world evangelization.[6] In his 1905 classic, *The Evangelization of the World in This Generation*, Mott reinterpreted the SVM watchword to the realities of the twentieth century.[7] He argued that "the evangelization of the world in this generation" does not mean all people need to be converted to Christianity in a decade or two. Rather the watchword implies that every person, in his/her own generation, has the opportunity and responsibility to make Christ known throughout the world.[8] By expanding the concept of evangelization beyond the premillennial emphasis on preaching to include mission schools, the distribution of literature and medical work, Mott made the watchword, and foreign missions in general, more accessible to a larger, less premillennial audience.[9]

Robert E. Speer is credited with being the greatest American missiologist after Rufus Anderson.[10] In many ways he was similar to Anderson in that he presented a balanced mission theory that emphasized the need to establish indigenous churches. As the secretary of the Board of Foreign Missions of the Presbyterian Church in the USA from 1891 to 1937, Speer had an important forum in which to formulate and implement his theories on mission.[11] Speer emphasized the need to establish indigenous national churches in the foreign mission fields.

> All of his writings gave much attention to the needs of the national church, its right to organize in its own way, to be the reasonable evangelistic agent in its own land, and to express the faith in its own style without any imitation of the West or domination by foreign missionaries. He was concerned that missionaries not take administrative office in the church or control its financial resources, and was likewise concerned about the fact that the younger churches had not yet produced the independent theology which could be expected of them.[12]

Although Speer emphasized that the primary goal of missions was to plant an indigenous church, he did allow for the imposition of Western cultural norms when the local culture was found to be less than "wholesome and clean."[13] His later writings, especially, indicate a wider acceptance of missionary involvement in social service.[14] Speer was thus unable to escape completely his own social context that held the Western, and especially Anglo-American, civilization as the preeminent Christian culture.

In the first decade of the twentieth century, Protestant foreign missions reached the apex of their popularity in the United States. The victory over Spain in the Spanish-American War added the Philippines and Puerto Rico to the territory of the United States. To spread Western Christian civilization was the justification for the expansion of the United States into foreign lands. President William McKinley, a devout Methodist, defended the annexation of the Philippines along moral and religious lines. He later described his decision to take the Philippines.

> I walked the floor of the White House night after night until midnight; and I am not ashamed to tell you, gentlemen, that I went down on my knees and prayed Almighty God for light and guidance more than one night. And one night late it came to me this way — I don't know how it was but it came:...that there was nothing left for us to do but to take them all, and to educate the Filipinos, and uplift and civilize and Christianize them, and by God's grace do the very best we could by them, as our fellow-men for whom Christ died.[15]

American expansionism saw a blending of religion, economics and politics at the turn of the century. Missionaries, businessmen and politicians focused their energies on the new foreign territories of the United States and often cooperated in their efforts to export American civilization.

> The missionary movement, the increasing concern of business with foreign markets, the political imperialism of American government were not unrelated. A bald and sometimes sordid economic and political imperialism certainly was made more palatable by the fact that Americans could clothe these drives in the altruistic terminology of the missionary who spoke of bringing Christianity and the advantages of western civilization to undeveloped areas.[16]

The cooperative spirit of American Protestant churches with business and government was exhibited at the Ecumenical Missionary Conference of 1900. Over 200,000 people attended the ten-day conference held in New York City in April of 1900. The Ecumenical Missionary Conference was larger than earlier missionary gatherings held in Europe and the United States. The primary role of American missionary organizations in the conference and the location of the gathering in New York City reflected the growing preeminence of American foreign missions over European efforts at the beginning of the twentieth century.[17]

A dominant theme at the Ecumenical Mission Conference was the important role of Protestant foreign missions in the spreading of Western Christian civilization. In the opening address, President William McKinley praised the accomplishments of American missionaries:

> I am glad of the opportunity to offer without stint my tribute of praise and respect to the missionary effort which has wrought such wonderful triumphs for civilization....Wielding the sword of the Spirit, they have conquered ignorance and prejudice. They have been among the pioneers of civilization.[18]

The president went on to applaud missionary efforts in education and saw mission schools as basic to the exportation of Western Christian civilization.

> [Missionaries] are placing in the hands of their brothers less fortunate than themselves the keys which unlock the treasuries of knowledge and open the mind to noble aspirations for better conditions. Education is one of the indispensable steps of mission enterprise, and in some form must precede all successful work.... Who can estimate [the missionaries'] value to the progress of nations? Their contribution to the onward and upward march of humanity is beyond all calculation. They have inculcated industry and taught the various trades. They have promoted concord and amity, and brought nations and races close together. They have made men better. They have increased the regard for home; have strengthened the sacred ties of family; have made the community well ordered, and their work has been a potent influence in the development of law and the establishment of government.[19]

McKinley was followed on the program by the governor of the state of New York, Theodore Roosevelt, and the former President Benjamin Harrison, who was honorary president of the conference.[20] The fact that two presidents of the United States and one future chief executive addressed the missionary meeting reflects the close identification of the American political agenda with foreign missions.

The culmination of the "Great Century" was the World

Missionary Conference held in Edinburgh in 1910. This gathering of missionary executives and theorists dealt with missionary strategy, consultation and cooperation, in the hopes of uniting all of Protestantism in the evangelization of the world. Edinburgh's priority on cooperative mission activities marks the beginning of the modern ecumenical movement.[21] Although it was billed as a "world" missionary conference, the vast majority of participants were from Britain and North America. There were only seventeen delegates from non-Western countries.[22] The significant presence of Americans in the World Missionary Conference was characteristic of the United States as the standard-bearer of foreign missions in 1910. John R. Mott, in particular, played a key role in the World Missionary Conference. He was the chairperson of both the Planning Committee and the Continuation Committee. Under Mott's watchful eye, the initiative of the World Missionary Conference would be carried forward into the founding of the International Missionary Council in 1914.[23]

In many ways Edinburgh 1910 marked the entrance into adulthood of Protestant foreign missions. For the first time, missionaries and mission administrators began to wrestle with questions of theory and theology in foreign missions in a systematic manner. The theological reflection begun at Edinburgh would continue throughout the twentieth century.

> The importance of Edinburgh 1910 for the theology of missions is that it provided the beginning of a process of thought, experience and organization in the missionary enterprise and in the life of the Church that would lead to a critical self-examination and systematic formulation of the theological presuppositions for the Christian mission.[24]

Reflecting the new seriousness of mission theology, Edinburgh 1910 resulted in the development of the Missionary Research Library in New York City, the *International Review of Missions*, and many seminary professorships in mission.[25] No longer were foreign missions the stepchild of activist groups in Protestantism. With a research facility, a new journal, and seminary professorships, foreign missions became central to American Protestantism.

\In the early decades of the twentieth century independent missionary societies were increasingly incorporated into denominational mission boards. Eventually the majority of American Protestant denominations would support general foreign mission boards as an organic structure of the church. The independent women's missionary societies were not overlooked in this process of centralization. Administrators of the general mission boards argued that the women's missionary societies had to be brought under the oversight of their boards.

> It was frequently alleged that the women were competing as rivals with the official church organizations. Money was supposedly deflected from the denominational budget. Pastors and higher central officials disliked their inability to control such funds, and this second line of giving went against the trend toward centralization. Many thought the church lost what the women gained.[26]

Eventually women lost the battle as their societies were incorporated into the general denominational mission boards. The incorporation undercut the independent voluntary associations of women in foreign mission work and ruined the particularity of women's work for women.[27] The subsequent loss of support by women at the grass-roots local church level meant a decline in the significance of women's missionary societies in American foreign missions in the twentieth century.

The triumphal attitude of American Protestants in foreign mission would continue until World War I. The outbreak of the war in 1914 saw Christian nations fighting against one another in the bloodiest conflict ever witnessed by the world. As a result, the presupposition that the West embodied the best of Christian civilization was called into question. Although the United States emerged on the winning side of the battle, America's confidence in itself as the provider of Christian moral truths was shaken. The number of American Protestant missionaries would continue to grow through the 1920s but the "Great Century" of missions was past.[28] The missionary enterprise following World War I no longer could assume uncritically that Western civilization was the hope of the world.

THE NATIONAL CHURCH IDEAL AND EPISCOPAL FOREIGN MISSION

Episcopal foreign mission activities increased more in the first two decades of the twentieth century than at any other time in the history of the church. In 1899 the Domestic and Foreign Missionary Society of the Protestant Episcopal Church supported 103 American missionaries in the three foreign missions located in Liberia, China and Japan. By 1919, 371 American Episcopalian missionaries were serving overseas in twelve foreign and five extra-continental missionary districts of the Episcopal Church.[29] What can explain this phenomenal growth in the number of Episcopalian missionaries and the expansion in the number of overseas missionary districts?

In the late 1800s and early 1900s the Episcopal Church increasingly saw itself as a unified body with a particular responsibility to the United States and the wider world. The Episcopal Church's experience of the Social Gospel combined with its tradition of Anglican establishmentarianism provided a new identity and missiological mandate for the church. The fusion of the Episcopal Church's new-found identity and mission with American supremacy in foreign missions at the turn of the century accounts for the phenomenal growth in Episcopal foreign mission activities from 1900-1919.

The Social Gospel and the Episcopal Church

The Episcopal Church participated actively in the Social Gospel movement of the late nineteenth and early twentieth centuries. The commitment of the Episcopal Church to health and educational ministries in the United States and abroad is directly related to the church's social consciousness raised by the Social Gospel. Women in particular played a primary role in the working out of the Social Gospel in the Episcopal Church. Through religious sisterhoods, a deaconess program and a host of female service agencies, Episcopalian women ministered to the social needs of an increasingly urban and industrialized America. The combination of the

Social Gospel and the expanding role of women in the mission outreach of the Episcopal Church significantly bolstered the civilizing emphasis of Episcopal foreign mission activities at the turn of the century.

The Anglican roots of the Episcopal Church's commitment to the Social Gospel are found in the writings of Frederick Denison Maurice (1805–1872) and Charles Kingsley (1819–1875).[30] Maurice and Kingsley are credited with founding the Christian Socialism movement in the Church of England in the mid-1800s.[31] Christian Socialism attempted to bring the incarnational reality of Jesus Christ to bear on the societal ills caused by the industrial revolution.

> Maurice had argued in *The Kingdom of Christ* (1837) that the incarnation provided a key to escaping a narrow personal understanding of faith. For Maurice, Christ's coming into flesh changed not only the character of persons, but human relationships and institutions and nature itself. Christian efforts to deal seriously with the corporate problems of a modern society were, therefore, not just a working out of the logical implication of a renewed soul; they were a participation in the incarnation.[32]

The stated aim of Christian Socialism was "to reach the unsocial Christians and the un-Christian socialists." Through the Society for the Promoting of Workingmen's Associations and the publication *The Christian Socialist*, Maurice and Kingsley dedicated themselves to the improvement of the lives and working conditions of the industrial laborer.[33]

In the last half of the nineteenth century, American Episcopalians became increasingly aware of the social mandate of the Gospel and how it related to the missionary work of the church. As a priest and educator, William Augustus Muhlenberg (1797-1877) was one of the first to combine the missionary and social mandates of the Episcopal Church. Muhlenberg was well acquainted with the mission structures of the church. As a young man he had been one of the three members of the Missionary Society of Pennsylvania who, along with Jackson Kemper and George Boyd, recommended the establishment of the Domestic and Foreign Missionary Society to the General Convention of 1820. From 1828 until 1846, Muhlenberg championed the model of a Christian preparatory school as the headmaster of the Flushing

Institute in Flushing, New York. In 1846 he was called to be the rector of the Church of the Holy Communion in New York City. As a self-professed evangelical-catholic, Muhlenberg combined high-church liturgical practices, such as morning and evening prayer and weekly eucharists, with a successful apostolate among the poor of New York City. With the assistance of the Sisterhood of the Holy Communion, a deaconess society founded in his parish, Muhlenberg helped to establish St. Luke's Hospital.[34] The social outreach begun by Muhlenberg at the Church of the Holy Communion would serve as a model for implementing the Social Gospel in Episcopal parishes throughout the United States.

> William A. Muhlenberg had created a design for the institutional parish in his Church of the Holy Communion, after which Grace Church and St. George's in New York were patterned in the closing years of the century. Here every conceivable form of social service was offered by a large staff with adequate facilities and supported by a powerful and enlightened preaching and interpretation of the gospel.[35]

In addition to parish-based social outreach, a variety of independent societies advanced the social agenda of the Episcopal Church. The Church Association for the Advancement of the Interests of Labor, the Christian Social Union, and the Society of Christian Socialists led by William D. P. Bliss were a few examples of the church organizations that lifted up the Social Gospel in the Episcopal Church in the late nineteenth and early twentieth centuries.[36]

Whereas men like Maurice and Muhlenberg are credited with developing a theology for the social consciousness of the church, Episcopalian women were the primary laborers in the vineyards of the Social Gospel movement. In her study of women's ministries in the Episcopal Church from 1850-1920, *A Different Call*, Mary Sudman Donovan argues that the Episcopal Church led the way in the Social Gospel because of the commitment of Episcopal women to social service.[37] Donovan believes that the unique blend of catholic and protestant traditions in the Episcopal Church pushed women Episcopalians into humanitarian activities. Whereas protestant leanings of the Episcopal Church emphasized the responsibility to share the gospel with others, the catholic stress on the ordained ministry limited evangelism to male clerics. Therefore the only available avenue for women's ministries in the Episcopal Church was in the social spheres of education and health care. In addition, social service as a valid form of Christian ministry complemented the upper-class attitudes of Episcopal women that prohibited gainful employment but encouraged benevolent activities. Donovan stresses that the significant efforts of Episcopal women in education and health contributed to the Episcopal Church's emphasis on social service over evangelism in its mission activities.

> The fact remains that the social-service programs and institutions begun and maintained by Episcopal women, both at home and in the mission field, placed far less stress on the conversion of clients than did those of other Protestant denominations. Education rather than evangelism was the primary focus. A key reason for this emphasis was that the Episcopal women did not feel qualified to evangelize; the Church gave them no authority to do so.

> Hence the Episcopal women who moved into social service did not focus on evangelism as the reason for their activities. One nursed the sick, aided the poor, and visited captives in prison because Christ had mandated such practices for his disciples — not to add members to the Episcopal Church.[38]

By the turn of the nineteenth century, Episcopal women, through such organizations as the Woman's Auxiliary, would provide the only consistent source of financial support for the Domestic and Foreign Missionary Society. This support, combined with the women's dedication to social service, had a direct effect on the type of mission activities pursued by the Episcopal Church.

Anglican Establismentarianism and the Episcopal Church

Closely allied to the social service emphasis is the establishmentarian tradition in Anglicanism. Historically, the Church of England has celebrated its identity as a church of the English people consistent with orthodox Western Christianity. As a church that prides itself on being both reformed and catholic, Anglicans see themselves as being the *via media* between Protestants and

Roman Catholics. The belief that Anglicanism, in its best form, is a local expression of the universal church has contributed to an establishmentarian ethic in the church. Establishmentarianism maintains that all Christians should be gathered together into a national church that serves as the Christian conscience of the nation. The mission of the national church is to Christianize the social and political order of a nation as a united body of Christ.

Anglican establishmentarianism has its roots in the theology and writings of Richard Hooker (c. 1554-1600). Hooker was the chief defender of the Elizabethan church against Puritan criticisms. In his *Treatise on the Laws of Ecclesiastical Polity*, Hooker opposed the authority of biblical literalism and argued for the existence of a God-given natural law. Hooker believed that all ecclesiastical and civil laws were to be ordered under this law of God. The role of the church was to discern the will of God in the context of a particular people or nation. While all churches were united under the law of God, each local church was to be an indigenous and autonomous expression of God's will. Hooker thus understood the church to be, above all, a national institution.

> [The church] should be so organized so that its influence would pervade the nation. It should be interwoven into the fabric of national life so that the church and the nation would be virtually inseparable. The church at prayer would be the nation at prayer...The nation existed as an institution within the church. The church's mission was to place a Christian stamp on the character and activities of a nation and of its people.[39]

This combination of crown and cross throughout the British empire contributed to the spread of worldwide Anglicanism.

Writing in the nineteenth century, F. D. Maurice also emphasized the social responsibilities of the national church. In keeping with Hooker, Maurice believed that the nation was to be ordered under God's law and that the state was to be the servant of God. For Maurice then, the national church was to be the *modus operandi* of the Christian nation.

> A National Church should mean a Church which exists to purify and elevate the mind of a nation; to give those who make and administer and obey its laws a sense of the grandeur of law and of the source whence it proceeds, to tell the rulers of the nation, and all members of the nation that all false ways are ruinous ways, that the truth is the only stability of our time

> or of any time...This should be the meaning of a National Church; a nation
> wants a Church for these purposes mainly; a Church is abusing its trust if
> it aims at any other or lower purpose.[40]

As a member of the Church of England, however, Maurice wrote in the context of an established national church.

In the United States the concept of a national church was foreign. Although an understanding of God-given natural law was fundamental to the founding of the United States, a single institutional national church was inimical to American religious and political experience. American Episcopalians were thus caught between their Anglican ideals and American experience. On one side American Episcopalians resonated with the idea of a national church but at the same time they realized that an organic union of church and state was impossible in the United States. The challenge for American Anglicans was to create a climate where Christians from all faiths could come together in a *de-facto* national church. This *de-facto* national church would be independent of the country's political structures but, in keeping with Maurice, would serve as the social conscience of the United States.

The Episcopal Church saw itself as the primary point of unity in American Christianity.

> Episcopalians believed that their church could play a leading role in the formation of a national church for several reasons. It was a national denomination, not divided into geographical areas (as were the Baptists, Methodists, and Presbyterians) or ethnic segments (as were the Lutherans). Its traditional strength was in the cities, which were increasingly replacing the farming areas as the hub of American life. It recognized and attempted to address serious American social problems. With a representative form of government and a commitment to a traditional Christian faith it already provided a model of what W. D. P. Bliss called "democracy organized in Christ."[41]

In addition, the Episcopal Church in the United States prided itself as being the only American church to incorporate protestant thought with catholic orthodoxy. Although high-church and low-church Episcopalians disagreed over theology and liturgical practices, the Episcopal Church, as a whole, celebrated the unity of both its protestant and catholic traditions. As a result, the Episcopal Church in the United States saw itself as the gathering point between Geneva and Rome for all American Christians. William Augustus Muhlenberg was one of the first to point out the national responsibility of the Episcopal Church. He believed that an authentic American Church, which was rooted in protestant evangelical truth yet maintained the structures of orthodox catholicism, could best minister to the social needs of the United States in the mid-nineteenth century. At the General Convention of 1853, Muhlenberg challenged the Episcopal Church to consider its social duty as the only American church that was both protestant and catholic. The resolution to the convention, commonly known as the Muhlenberg Memorial, read in part:

> The actual posture of our Church, with reference to the great moral and social necessities of the day, presents to the minds of the undersigned a subject of grave and anxious thought...The divided and distracted state of our American Protestant Christianity; the new and subtle forms of unbelief, adapting themselves with fatal success to the spirit of the age; the consolidated forces of Romanism, bearing with renewed skill and activity against the Protestant faith; and, as more or less the consequence of these, the utter ignorance of the Gospel among so large a portion of the lower classes of our population, making a heathen world in our midst; are among the consolidations which induce your memorialists to present the inquiry whether the period has not yet arrived for the adoption of measures, to meet the exigencies of the times, more comprehensive than any yet provided for by our present ecclesiastical system; in other words, whether the Protestant Episcopal Church, with only her present canonical means and appliances, her fixed and invariable modes of public worship, her traditional customs and usages, is competent to the work of preaching and dispensing the Gospel to all sorts and conditions of men, and so adequate to do the work of the Lord in this land and in this age?[42]

The House of Bishops responded to the memorial (resolution) by appointing a committee, headed by Bishop Alonzo Potter of Pennsylvania, to consider its suggestions and report to the next General Convention. Unfortunately the prophetic vision of the memorial was lost in the work of the study committee. The memorial deserves credit, however, for initiating ecumenical discussions in the Episcopal Church. Many of the Episcopal Church's liturgical and canonical changes in the late nineteenth century intended to foster Christian unity had their origin in the Muhlenberg Memorial.[43]

The foremost proponent of a national non-established church in the United states was William Reed Huntington. Huntington was a product of the Episcopal Church in Massachusetts. Born in Lowell in 1838, he prepared for ministry at Harvard, graduating in 1859. Following his ordination to the priesthood in 1862, Huntington served as rector of All Saints' in Worcester, Massachusetts, for 21 years. He left Massachusetts in 1883 to become rector of the highly influential parish of Grace Church in New York. Huntington remained at Grace Church until his death in 1909 at the age of 70. On numerous occasions he declined episcopal election, preferring to remain pastor of a parish. From 1871 to 1907, Huntington was the leading spokesperson in the House of Deputies and led the way in many church reforms including the canonical authorization of deaconesses. Huntington's leadership in the Episcopal Church earned him the unofficial title of "first presbyter of the Church."[44]

Huntington believed strongly that the United States needed a national church to serve as the Christian conscience of the country. He argued that the Episcopal Church was in the best position to offer the leadership necessary for the development of such a national church. In his 1870 classic, *The Church Idea: An Essay Towards Unity*, Huntington first outlined the particularities of American Christianity and wondered how there could be Christian unity given the separation of church and state in the United States.

> We are thus brought face to face with the American Problem, which is this: Given a country constituted like ours, how is the Church of Christ therein planted to achieve and to maintain her proper unity?[45]

Huntington maintained that neither "Romanism, Puritanism, nor Liberalism" was wide enough to serve as the foundation of a national church. Instead he emphasized that four pillars of Anglicanism could serve to unite American Christianity. For Huntington these four pillars were:

1. The Holy Scriptures as the word of God.
2. The Primitive Creeds as the Rule of Faith.

3. The two Sacraments ordained by Christ himself.
4. The Episcopate as the key-stone of Governmental Unity.[46]

In the late 1880s both the General Convention of the Episcopal Church and the Lambeth Conference affirmed Huntington's four principles as the basis for Christian unity. Today, the Chicago-Lambeth Quadrilateral continues to serve as the basic document for Anglican ecumenical conversations.[47]

The concept of a non-established national church was articulated further by Huntington in his book, *A National Church*, published in 1898. By the turn of the century Huntington was convinced that the Episcopal Church had a unique role to play as a unifying force in American Christianity.

> The Episcopal Church in this new world stands, at the present moment, at the parting of the ways. After a century of infancy, a century of childhood, and a century of adolescence, she has come at last to her majority, and reports for duty. "For duty," and towards whom? Towards all, no doubt, whom her voice can reach or her hand help, but in a special sense towards those twenty millions of believers who among our sixty or seventy millions of population have with their own mouth and consent openly acknowledged Christ. Her errand to these is the errand of the reconciler and the peacemaker.[48]

It was Huntington who helped the Episcopal Church to appreciate fully its unique calling in American Protestantism at home and abroad.

> Huntington argued that the mission of the Episcopal Church was to unite all non-Roman Christianity in this nation and thus to shape and mold the Christian character of the nation. The Episcopal Church's identity was simply to be that national church which would be both catholic and apostolic. And Huntington argued, as William Augustus Muhlenberg had done two generations earlier, that [the Episcopal Church's] self-understanding would have to change drastically to fulfill that mission.[49]

By the dawn of the twentieth century the Episcopal Church was growing rapidly in both numbers and national prestige. Increasingly the church saw itself as the *de-facto* national church of the United States. The most poignant example of this self-identification as the national church is the development of the "National Cathedral" in Washington, D. C. Construction on the

Cathedral of St. Peter and St. Paul began in 1907. From its inception the cathedral understood its ministry as both a national house of prayer for all people and a see church for the Episcopal Diocese of Washington. Eventually the cathedral would become the official seat of the Presiding Bishop of the Episcopal Church. Sitting high on a hill above the nation's capital, the cathedral was to stand as a symbol of the Christian virtues underlying American democracy. In time presidents of the United States would come to the "National Cathedral" to honor, and be honored, in both civil and religious celebrations. The Cathedral of St. Peter and St. Paul towers above the seat of American government as a tangible expression of the Episcopal Church's emerging sense of itself as a national church.

The National Church Ideal

The Episcopal Church's experience of the Social Gospel fortified by its tradition of Anglican establishmentarianism gave birth to a national church ideal.[50] Episcopalians increasingly saw themselves as a unified body called to impart the riches of American society and the richness of Anglican tradition at home and overseas. The mission of the Episcopal Church, in the United States and around the world, was not evangelization and conversion but rather social regeneration through Christian moral truths and American democracy. The Episcopal Church would be the leaven that raises the United States, and other nations, to new heights of goodness and virtue.

It must be emphasized that the national church ideal was not a specific goal to be achieved but rather a general motivating tenet in the mission work of the Episcopal Church. Episcopalians never believed that the United States government would recognize their church as the official church of the country. In the same way, Episcopal foreign missions did not attempt to set up established state churches in overseas jurisdictions. Rather, the Episcopal Church saw itself as providing the best model for the "one holy catholic and apostolic Church" both in the United States and abroad. The primacy of the apostolic episcopate, guaranteed through missionary bishops, and the importance of a dignified and ordered form of worship as found in the Book of Common Prayer, were celebrated as the Episcopal Church's legacy. Episcopalians believed that all Christians, Catholic and Protestant, could find a point of unity in the Chicago-Lambeth Quadrilateral. The Episcopal Church thus saw itself as sent into the world to gather together all Christians in loving service to God and neighbor. Building up the church catholic in order to minister better to the spiritual and temporal needs of the world was the missiological imperative of the national church ideal.

The belief that the Episcopal Church had a unique mission in both the United States and the world was a fundamental aspect of the national church ideal. Episcopalians, such as Muhlenberg and Huntington, maintained that only in Anglican tradition could one find catholic orthodoxy combined with reformed thought. And only in the Episcopal Church in the United States was this unique combination fused with a commitment to American democracy and freedom. What resulted was a view of the Episcopal Church as a chosen people among an elect nation. The Episcopal Church thus began to see itself as the true church within the true Christian nation.

One of the earliest works promoting the uniqueness of the Episcopal Church was Calvin Colton's *The Genius and Mission of the Protestant Episcopal Church in the United States*, published in 1853. Colton believed that the distinctiveness of the Episcopal Church was the blending of catholic orthodoxy, including the centrality of Scripture and the authority of the apostolic episcopate, with the polity of an autonomous, democratically controlled, American church. The genius of the Episcopal Church was that it was catholic in theology yet republican in organization, "the Catholic Church, under the Protestant banner."[51]

It is among the main purposes of this work to show, that the American Episcopal Church occupies a new position in history, different from that of any other Church that ever existed; that it is a position of exceeding interest, in its aspects on the future of the American continent, of eminent importance in relation to that future, and mediately so in relation to the world; that she is entirely independent; that she derived nothing from the past obligatory upon her, except the Bible, Creeds, her Episcopacy...that her organization, and consequently her structure, are in their adaptations, different from that of any other Church; and consequently, that her genius is different from that of all others.[52]

For Colton the mission of the Episcopal Church was to "preserve the integrity and soundness of the Catholic faith" while reaching out to Protestant brothers and sisters.[53] Colton believed that only in the American Episcopal Church could the best of catholic and protestant traditions be brought together. Only in the Episcopal Church could American Christians come together to achieve their true greatness as the new Israel. Colton thus saw the Episcopal Church playing a key role in the expansion of American civilization in the imperial era. He closes his book with an observation of the unique calling of the Episcopal Church in the American empire in the last half of the nineteenth century.

> Finally: The most interesting and most important part of the Mission of the American Episcopal Church, remains to be seen in the vast field of Christian enterprise, which is opened by the extended and growing empire of American freedom and American institutions....from our Pacific border, we now look out on a new Western world of vast interest and attraction, in the waters and islands of the Pacific, and in the Eastern nations of Asia. North America is capable of sustaining some hundreds of millions of people, in the use only of the present arts of life. But the arts of life are improving more rapidly than the increase of population on the globe. What a prospect is this for the American empire! And that same empire is the future Missionary domain of the American Episcopal Church.[54]

The belief that the Episcopal Church offered an American model of national churches, different from the combination of crown and church found in England, became an implicit part of the national church ideal in the first decade of the twentieth century. At the first Pan-Anglican Congress of 1908, Bishop Edward M. Parker of New Hampshire noted the unique offering of the Episcopal Church in Anglican missions. He asserted:

> "there was a great tendency in that Congress to identify the Anglican Communion with the British Empire. I do not say it is consciously done,...but it seems to me that the best line for the American Church to take is to stand rather stiffly for the position of national Churches which do not belong to the British Empire."[55]

The national church ideal of the Episcopal Church maintained that the development of national churches in the Anglican Communion should be based upon American democracy rather than British monarchy.

Writing in 1916, the educational secretary of the Domestic and Foreign Missionary Society, Arthur R. Gray, echoed the unique calling of the Episcopal Church. In his book, *The New World*, Gray emphasized that the Episcopal Church had a distinct role to play in the future of the United States and Latin America. Gray believed that the Episcopal Church stood for the best of Western Christianity, both catholic and protestant. In addition, Gray maintained that the Episcopal Church was solidly located within the highest form of political governance, that of American democracy. The mission of the Episcopal Church in the New World was thus to nurture American democratic ideals at home and abroad through national Anglican churches loyal to the catholic faith but reformed by protestant thought.

> Yes, the New World is one world and the New World has a contribution to make to the peoples of the rest of the world. It is surrounded by a cloud of witnesses who are watching the great experiment which it is making in government.
>
> Just because this New World of ours has this brave task imposed upon it, each and every citizen should feel responsible for the progress of the whole of it. And specially those of us to whom has been entrusted the knowledge of the true relation between catholicity and individualism, between authority and liberty, between dogma and scholarship, — we to whom this precious gospel has been given owe a double duty to every nation in the New World as it struggles towards the ideals set up by Washington and Bolivar. Without our message their ambitions will never be realized. God give us wisdom and power so to play our part that the labors of the Conquistadores and the struggles of the liberators may be justified and the New World made an exemplar of Christian Democracy among the nations of the earth.[56]

The national church ideal resulted in the Episcopal Church's perceived role of building up Christian democracies throughout the "New World."[57]

The goal of the national church ideal was thus to export Western civilization and Christian truths as found in the history and the experience of the Episcopal Church in the United States. The closing words of the 1899 Annual Report of the Domestic and Foreign Missionary Society set the agenda for the church's foreign mission work in the next century.

> It is evident [that the people of Africa, China, and Japan] have at last reached the point where they have seen that Western learning and civilization are the sole conditions of the continuance of their political power and stability, and are rapidly adopting these methods, and readjusting their former customs and habits to the more enlightened knowledge that has dawned upon them....With Africa rapidly opening its vast and heretofore almost inaccessible territory to the ingress of civilization, and with its people becoming evangelized through the instrumentality of a native ministry preaching the Gospel of Jesus Christ; with China awakening out of her slumbers of centuries, casting off the fetters that have impeded her liberty and progress, and issuing royal edicts for the adoption of Western civilization and proclaiming religious liberty to all her citizens; with Japan now admitted into the family of civilized nations, opening the whole empire to the foreigner with the same privileges of the rights of residence and ownership of property as are extended to its own people, and with the free and open privilege to preach the Christian religion throughout its domains — a crisis presents itself that makes it the imperative duty of the Church of God to go at once and possess these lands in the name of Christ. The doors are now open wide and many, yea hundreds, are lifting up their hands and asking for our religion, our civilization, our schools.[58]

The drive to spread "our religion, our civilization, our schools" epitomized the national church ideal of Episcopal foreign mission and led to a dramatic increase in the church's missionary activities in the first two decades of the twentieth century.

New Foreign Missionary Districts

At the end of the nineteenth century the foreign mission work of the Episcopal Church was in a state of transition. The development of Episcopal Churches in West Africa, China and Japan was progressing well. Under the episcopal oversight of missionary bishops, new schools, hospitals and churches were constructed in each of the foreign missionary districts.[59] There were fledgling efforts to establish autonomous Anglican churches in the foreign fields and in 1874 the *Nippon Sei Ko Kai* (the Holy Catholic Church in Japan) was formed from British and American Anglican missions. Other missions such as Greece and Constantinople were not elevated to missionary districts and were closed in 1898 and 1850, respectively. In 1877 the American Church Missionary Society became an auxiliary to the Domestic and Foreign Missionary Society. Increasingly the foreign mission activities of the ACMS in Cuba and Brazil came under the oversight of the church's "official" Missionary Society. With the addition of new territories to the United States following the Spanish-American War, the Episcopal Church, like other American Protestant churches, stood ready to increase its foreign mission activities in the early years of the twentieth century.

The year 1901 could be considered a landmark year in the foreign mission work of the Episcopal Church. In one year the church established new missionary districts in Puerto Rico, the Philippines and Honolulu. In addition, the China mission was expanded and a second missionary district, that of Hankow, was formed. All of these new efforts were supported financially by a new system of appropriations that tied the Board of Missions of the Missionary Society more closely to the dioceses of the Episcopal Church.

Like most American Protestants, Episcopalians believed that God's hand was at work in the American victory in the Spanish-American War. In a sermon preached at Grace Church, New York City, on the Sunday after the breaking out of hostilities between the United States and Spain, William Reed Huntington preached on the reality of God's will in the ordering of the events of the war. He believed

> that God is both on the throne and in the field, that the course of this world is, in a lofty and true sense, ordered by His governance, and that quite apart from the mixed motives which sway the wills of congresses and parliaments, cabinets and council-boards, He has a purpose of His own, a clear intention, an infallible plan of campaign the issue of which, when it comes, will be known and read by all men.[60]

Huntington and others thus believed that God had a hand in the outcome of the Spanish-American War. The American victory in the war fortified the mission of national church ideal. The leadership of the Domestic and Foreign Missionary Society believed that American Episcopalians were now called to go to Cuba, the

Philippines and Puerto Rico to bring the best of American democracy and American Christianity to the "down-trodden and unhappy
people."

> This fact was never made more prominent than in our late war with Spain,
> and the causes which led up to it and made the interference of this gov-
> ernment imperative. It was not the greed of the empire but the impulse of
> brotherhood that prompted the United States to extend to the down-trod-
> den and unhappy people of Cuba liberty, law, peace and prosperity. Having,
> therefore, assumed this responsibility, and having succeeded in planting the
> flag of this mighty Republic upon those and other foreign shores, (the
> Philippines and Puerto Rico) it becomes our bounden duty and service to
> instill into the hearts and minds of the more than ten millions of people
> who have been brought under the protecting folds of our flag, the high and
> noble principles of truth and justice, religion and piety.[61]

The close connection between the church's missionary activities and the political agenda of the American government is stated unabashedly in the triennial report of the Domestic and
Foreign Missionary Society to the General Convention of 1907.

> In all the dependencies [missionary districts] the need for men is empha-
> sized by the fact of the singular obligation resting upon the Church to assist
> the Government in making the peoples competent for the administration
> of their own affairs. The American Church [the Episcopal Church] has
> more than it realizes to do with deciding when methods characteristic of
> the old civilizations shall give place to Christian institutions.[62]

The fact that the Episcopal Church saw itself as being the
"American Church" called to assist the government in raising up
new Christian institutions in the "dependencies" epitomizes the
national church ideal of Episcopal missions in the early twentieth
century.

The national church ideal also maintained that the Episcopal
Church was the only heir to catholic orthodoxy in American
Christianity. This belief played an important role in the development of Episcopal missions in the previously Spanish colonies. At
first, Episcopal missionaries were sent to the Philippines and
Puerto Rico as chaplains to the American citizens and military
personnel living in the new American territories. Eventually these
chaplains widened their ministry to include mission to the indigenous Roman Catholics. Unlike other American Protestant denominations, Episcopalians did consider the Roman Catholics to be

Christians, but Christians that needed to be purified of their popish truancies. This fact was emphasized in the triennial report of the Domestic and Foreign Missionary Society to the General Convention of 1901.

> And especially in the Philippine Islands, the services held by the chaplain soon attracted the attention of the native people, to whom the yoke of Roman oppression, with its unauthorized terms of communion, and its association with the tyranny of some of the religious orders, had become a bondage which neither "their fathers nor they were able to bear." The Managers are not disposed to raise the vexed question of what some people are inclined to count intrusion, into the countries claimed by the Roman communion as owing allegiance to the Bishop of Rome. The policy of this Church is plainly and positively settled now. It takes in the oversight of the struggling native Church in Mexico, the mission planted in the Island of Cuba, and, more recently the sending of priests to Porto Rico [sic] and Manila to preach the pure Gospel, to administer the Sacraments on the primitive terms of communion, and to set the example of a higher morality in the Priesthood and among the people.[63]

In order to minister to American citizens and "misdirected Roman Catholics," the 1901 General Convention of the Episcopal Church officially established missionary districts in the Philippine Islands and in Puerto Rico (known as Porto Rico). The 1901 Convention elected Charles Henry Brent as missionary bishop for the Philippines and the following year Charles H. Van Buren was elected for Puerto Rico. Since both of these new missionary districts were in territories of the United States government, they were not considered foreign missions but rather domestic fields. In time these "overseas domestic missions" would be known as Extra-Continental Missionary Districts and would be treated in the same manner as other foreign missions of the Episcopal Church.[64]

In addition to the Philippines and Puerto Rico, Honolulu and Alaska were added as "overseas domestic missions" at the turn of the century. Although Alaska became a territory of the United States in 1867, following its purchase from Russia, Episcopal mission work did not begin in the northern region for almost two decades. The first Episcopal missionary to Alaska was the Rev. John W. Chapman, who began work among the Eskimos at Anvik, 300 miles inland on the Yukon River, in the 1880s.[65] In the 1890s other Episcopal missions were opened in Point Hope and Tanana.[66] Although a bishop for Alaska had been called for in 1883, the mission was without a missionary episcopate until the mid 1890s.[67] As a result, one missionary referred to the Alaska effort as "our Presbyterian mission." In 1890 the House of Bishops held a special session and elected Chapman bishop, but he declined the election.[68] Although a missionary bishop for Alaska was called for at the 1892 General Convention, the mission had to wait until 1895 when the convention elected Peter Trimble Rowe to the episcopate. Under Rowe's leadership, Episcopal missionary activities grew among the native Eskimos as well as with white settlers who had moved to Alaska in the Klondike Gold Rush. For the next seventy-five years Alaska would be considered an "extra-continental" or "overseas" missionary district of the Episcopal Church.

In 1901 Honolulu was made a missionary district of the Episcopal Church. There had been an Anglican presence in Hawaii since the early 1800s. The Church of England first began mission work in Hawaii in 1833, and in 1862 the Right Rev. Thomas N. Staley was sent from England as the first missionary bishop. The appointment of Staley was made in response to a request for episcopal oversight of the Islands from the King of Hawaii, Kamehameha IV. King Kamehameha and his wife Emma were Christian benevolent rulers.[69] Although already a Congregationalist, Kamehameha's interest in Anglicanism "came through a boyhood tour of England where he had seen, in the stately beauty of Anglican liturgy, a quality that seemed attuned to the gentle beauty of the Hawaiian spirit."[70] Under Bishop Staley and his successor the Right Rev. Alfred Willis, who became bishop in 1872, the Anglican Church ministered to indigenous Hawaiians as well as immigrant Chinese, Japanese and Americans. When Hawaii was annexed by the United States in 1898, becoming a territory in 1901, provision was made for the transfer of Anglican mission work from the Church of England to the Episcopal Church. Hawaii became a missionary district of the Episcopal Church in 1901 and the first American Episcopal missionary bishop, the Right Rev. Henry B. Restarick, was elected April 16, 1902.

Through schools and churches, the Episcopal Church under Restarick continued to minister to the many diverse nationalities found in Hawaii.

In the city of Honolulu, on Oahu Island, St. Andrew's Cathedral was the missionary center, with two organized congregations, Hawaiian and Anglo-American. Close by was St. Andrew's Priory, a boarding- and day-school for girls, of whom nine-tenths were then of native blood. More interesting in their racial variety were the three hundred boys in Iolani School, where eight nationalities were represented. St. Luke's mission ministered to the Koreans, St. Peter's to the Chinese, and Trinity to the Japanese — each with a school attached to the church.[71]

Restarick served the missionary district for eighteen years during which time membership in the Episcopal Church in Hawaii grew ten times faster than the island population.[72]

The turn of the century saw significant challenges placed before the Episcopal mission in China. On one hand, the work of the Episcopal Church in China was progressing rapidly. In 1900 the missionary district of Shanghai was the largest foreign mission field of the Episcopal Church both in total valuation of property and in number of missionaries.[73] With mission activity stretching 600 miles up the Yang-tse River from Shanghai to Hankow, the Shanghai mission was becoming too big to manage effectively as one unit. On the other hand, in 1900 Chinese nationalists led a violent struggle to overthrow foreign control of their country. This movement was known to Westerners as the Boxer Rebellion for its symbol of the clenched fist. Missionaries and Chinese Christians, who were considered traitors to their country, were targets of the uprising. During the rebellion 30,000 Chinese Christians lost their lives. Foreign missionaries also were killed and suffered losses in property.[74] By late summer 1900, the uprising had been put down by an international armed force. The Boxer Rebellion brought increased attention to China, and the victory over the nationalists was seen as a sign of hope for Christian mission. In its report to the General Convention of 1901, the Board of Managers of the Domestic and Foreign Missionary Society spoke triumphantly about the China mission.

The Bishop of Shanghai, with a wise courage and fearless prudence, faced and met the threatenings of danger, withdrawing the workers from certain points, and watching the opportunities for their return. In the good providence of God, no personal harm was done to any of our missionaries, who showed, through all the anxious hours of surrounding violence, self-control and steadiness, and who have been fully vindicated, by the testimony of witnesses of every sort from the attacks and imputations sedulously circulated by the opponents of Christianity. The final seal of sincerity and earnestness has been set upon the missionary work in China, by the readiness with which great numbers of native Christians laid down their lives rather than renounce their faith. And now, when the first violence of the outbreak has subsided, at least for the time, the work in the stations, in the schools, in the college, and in the hospitals is quietly resumed, with increasing numbers of worshippers and students, and a confidence and purpose never more sanguine and determined, to preach the everlasting Gospel. The founding of a new episcopal see and the sending of another Bishop to China [if this be done] may well be counted as part of the progress of last year[75]

And so the General Convention of 1901 created a second missionary district in China, that of Hankow, and elected J. Addison Ingle missionary bishop. Bishop Ingle was consecrated on February 24, 1902 in St. Paul's Church, Hankow, but served only ten months before dying in December of 1902.

At the General Convention of 1904, held in Boston, Massachusetts, it became increasingly clear that the Episcopal Church was looking towards Latin America. Although discussions about Cuba and Mexico had begun three years earlier, the General Convention of 1904 officially assumed control of early Episcopal work in these countries and created the missionary districts of Cuba and Mexico. In addition, the General Convention placed the Canal Zone in Panama under the jurisdiction of the Presiding Bishop. Consistent with its national church ideal, the Episcopal Church felt called to both U.S. citizens and Latin American Roman Catholics in the new missionary districts.

Episcopal mission work in Mexico began when a group of reformist priests and lay people split off from the Roman Catholic Church in the early 1860s. Desiring assistance from the Episcopal Church, these priests corresponded with the Rev. Angel Herrerros, an Episcopal priest in New York. Through Herrerros, the Mexican priests requested assistance in their breakaway efforts from the Foreign Committee of the Domestic and Foreign Missionary

Society. The national church ideal and its emphasis on the reformed and catholic nature of the Episcopal Church provided a justification for the Episcopal Church's involvement in Mexico.

> We shall greatly fail in our duty if we leave these men to themselves, or cause them through our neglect to turn for aid to those who, however much good they may do them, will not enable them to make the Reformed Church of Mexico a Church which shall combine evangelical truth with apostolic order.[76]

In 1864 the Missionary Society sent the Rev. E. J. Nicholson to survey the situation in Mexico. Working in cooperation with the leader of the reformist priests, by the name of Aguilar, they founded *La Sociedad Catolica Apostolica Mexicana* (Mexican Catholic Apostolic Society) later named *La Iglesia de Jesus* (The Church of Jesus).[77] Support from the Episcopal Church for *La Iglesia de Jesus* was small, although missionaries and funds were received from various independent mission organizations such as a newly formed Mexican Missionary Society and the American Church Missionary Society (which adopted Mexico as a mission in 1872).[78] Lacking an episcopate, the reformed church in Mexico petitioned the General Convention of 1874 and asked that a bishop be sent to Mexico. Three years later, in 1877 the Episcopal Church consecrated the Rev. Henry Chauncey Riley bishop of *La Iglesia de Jesus*. Riley had been a missionary in Mexico since 1869; because of his background he seemed like the perfect person to lead the new church. He was a man of independent fortune and English citizenship who had been raised in Chile and educated in Spain. Previous to his missionary service in Mexico, Riley had served as a rector of a Spanish-speaking Episcopal Church in New York. Unfortunately, the task of governing *La Iglesia de Jesus* proved to be too much for him. Poor administration of finances combined with a schism in the church left the reformed church movement in Mexico in confusion. Unable to overcome these difficulties, Riley resigned his post in 1884. For the next two decades, the Episcopal Church maintained a low profile in the affairs of the independent Mexican church. There were dedicated individuals, however, such as the Rev. W. B. Gordon, the Rev. Henry Forrester and Mrs. M. J. Hooker who continued to serve as Episcopal missionaries in Mexico.[79]

With the increased commitment of the Episcopal Church to Spanish-speaking mission fields following the Spanish-American War, the General Convention of 1904 elevated the Mexican mission to a missionary district and elected Henry D. Aves missionary bishop. Although the primary charge to Aves was to care for the Anglo-Americans in Mexico, he could not turn his back on the reformed Mexican church that had struggled for over four decades. As a result, Aves "undertook to care for the 'thirty-two or more congregations' of natives who appealed to him to be their chief pastor."[80] The political turmoil of the Mexican Revolution, however, resulted in the suspension of Episcopal missionary activities in 1913. A reinvestment of the energies of the Episcopal Church in the Mexican mission would have to wait until the 1930s.

As in Mexico, Episcopal mission work in Cuba at the turn of the century suffered from disorganization and poor funding. The American Church Missionary Society had labored in the field for over two decades and had achieved only modest success. Although the ACMS was now an Auxiliary to the Domestic and Foreign Missionary Society, support for the Cuban Mission continued to be inadequate. The annual report of the American Church Missionary Society for the year 1900 emphasized the weak commitment of the Episcopal Church to Cuba. It challenged the Episcopal Church, as the only church that embodies both catholic traditions and protestant inspirations, to support missionary work in Cuba.

> An opportunity is slipping away from the Church, and simply because of failure to accept it, meet its conditions and establish ourselves....There are many thousand people in Cuba unassociated with any Church, in fact without any religion. Their reaction from the Roman Communion has been so violent and radical that there is not a hope of their return to it. Their reformation must be had through our Churches. We appeal to them because of our identity with their traditions and education and ecclesiastical use as no other may. Their civilization with its crushed ideals and lost ambition is ready and ripe for a new inspiration. That inspiration must come from a Protestant body, and we are in the very nature of things that body.[81]

The opinion at the start of the twentieth century was that "something radical had to be done. There was no use trifling any longer. The work needed a bishop and a regular ecclesiastical organization."[82]

The elevation of Cuba to missionary district status was discussed at the General Convention of 1901, but it was not until the next convention in 1904 that the Rev. Albion W. Knight was elected bishop of Cuba. Bishop Knight believed that the Episcopal Church had a three-fold mission in Cuba. First, the church was to be a chaplain to North Americans working in the mining, sugar and citrus industries on the island. Second, the Episcopal Church was to minister to other English-speaking residents in Cuba such as Canadians and individuals from England. Finally, the Episcopal Church was to reach out to lapsed Roman Catholics. In the words of Bishop Knight:

> The work therefore of the Episcopal Church among these people is to gather together as far as possible, those who may come to it through the excitement of renewal of their interest in religious matters, and also to create such an atmosphere as will help the old Church [Roman Catholics] to do its work more efficiently and more effectively.[83]

The new commitment of the Episcopal Church to Cuba as a missionary district and the concomitant increase in funds and missionary appointments for the island had marked results. Ten years after Bishop Knight's consecration, the church had grown from six to thirty-seven congregations. The number of Cuban clergy had increased from two to twenty-four, and the total number of communicants from 200 to more than 1,700. In addition, the number of children enrolled in schools supported by the Episcopal Church had increased from seventy-five to more than three hundred.[84] The church's educational work was expanded during the episcopacy of Bishop Hiram R. Hulse, who succeeded Knight as missionary bishop in 1915. Hulse opened dozens of church-supported schools and significantly expanded the Cathedral School for Girls in Havana and All Saints' School at Guantánamo.[85]

The adoption of Cuba as a missionary district in 1904 began the official transfer of the foreign mission fields of the American Church Missionary Society to the Domestic and Foreign Missionary Society. The dwindling ACMS constituency could no longer support the work in Cuba and Brazil and so it transferred all of its foreign mission activities to the Domestic and Foreign Missionary Society in 1905. In addition, the Rev. Arthur S. Lloyd, General Secretary of the D&FMS, was elected general secretary of the ACMS. The election of Lloyd as general secretary of the ACMS and the transfer of Cuba and Brazil was the death knell for the ACMS as an auxiliary. Without a separate organization and its own foreign mission fields, the ACMS would be subsumed under the growing presence of the church's "official" Missionary Society. The tendency to centralization of the national church ideal was too strong for the weakened voluntary missionary society.[86]

The official transfer of Brazil from the American Church Missionary Society to the Domestic and Foreign Missionary Society in 1905 resulted in a problematic ecclesiastical situation. ACMS mission activities in Brazil were organized under the semi-independent *Egreja Brasileira Episcopal* (Brazilian Episcopal Church) in 1893. Because the American Church Missionary Society embraced an evangelical low-church ecclesiology, the securing of a missionary bishop was not a high priority. As a result the Brazilian Episcopal Church existed for six years before electing Lucien L. Kinsolving its first bishop in 1899. The transfer of the Brazilian mission from the ACMS to the D&FMS posed a problem for the *Egreja Brasileira Episcopal*. The Domestic and Foreign Missionary Society was unwilling to acknowledge the authenticity of the *Egreja Brasileira Episcopal* since it had been founded outside of the auspices of the society. To resolve these problems, the Episcopal Church maneuvered to have Kinsolving resign as bishop of the *Egreja Brasileira Episcopal*. Following his resignation and the ensuing dismantling of the Brazilian Episcopal Church, the General Convention of 1907 inaugurated the Missionary District of Southern Brazil and elected Kinsolving its missionary bishop.[87] The co-option of *Egreja Brasileira Episcopal* by the missionary superstructure of the Episcopal Church reflects the strong central control of the official Missionary Society under the national church ideal. Although the Episcopal Church stated that the founding of independent national Episcopal churches was the goal of its mission work, if the initiative for independence did not originate with the leadership of the Domestic and Foreign Missionary Society in New York, then efforts towards autonomy were not considered genuine. It would be five decades before the missionary district of Southern Brazil was encouraged by the Episcopal Church in the United States to venture forth as the autonomous *Igreja Episcopal Do Brasil* (Episcopal Church of Brazil).

In the first decade of the twentieth century China continued to be the preeminent foreign mission of the Episcopal Church. More funds and more missionaries were sent to the two missionary districts of Shanghai and Hankow than to any other mission field. With a growing number of schools, hospitals and churches to administer, pressure to form a third missionary district in China increased. Thus in 1910, the General Convention carved out a new missionary district of Wuhu from Hankow. The Rev. F. L. Hawks Pott, the president of St. John's College in Shanghai, was elected bishop of the new district. Pott, however, declined the position, choosing instead to continue his work at St. John's.[88] Bishop Roots of Hankow provided episcopal oversight of the new missionary district until March of 1912 when the Rev. D. Trumbull Huntington was consecrated missionary bishop of Wuhu. The following year the name of the missionary district was changed from Wuhu to Anking, reflecting the primacy of the see city of the district.

The Episcopal Church's commitment to meeting the social, political and spiritual needs of the Chinese people was increasingly affirmed following the revolution of 1911-1912. Annual reports of the Domestic and Foreign Missionary Society celebrated the role of the church in the founding of a new Chinese society.

> Draw back the curtain and look at China. What is the meaning of that great movement that is touching every department of social and public life — the cry for a constitutional government; for western education; for the prohibition of opium; anti-footbinding; new journalism; post-office extension; railroad extension; currency reform; reorganization of army and navy; growth of a national spirit. It is certainly a most significant sign of the times when China discards forever the system by which her young men have been educated for thousands of years, and replaces that system by the

school and college system of the Christian world....To the real reformers of China, the sober, thinking, right-minded citizens of that mighty race, the conviction that Christianity, and Christianity alone, is the solution to their social, political and moral problems is rapidly gaining ground, and, to a great degree, has indeed become not only a conviction but an absolute conclusion.[89]

Paralleling the efforts of Chinese nationalists following the revolution and consistent with the national church ideal, Episcopalians in China pushed for an independent national Anglican Church in China along the lines of the Episcopal Church in the United States. In 1912, American, English and Canadian Anglican missionaries combined their efforts to form the *Chung Hua Sheng Kung Hui* (The Holy Catholic Church in China). As reported to the General Convention of 1913:

> The year 1912 will always be memorable in China's history, because in April of that year the first *national* Church for China was organized, and a new national branch was added to the fellowship of the world-wide Anglican Communion. (Italics added)[90]

The organization of the *Chung Hua Sheng Kung Hui* followed that of the *Nippon Sei Ko Kai* founded in Japan in 1874. The four tenets of the Chicago-Lambeth Quadrilateral were the guiding principles around which the Anglicans in China organized themselves. But like the Holy Catholic Church in Japan, the leadership of the Holy Catholic Church in China remained firmly in Western hands. The bishops of the new Anglican Church continued to be missionary bishops sent out from England, Canada and the United States. There was little change in the administration of the mission in China. Shanghai, Hankow and Anking continued to be missionary districts of the Episcopal Church. The founding of the *Chung Hua Sheng Kung Hui* was applauded as a true national Chinese Anglican Church. In practice, little had changed.

Whereas the establishment of the *Chung Hua Sheng Kung Hui* in 1912 added a church to the Anglican Communion, the absorption of *L'Eglise Orthodoxe Apostolique Hatienne* (The Haitian Orthodox Apostolic Church) into the Episcopal foreign mission fold in 1913 reduced by one the number of autonomous Anglican churches in the world. *L'Eglise Orthodoxe Apostolique Hatienne* became a missionary district of the Episcopal Church because racial, economic and political forces of the national church ideal pushed the Haitian Church into the growing domain of the centralized Episcopal mission organization.

The birth of Anglicanism in Haiti occurred in May of 1861 when an African-American Episcopal priest named James Theodore Holly led 110 fellow African-American Episcopalians in their immigration to the "Black Republic." As a priest of the Episcopal Church, serving at St. Luke's in New Haven, Connecticut, Holly had experienced first-hand the racism of American society and the Episcopal Church in the mid-1800s. Holly believed that men and women of African descent would never be completely free in the United States and so advocated emigration of African-Americans to Africa and the West Indies. Combining his service to the Episcopal Church with his emigration platform, Holly applied to the Domestic and Foreign Missionary Society to become a missionary to Haiti. The Missionary Society, however, denied his application two times. The society's hesitation to support Holly and his work in Haiti was to be a common story throughout the nineteenth century.[91]

Holly, however, was undaunted by the lack of support he received from the Domestic and Foreign Missionary Society. Once in Haiti, he turned to the American Church Missionary Society for assistance. The ACMS provided modest funds to Holly for the first five years of his work.[92] During these early years, the parish of Holy Trinity in Port-au-Prince was founded and steps were taken to form an indigenous ministry. The beginning by Holly was so successful that the Domestic and Foreign Missionary Society could no longer turn its back on his work, and in 1866 the society sent Bishop George Burgess to the island to review Holly's efforts. During his episcopal visit, Burgess consecrated three other parishes and ordained two Haitians, one to the priesthood and the other to the diaconate.[93] Burgess's episcopal acts reinforced Holly's belief that the church in Haiti needed to have its own missionary bishop. And so he began to petition the Episcopal Church in the United States for a Haitian Episcopate. The General Convention was slow to respond but did appoint Arthur C. Coxe, bishop of Western New York, bishop-in-charge of Haiti. When Coxe visited

Haiti in 1872, Holly convinced him of the appropriateness and political rightness of the Haitian church's organizing itself as an independent Anglican Church with its own indigenous episcopate. Holly's request was in keeping with the national church ideal. Coxe's report to the General Convention of 1874 reflected this although his initial belief that a white missionary bishop would be best for Haiti reflected the endemic racism of the time.

(1) We believe that the Haitien [sic] Mission must be made a National Haitien Church, as speedily as possible. As a mere Mission, it will always be a foreign interest among Haitiens [sic]...it will languish and fail to command the sympathy and affection of the natives. It will be regarded as the church of certain American residents but will never spread among the people. The fact that its clergy are all Haitiens, and that for several years they have presented themselves to popular attention as the seed of a National Church, has already operated favorably on the minds of many intelligent Haitiens and has been felt in their National Councils.

(2) Your committee were at first disposed to believe that a Bishop of the white race and a citizen of the United States going out, like our other foreign Missionary Bishops, to preside over the work would be able to secure many advantages which a co-citizen of the Haitiens would not be likely to command. To be brief, however they found many considerations of great weight on the other side; and recent changes in Haitien affairs have led them to regard such considerations as preponderating and decisive. By an article of the Constitution of Haiti the superior ecclesiastics of any form of religion, established on the Isle, must be Haitien citizens...it is essential that the person selected [to be bishop] should be of the colored race, and one willing to identify himself with the Haitien people, as a fellow citizen, if not already a native or naturalized citizen of that republic. Let such a Bishop be sent out as a Missionary Bishop of our Church; and then, let him as speedily as possible give to the Mission such a national organization as we have proposed.[94]

And so the General Convention of 1874 elected James Theodore Holly as bishop of *L'Eglise Orthodoxe Apostolique Hatienne*. Holly was the first bishop of African heritage ordained by the Episcopal Church and the second black bishop of the Anglican Communion.[95]

For close to fifty years James Theodore Holly worked to plant the Church in his adopted land. By the time of his death in 1911 *L'Eglise Orthodoxe Apostolique Hatienne* had developed an extensive ministry in education and health care with twenty-six congregations, close to fifty schools, and an indigenous Haitian clergy of twelve priests and two deacons.[96] The Haitian Anglican church, however, never achieved a firm financial base but continued to rely on the goodwill offerings of friends in the United States. For five years following Holly's death, *L'Eglise Orthodoxe Apostolique Hatienne* struggled without episcopal oversight. At the same time American political and economic interests in Haiti increased, resulting in an occupation of the island nation by the United States government from 1915 until 1934. Because of the financial hardship of the Haitian church and the vacuum of episcopal leadership, the 1913 General Convention stepped in to take over the work of the indigenous Haitian Anglican Church. The *L'Eglise Orthodoxe Apostolique Hatienne* was disbanded and the church was made a missionary district of the Episcopal Church with the stipulation that a white American bishop be given charge of the work in Haiti. The triennial report of the Board of Missions emphasized this fact.

> The deputation [sent to visit Haiti after Holly's death] also recommended that a white Bishop should have supervision of the Haitien Church. [*sic*] The Board heartily concurs in this opinion, if Haiti is to be received as a foreign Missionary District, or if the Church in this country is expected to continue its financial aid to the Church in Haiti.[97]

The 1913 General Convention placed the new missionary district under the care of the missionary bishop of Puerto Rico. In addition, the General Convention extended the jurisdiction of the bishop of Puerto Rico over the whole island of Santo Domingo, placing "such Christian people in Santo Domingo [The Dominican Republic] as may have asked or may hereafter ask for his pastoral oversight" under his care.[98]

The missionary district in Haiti was without an American missionary bishop for over a decade. In 1923, during the American occupation of Haiti when the prohibition against non-Haitian church leaders was relaxed, the General Convention elected the Right Rev. Harry R. Carson, missionary bishop of Haiti. Although the Haitian Anglicans had become a missionary district of the Episcopal Church with a white American expatriate bishop, they never lost their identity as an autonomous Haitian church preferring to call themselves the Episcopal Church *of* Haiti and not the

Episcopal Church *in* Haiti.

With the growing interest of the American Episcopal Church in Latin America and the Caribbean, the General Convention of 1913 appointed a committee to study the possibility of establishing a missionary district of Central America. At the next General Convention, the Board of Missions recommended that the Episcopal Church assume responsibilities for the work of the Church of England in Central America. The Board reported:

> There is in many quarters a deep feeling that we should not only come to the aid of the Church of England by relieving her of her responsibility for Central America, but also should recognize our own growing duty in the Western Hemisphere.[99]

The establishment of a missionary district in Central America, however, did not occur. The only transfer of missions from the Church of England to the Episcopal Church was the work among English-speaking West Indians of African descent in the Virgin Islands. This occurred in 1918, one year after the United States purchased the Virgin Islands from Denmark. The three Anglican congregations in the Virgin Islands did not warrant the status of a missionary district and so were placed under the episcopate of Puerto Rico.[100] As bishop of Puerto Rico, the Right Rev. Charles B. Colmore now had responsibility for Haiti, the Dominican Republic and the Virgin Islands as well as his own missionary district.

The Panama Canal Zone was the final "foreign" missionary district added to the Episcopal Church in the first two decades of the twentieth century. Since the mid-nineteenth century, the work of the Episcopal Church in Panama was closely associated with American economic interests in the region. In 1848 a New York businessman, William H. Aspinwall, secured the rights to build a railroad across the isthmus. Aspinwall was a faithful Episcopalian who arranged for his church to provide a chaplain to the managers of his railroad company and to the many English-speaking West Indians employed in the building of the railroad.[101] Episcopal endeavors in this early era were focused at Christ Church located in the city of Aspinwall (later Colon). The church was a beautiful, gothic structure built by Aspinwall and consecrated by Alonzo Potter, bishop of Pennsylvania, on his trip through Panama to San Francisco in 1865.[102] For twenty-five years the Episcopal Church served as chaplain to Aspinwall's railroad company, and no less than nine priests served the chaplaincy under the patronage of Aspinwall and the Domestic and Foreign Missionary Society.[103] When the importance of the railroad company gave way to the growing banana plantations and the building of the Panama Canal in the 1880s, Episcopal work in the region was slowly transferred to missionaries from the Church of England who were ministering to the farm and canal workers.

The purchase of the Canal Zone from the Republic of Panama by the United States in 1903 resulted in renewed Episcopal interest in the isthmus. In 1904, the Board of Managers of the Missionary Society recommended that the Episcopal Church request jurisdiction of the Canal Zone from the English bishop of Honduras, who had episcopal oversight of the region. The General Convention of 1904 officially assumed responsibility for the Canal Zone from the Church of England and the Presiding Bishop appointed Bishop H. Y. Satterlee of Washington as his commissary in charge of the Zone.[104] In 1908, episcopal oversight for the Canal Zone was transferred to the Right Rev. A. W. Knight, missionary bishop of Cuba, who served in this capacity until 1919. During this time the Episcopal Church served primarily as a chaplaincy to the Americans involved with the administration of the Canal. In addition, the United States government looked to the Episcopal Church to provide education to the West Indian laborers who were building the Canal.[105] The fact that the Episcopal Church and the American government worked hand in hand to provide social services for the Canal workers was consistent with the national church ideal. By 1919, the work of the Episcopal Church in the region had grown sufficiently to justify making the Canal Zone a full missionary district of the Episcopal Church. The General Convention of 1919 thus created the extra-continental missionary district of the Panama Canal Zone with the Right Rev. James C. Morris its first resident missionary bishop.[106] One month after his consecration, responsibility for Haiti was transferred to Morris from the missionary bishop of Puerto Rico.

The addition of the Panama Canal Zone as a missionary district of the Episcopal Church completed the expansion of the Episcopal Church's foreign mission activities in the first two decades of the twentieth century. Entering the 1900s the Episcopal Church had only four foreign missionary districts: Cape Palmas in Liberia, Shanghai in China, and Tokyo and Kyoto in Japan; and the one extra-continental missionary district of Alaska. By 1920 the Episcopal Church supported the eleven foreign missionary districts of: Anking, Hankow and Shanghai in China; Liberia; Brazil, Cuba, the Dominican Republic, and Haiti; Kyoto and Tokyo in Japan; and Mexico. Four more extra-continental "foreign" missionary districts had been added in the first two decades of the twentieth century. Honolulu, the Panama Canal Zone, the Philippine Islands and Puerto Rico joined Alaska as missionary districts in American territories lying outside the continental United States. These eleven foreign and five extra-continental missionary districts would be the primary focus of the foreign mission work of the Episcopal Church for the next four decades.

New Resources and New Structures for Mission

The growth in mission activity of the Episcopal Church in the first two decades of the twentieth century added to the expenses of the Domestic and Foreign Missionary Society. To meet the new budget demands, the Missionary Society undertook new fundraising and educational programs in support of the church's mission work. In addition, the different offices of the society became increasingly consolidated in a central, national structure. This centralization bolstered the national church ideal by providing a national identity for the Episcopal Church and its ministries in the United States and beyond.

Although since 1835 every Episcopalian had been considered a member of the Domestic and Foreign Missionary Society by virtue of his/her baptism, no systematic process by which every Episcopalian shared in the financial responsibility of the church's mission work had been established. Throughout the nineteenth century the domestic and foreign missions of the Episcopal Church relied solely on voluntary contributions and occasional legacies. Annual reports of the Missionary Society continually stressed that the only inhibiting factor to the advance of the church's missionary endeavors was the paucity of funds provided by Episcopalians. Expenditures for the support of missionaries, mission schools, and hospitals always outran the income produced by voluntary contributions. With the addition of new mission fields at the turn of the century, the gap between income and costs for missions widened enormously. For example, during the fiscal year September 1900 through September 1901, appropriations of the Domestic and Foreign Missionary Society reached $712,170. Income from contributions, legacies and special gifts, however, amounted to only $609,450. This left a deficit of $102,720 for the Missionary Society at the end of the year.[107] Clearly, something had to be done. The Domestic and Foreign Missionary Society could no longer afford to run a deficit budget and so recommended a 10% cut in appropriations for the following year.[108]

The 1901 General Convention in San Francisco was hesitant to cut back on missionary activities. With new territories added to the United States following the Spanish-American War, the times called for an advance — not a retreat — in foreign missions. To meet the deficit and to pay for the new missionary districts in Honolulu, the Philippines, Puerto Rico, and Hankow, as well as Western Kansas and Salina in the United States, the General Convention implemented the Apportionment Plan for mission giving. Under the new system, the Missionary Society suggested to each Episcopal Church diocese its fair share for the support of the church's missionary endeavors. It was expected that each diocese would then divide up its apportionment among its parishes, with an additional asking for diocesan missions.[109] The adoption of the Apportionment Plan meant that for the first time in the history of the Episcopal Church, the Missionary Society had a systematic giving process by which, in theory, every Episcopalian participated in the support of the missionary work of the church.

The Apportionment Plan was successful at first. In the first two years of the plan, the number of parishes contributing to the Missionary Society doubled from one third to almost two thirds of all Episcopal congregations. As a result, the funds received for foreign and domestic missions also doubled. The Apportionment Plan was hailed as a major breakthrough in overcoming the parochial mindset that had inhibited contributions to the Missionary Society throughout the nineteenth century.

> For the year 1901, the last fiscal year before the adoption of the Plan, the Board received congregational offerings, amounting to $235,993.81 applicable on the appropriations from 2,226 congregations as out of a total of 6,546. For the year just closed, [1904] the record has been $413,224.36 applicable on the appropriations from 4,190 congregations. Even more important than the present financial returns is the deepened recognition of responsibility, shown by many congregations, for the payment of pledges made to the missions in the name of the Church....
>
> The weak point in our giving has been the parochial congregations. The Apportionment Plan was intended to correct this condition, by throwing the chief responsibility for missionary support where it belongs, upon all the congregations which make up the body of the Church. Its success is evidenced by the large increase in the amount of congregational offerings and in the number of congregations from which those offerings have come.[110]

With the appointment of additional missionaries to the new missionary districts, the costs for the support of the Episcopal Church's missionary work continued to rise. Although the apportionment system increased missionary giving, income received continued to be insufficient to cover the appropriations made by the Domestic and Foreign Missionary Society. Leadership of the society believed that the inhibiting factor in contributions to the missionary work of the church was that some dioceses and parishes saw the Apportionment Plan as a tax levied upon them.

> While in some places [the apportionment] seems to be still regarded as a tax laid upon them [parishes and dioceses] for operations in which they are not concerned, there is an increasing recognition in the Church that the Board of Missions is really the Church's agent appointed to enable them to meet their obligation. From this point of view alone the wisdom of the Church seems to be demonstrated in adopting the policy of apportioning to the various dioceses and missionary districts the amount necessary to carry on the Church's missionary operations, and it is believed that once it is fairly understood that the Church's Mission was committed to the Church

and not to the Board of Missions, there will be no further trouble in meeting its financial obligations.[111]

To help Episcopalians better understand their responsibility to the mission of the church, the Missionary Society enlarged its educational programs.

One of the most important channels for publicizing the missionary work of the Episcopal Church was the missionary conference. The idea of missionary conferences was not new. Since the mid-nineteenth century, the Domestic and Foreign Missionary Society had sponsored conferences to generate interest in the missionary work of the Episcopal Church. To aid the functioning of the Apportionment Plan, the General Convention of 1901 divided the church into eight geographic districts.[112] Each district was to be under the leadership of a district secretary, who served without pay. The secretaries functioned as a liaison between the Missionary Society and the dioceses. In particular, the district secretaries helped to coordinate missionary conferences and encouraged participation in the Apportionment Plan. In 1904 the Domestic and Foreign Missionary Society added an educational department "to organize study classes, arrange missionary meetings and make a study of the Mission field."[113] The Rev. Everett P. Smith was called as the first educational secretary. It was hoped that the efforts of the educational secretary and the increased coordination of the missionary conferences would elicit from Episcopalians a greater commitment to the church's missionary endeavors.

Although the missionary conferences and work of the educational secretary improved the understanding of mission in the Episcopal Church, financial contributions from parishes and dioceses continued to remain below appropriations. Each year offerings from congregations, received through the dioceses, were less than that asked for by the Apportionment Plan; thus the Missionary Society continued to run a deficit. One segment of the Episcopal Church, however, gave generously to the mission activities of the church. Through the Woman's Auxiliary, Episcopalian women continued to be a major source of funding for the missionary work of the church. The key role of the Woman's Auxiliary in paying for Episcopal missions was generally acknowledged. When the Apportionment Plan was instituted in 1901, it was decided to keep the financial request to the Woman's Auxiliary and the Sunday-School Auxiliary separate from the general askings of congregations. The Missionary Society feared that if the askings to the auxiliaries were merged with the diocesan requests, the vitality of Episcopal women's commitment to mission might be lost.

> It seemed to the Board wise to keep the offerings of the Woman's Auxiliary and of the Sunday-School Auxiliary distinct from the offerings of congregations. It was feared that if the gifts of these Auxiliaries were not kept apart, the zeal which now marks their efforts would be endangered, because they would be converted from general to diocesan or parochial organizations. At, present they tend to obliterate diocesan and parochial lines, an important consideration when it is remembered that among the chief obstacles to the Church's Mission are diocesanism and parochialism. For many years both Auxiliaries have steadily increased their offerings.[114]

By 1907, the financial gifts of the Woman's Auxiliary to the Apportionment Plan amounted to $137,905, almost 39% above the asking of $100,000. In the same year contributions from congregations and individuals equaled $466,977, 29% below the requested $656,675.[115] In addition, the funds given to the apportionment by Episcopal women did not include the support for women missionaries provided by the Auxiliary's United Offering. In 1907, the Woman's Auxiliary sponsored eighty-three women missionaries through its United Offering. These United Offering missionaries, most of whom were single women, represented almost one third of the total number of American Episcopal missionaries serving overseas at the time.[116]

The financial and personal contributions of Episcopal men to the mission work of the Episcopal Church paled in comparison to that of the women. Efforts were made, however, to excite and organize the men of the church for a greater involvement in the church's missionary activities. Following the lead of the women's United Offering, a plan for a Men's Thank Offering was suggested at the General Convention of 1904. The Offering was to be presented at the next General Convention to commemorate the planting of the church at Jamestown, Virginia, 300 years before.[117]

When the convention met in Richmond in 1907, the men of the church brought forward only $775,000 of the hoped-for million. Although the offering produced less than expected, a suggestion was made to continue the Men's Thank Offering. The bishops vetoed the idea, fearing that it would interfere with the yearly offerings to the apportionment.[118]

A second effort to involve Episcopal men in the outreach of the church was the One Day's Income Plan, begun in 1915. This plan was conceived originally as a fund-raising program to meet the deficit of the Missionary Society that totaled over a quarter of a million dollars. Under the plan each Episcopalian was to set aside one day's income for the support of the mission activities of the church.[119] The One Day's Income Plan was a success and raised $416,211, freeing the Missionary Society from its debts. In order to capitalize on the accomplishments of the One Day's Income Plan, the General Convention of 1916 approved an annual program for a day of giving and prayer for the Missionary Society.[120]

The most significant program to stir the hearts and minds of Episcopal men for mission was the Laymen's Forward Movement. The Laymen's Forward Movement began in 1904 under the leadership of the Rev. Rufus W. Clark. In order to promote interest in and giving to the church's missions, Clark organized conferences, prayer meetings, and other educational activities for laymen in twelve Midwestern dioceses.[121] Because of his efforts, significant advances in men's commitment to mission activities were achieved. The leadership of the Domestic and Foreign Missionary Society recognized that Clark's campaign among the men of the Midwest could be replicated throughout the Episcopal Church. The General Convention of 1907 noted the important contributions of the Laymen's Forward Movement.

> An interesting development in the Church during the past three years has been the Laymen's Forward Movement, which had its beginning in 1904 on the initiative of the Rev. Dr. Clark, then secretary of the Fifth Department. Within this department several conferences of this Movement have been held. It would be well for the Church if this movement were extended throughout its borders, thus helping the men of the Church to realize more fully that the obligation for the Church's extension rests with themselves, and not with their wives and children.[122]

In the next decade the Laymen's Forward Movement would grow to become a major educational and fund-raising campaign that would touch every member of the Episcopal Church. At a "National Missionary Congress" held in Chicago in May 1910, it was suggested that every Episcopalian be individually canvassed to support the missionary work of the Episcopal Church. It was suggested that:

> "the time has come for the general adoption of the plan of an every-member canvass of the congregation for definite personal subscriptions to our mission work. Such a canvass gives to the congregation a new vision of the Mission of the Church. It brings out latent energies by giving the people some really large thing to do. It deepens the spiritual life of those engaged in the work. It puts those opposed to missions on the defensive. It increases interest in and contributions to the work at home. It gives courage and confidence to the clergy at home and the missionaries in the field by making them feel that they have the men of the Church behind them."[123]

The leadership of the Missionary Society welcomed the suggestion of an "every-member canvass" and looked to the Laymen's Forward Movement as the best vehicle to implement such a program. In 1910 the word "Laymen" was dropped from the title and the larger Forward Movement was begun. Soon diocesan Forward Movement Committees were established in each diocese.[124] Double-pocket envelopes that made provisions for offerings to the local parish as well as the Domestic and Foreign Missionary Society were provided to each Episcopalian in the pew.[125] By 1913, the Forward Movement and "every-member canvass" was celebrated as a major force in advancing the Episcopal Church at home and overseas.

> In undertaking this work under the name of the Forward Movement, the Board has endeavored to emphasize the importance of organization and the enlistment of personal service. About 1,200 congregations in all parts of the country have put these plans into operation more or less completely. Wherever the methods that experience has shown to be the best have been applied, the results have been little short of startling. Not only have missionary offerings largely increased, but money has come freely for Parish expenses and Parish improvements. Larger gifts have been made for diocesan missions because larger offerings have been made for the extension of the Church in the general field. Debts have been wiped out, churches, parish houses and rectories have been erected, and new plans, heretofore impossible, have been carried through triumphantly because of the more

generous spirit developed in the course of a canvass of the congregation for offerings for the Church's work beyond the Parish. In many instances congregations have been permanently enlarged, confirmation classes have increased in size, and negligent Churchmen have been brought back to Communion as a result of this work.[126]

Three years later, an expanded Forward Movement Campaign was planned to raise capital funds for foreign and domestic missions. The campaign, however, never materialized fully as it was begun the same month that the United States entered World War I. For the next few years Episcopalians were consumed with the conflict in Europe rather than raising money for missions. Following the war, the Forward Movement Campaign would throw its efforts behind a new Nation-Wide Campaign, the largest fund-raising program in its history of the Episcopal Church.[127]

Paralleling the growth in missionary districts and fund-raising programs in the first two decades of the twentieth century was an increasing consolidation of the symbolic and canonical powers of the Domestic and Foreign Missionary Society. Increasingly, the national church ideal necessitated a national institution to which all Episcopalians could point as the locus of their corporate identity. As the only body claiming to represent every member of the Episcopal Church, the Missionary Society began to fill the emerging role of the church's national organization.

One of the most important national church symbols of the Missionary Society was the construction of a national "Church Missions House" in the last decade of the nineteenth century. In 1888, the Rev. William Langford, General Secretary of the Missionary Society, argued that the Episcopal Church needed a headquarters from which all of its missionary activities could be centrally administered. He believed that a "missions house" would be "a symbol and embodiment of the missionary idea" and that the society "had earned a right to permanent headquarters, testifying to its stability and value."[128] Six years later, in 1894, the Domestic and Foreign Missionary Society entered its own headquarters on 281 Fourth Avenue in New York City, leaving behind forever its years as a tenant in various buildings in New York and Philadelphia. From its conception, the "Church Missions House" was to be a facility where all of the various mission activities of the Episcopal Church could come together under one roof.

In this House, from the first, the Woman's Auxiliary was made freely at home, but rented rooms also — for a Church book store on the ground floor, and for the purposes of the American Church Missionary Society, the American Church Building Fund, the Society for the Promoting of Christianity among the Jews, the Church Temperance Society, the Church Periodical Club, and the Brotherhood of Saint Andrew — were a partial fulfillment of the long time vision that the Missions House might be a real Church center to which any and every Churchman pilgrimaging to New York might turn for friendliness, help and convenience, and where a strong sense of unity and mutual interdependence might be engendered. Here also at last the Missionary Society had an altar of its own, where its officers and those at daily work within the house, the missionaries going to the field and returning — any and all of its members — might gather for intercession and thanksgiving, for closer union with their Lord and a renewal of their spiritual life.[129]

As a place of worship and mission administration, the Church Missions House would come to be known as both the "Church Center" and "281" for its street address.

In the first two decades of the twentieth century, significant canonical changes increased and centralized the powers of the Domestic and Foreign Missionary Society. The first canonical change occurred at the 1904 General Convention when the Board of Managers and the Board of Missions of the Missionary Society were combined. Since 1877 the society had been saddled with a complex structure that included the two boards. In theory the Board of Missions was a standing body that represented the General Convention (and by extension all Episcopalians) between meetings of the church's national convention. The Board of Missions, however, had no clear constitutional power but was in fact "nothing in the world but a committee of the whole, of doubtful constitutionality."[130] The Board of Managers, on the other hand, was the executive committee of the Missionary Society and was responsible for general oversight of its workings. William Reed Huntington called the complex and confusing relationship between the Board of Missions and the Board of Managers "the opprobrium of our Missionary Canon."[131] He suggested instead that the two boards be merged into one true "Board of Missions" to serve as the central administrative head of the Missionary Society. A finely tuned and centralized missionary society was consistent with Huntington's emphasis on Christian unity and the national church ideal.

The General Convention of 1904 implemented a new missionary canon resulting in a more efficient and more centralized administration of Episcopal mission initiatives. As suggested by Huntington (who was the chair of the Committee on the Constitution at the General Convention), the Board of Managers and the Board of Missions were merged into one Board of Missions. This Board was made up of fifteen bishops, fifteen presbyters and fifteen laymen, elected by the General Convention, with the Presiding Bishop as the *ex officio* president. The new Board of Missions was empowered to make all policy and administrative decisions for the Domestic and Foreign Missionary Society. In addition the new by-laws of the Board of Missions utilized a new method to oversee promotion of the missionary work of the Episcopal Church. The eight regions or missionary districts of the United States (organized in 1901) were instituted as Missionary Departments of the Society. Like the earlier districts, the departments were to serve as conduits of mission education and funding between the dioceses and the central Board of Missions. Each department would be administered by department secretaries replacing the earlier district secretaries. At first the Missionary Society provided for only three paid department secretaries, one of whom was the Rev. Rufus W. Clark. It was while serving as the secretary of the Department of the Mid-West that Clark organized the men of his twelve dioceses into a vital mission force and thus founded the Laymen's Forward Movement.

By 1907, the effectiveness of the missionary departments as important vehicles for the promotion of the missionary work of the Episcopal Church was widely acknowledged. In order to give the missionary departments formal authority and to link them in an organized structure to the Board of Missions, the General Convention of 1907 amended the canons of the Episcopal Church and formally constituted the missionary departments as part of the machinery of the church's mission administration.

> The General Convention grouped all of the dioceses and missionary districts in the United States into eight departments and made provision for the organization of a missionary council in each department to be auxiliary to the Board of Missions.

> The missionary council was given power to elect a department secretary, subject to the approval of the Board of Missions, his compensation to be fixed and paid by the Board of Missions; to select an additional representative to attend meetings of the Board of Missions with the privileges of the floor, but without the right to vote; to promote the holding of the missionary meetings and to foster missionary interest in the department; and the right to require the Board of Missions to make the annual apportionment in gross to the department, to be divided among the diocese and missionary districts by the council.[132]

As a result of the canonical amendment of 1907, the Board of Missions gained a greater identity as a representative body of the national Episcopal Church. This identity was strengthened even more in 1910 when the General Convention once again changed the Missionary Canon of the Episcopal Church.

> Instead of the whole body of the Board [of Missions] being chosen by the General Convention, it was divided, eight bishops, eight presbyters and eight laymen being chosen by the General Convention, and three members, one of each order, being chosen by each of the Missionary Departments with the purpose of giving the whole Church a voice in the administration of its work.[133]

In addition the General Convention of 1910 elevated the office of general secretary of the Board of Missions to that of president of the Board. The president was to be elected by the General Convention and was to hold office for six years. The new president of the Board would be the executive head of the Board of Missions and would be entrusted with the oversight of all of its administrative affairs. "The Board of Missions at once realized that in the placing of a real executive at the headquarters, a new force had been introduced."[134]

While the Board of Missions was increasingly consolidating its power and identity as a national body of the Episcopal Church, a parallel movement to raise the office of the Presiding Bishop to that of executive officer for the whole Episcopal Church was in the works. For over a century the Presiding Bishop had been the senior bishop in the House of Bishops of the General Convention. His responsibilities were primarily parliamentary and ceremonial, presiding at the meetings of the House and at the consecration of other bishops. As *ex officio* president of the Board of Managers of the Domestic and Foreign Missionary Society, the Presiding Bishop's main duty was to receive annual reports from the missionary bishops and transmit them to the Board of Managers.[135] By the turn of the century, however, the responsibilities on the Presiding Bishop had increased to the point of becoming too weighty for the senior bishop, who was usually advanced in years. In his address to the House of Bishops at the 1901 General Convention, Presiding Bishop Thomas March Clark noted that the work of the Presiding Bishop was too important for the elderly senior bishop to administer. To resolve this predicament Clark suggested that a careful study be done to define that nature of the office and that "the office of the Presiding Bishop be elective, instead of leaving it to be determined by the simple act of seniority."[136] There was much debate in both the House of Bishops and the House of Deputies about making the office of Presiding Bishop elective. Eventually an amendment to the church's constitution was introduced that allowed for the election of the Presiding Bishop by the House of Bishops, subject to the confirmation of the House of Deputies.

For the amendment to be passed, it had to be ratified by both houses at the next General Convention. By that time Bishop Clark had died and the Right Rev. Daniel Sylvester Tuttle had assumed the office of Presiding Bishop. Bishop Tuttle was a staunch advocate of the position that the senior bishop should be the Presiding Bishop. Under his leadership the 1904 General Convention failed to ratify the 1901 amendment although a committee to study the question of an elected Presiding Bishop was established. The next three General Conventions would wrestle with the issue. The Episcopal Church, however, was unable to be of one mind for two consecutive meetings and so the question of an elected Presiding Bishop was left open.

The General Convention of 1913 was significant for it brought together the issue of the growing national power of the Board of Missions and the question of an elected Presiding Bishop. To begin with, the convention passed a new canon that replaced the missionary departments with eight provinces in the church. Whereas the missionary departments were concerned primarily with missionary activities, the new provinces were to add the Episcopal Church's involvement in religious education and social service to their domain. The merging of religious education, social service and missionary activities under the provincial system reflected the greater centralization of the Episcopal Church's ministries into one national administrative structure. The new structure, however, raised the question of the appropriateness of the church's work in religious education and social service coming under the oversight of the Board of Missions. And so, at the initiative of the Board of Missions, the General Convention created a commission to reconsider the whole question of the Episcopal Church's missionary organization with particular attention to the role of the Presiding Bishop.

The Commission of Missionary Organization and Administration worked hard for the next three years and presented an extensive report to the General Convention of 1916. The report was accepted but the subject was re-committed for further action until the next General Convention. It was not a good time for a drastic revision of the structures of the church since, like most Americans, the majority of Episcopalians were preoccupied with the entrance of the United States into World War I.[137] At the General Convention of 1916, however, both houses finally concurred in adopting an amendment providing for the election of a Presiding Bishop. It was necessary for the next Convention to approve the amendment before it could become a part of the church's constitution.[138] And so the stage was set. The Episcopal Church was prepared to establish a new unified national structure with an elected Presiding Bishop as its head. The national church ideal celebrating a "national church," under which all Episcopalian mission activities would be united, was about to be realized.

NOTES

[1]Charles W. Forman, "A History of Foreign Mission Theory in America," in *American Missions in Bicentennial Perspective*, ed. R. Pierce Beaver (South Pasadena, Calif.: William Carey Library, 1976), 84.

[2]Anderson, "American Protestants in Pursuit of Mission: 1886-1986," *International Bulletin of Missionary Research* 12 (July 1988): 101.

[3]Paul A. Varg, "Motives in Protestant Missions: 1890-1917," *Church History* 23 (March 1954): 74-75.

[4]Anderson, 106.

[5]Dana L. Robert, "The Origin of the Student Volunteer Watchword: 'The Evangelization of the World in This Generation,'" *International Bulletin of Missionary Research* 10 (October 1986): 146.

[6]Forman, 91.

[7]John R. Mott, *The Evangelization of the World in This Generation* (New York: The Student Volunteer Movement, 1905).

[8]Robert, 148-149.

[9]William R. Hutchison, *Errand to the World: American Protestant Thought and Foreign Missions* (Chicago: The University of Chicago Press, 1987), 120.

[10]Forman, 91, and Hutchison, 121-124.

[11]Anderson, 101.

[12]Forman, 92.

[13]Hutchison, 123.

[14]Foreman, 93.

[15]Anderson, 101.

[16]Varg, 72-73.

[17]Kenneth Scott Latourette, *A History of the Expansion of Christianity* (New York: Harper & Brothers, 1941), vol. iv, *The Great Century: 1800-1914*, 106.

[18]Eccumenical Missionary Conference, *Report of the Ecumenical Conference on Foreign Missions, New York, 1900*, vol. 1 (New York: American Tract Society, 1900), 39.

[19]Ibid., 39-40.

[20]Anderson, 102.

[21]William Richey Hogg has traced the fundamental role the Edinburgh Conference played in the development of the modern ecumenical movement. See: William Richey Hogg, *Ecumenical Foundations: A History of the International Missionary Council and Its Nineteenth-Century Background* (New York: Harper and Brothers, Publishes, 1952), 98-143.

[22]Hutchison, 135.

[23]Latourette, 106.

[24]Gerald Anderson, "The Theology of Missions: 1928-1958" (Ph.D. diss., Boston University, 1960), 13.

[25]Anderson, "American Protestants in Pursuit of Mission: 1886-1986," 104.

[26]R. Pierce Beaver, *All Loves Excelling: American Protestant Women in World Mission* (Grand Rapids, Mich.: William B. Eerdmans Publishing Co., 1968), 178.

[27]Patricia R. Hill, *The World Their Household: The American Woman's Foreign Mission Movement and Cultural Transformation, 1870-1920* (Ann Arbor: University of Michigan Press, 1985), 5-6.

[28]Latourette marks the end of the "Great Century" of mission with the outbreak of World War I in 1914. See Latourette, 7.

[29]The missionary numbers quoted here represent men and women American Episcopalians who were appointed by the Domestic and Foreign Missionary Society of the Protestant Episcopal Church. The figures do not include indigenous church workers and wives of American missionaries. Indigenous church workers, however, were listed as missionary personnel in the Annual Reports. Wives, on the other hand, were only listed as missionary personnel if they had a specific appointment such as teacher or a nurse. See: Domestic and Foreign Missionary Society of the Protestant Episcopal Church in the United States of America, *Annual Report of the Domestic and Foreign Missionary Society of the Protestant Episcopal Church in the United States of America, 1899* (New York: The Domestic and Foreign Missionary Society of the Protestant Episcopal Church in the United States of America, 1899) and, Protestant Episcopal Church in the United States of America, Board of Missions, *Annual Report of the Board of Missions of the Protestant Episcopal Church in the United States of America, 1919* (New York: The Domestic and Foreign Missionary Society of the Protestant Episcopal Church in the United States of America, 1919).

[30]Ahlstrom states that Maurice and Kingsley played a leading role in the American Social Gospel Movement. See: Sydney E. Ahlstrom, *A Religious History of the American People* (New Haven, Conn., and London: Yale University Press, 1972), 632.

[31]William W. Manross, *A History of the American Episcopal Church* (New York: Morehouse-Gorham Co., 1950), 318.

[32]Robert W. Prichard, *A History of the Episcopal Church* (Harrisburg, Va.: Morehouse Publishing, 1991), 153.

[33]James Thayer Addison, *The Episcopal Church in the United States: 1789-1931* (New York: Scribner, 1951), 284.

[34]Ahlstrom, 629-630.

[35]Raymond W. Albright, *A History of the Protestant Episcopal Church* (New York: Macmillan Co., 1964), 314.

[36]Addison, 286-287.

[37]See: Mary Sudman Donovan, *A Different Call: Women's Ministries in the Episcopal Church, 1850-1920* (Wilton, Conn.: Morehouse-Barlow, 1986).

[38]Donovan, 16-17.

[39]Frank Sugeno, "The Establishmentarian Ideal and the Mission of the Episcopal Church," *Historical Magazine of the Protestant Episcopal Church* 53 (December 1984) 286. I am deeply indebted to Sugeno for his ground-breaking work on establishmentarianism in the context of the Episcopal Church, USA.

[40]F. D. Maurice, *Lincoln's Inn Sermons*, II, 93 ff., quoted in Stephen Neill, *Anglicanism* 4th ed., (New York: Oxford University Press, 1978), 252.

[41]Prichard, 188.

[42]S. D. McConnell, *History of the American Episcopal Church* (Milwaukee, Wis.: Morehouse Publishing, 1916), 344-345.

[43]Albright, 312.

[44]General Convention of the Episcopal Church, *The Proper for the Lesser Feasts and Fasts* (New York: Church Hymnal Corporation, 1988), 288.

[45]William Reed Huntington, *The Church-Idea: An Essay Towards Unity* 5th ed., (Boston and New York: Houghton Mifflin Company, 1928), 109-110.

[46]Ibid., 125-126.

[47]The "Quadrilateral" is found in the back of the Episcopal Prayer Book. See: Episcopal Church, The Book of Common Prayer (New York: The Church Hymnal Corporation, 1979), 876-877.

[48]William Reed Huntington, *A National Church* (New York: Charles Scribner's Sons, 1898), 71.

[49]Guy Roland Foster, "William Reed Huntington and the National Church," *The Episcopalian* (December 1989): 18-19.

[50]Frank Sugeno refers to a similar phenomenon but uses the term "establishmentarian ideal" not "national church ideal." See: Frank Sugeno, "The Establishmentarian Ideal and the Mission of the Episcopal Church."

[51]Calvin Colton, *The Genius and Mission of the Protestant Episcopal Church in the United States* (New York: Stanford & Swords, 1853), 292.

[52]Ibid., 250.

[53]Ibid., 293-304.

[54]Ibid., 305-306.

[55]Quoted in Robert S. Bosher, "The Pan-Anglican Congress of 1908," *Historical Magazine of the Protestant Episcopal Church* 13 (June 1954): 137.

[56]Arthur R. Gray, *The New World* (New York: The Domestic and Foreign Missionary Society, [1916]), vii.

[57]The inclusion of "The Monroe Doctrine" as an appendix in Gray's book represents the close identification of the mission work of the Episcopal Church with the political agenda of the United States government in Latin America.

[58]*Annual Report of the Domestic and Foreign Missionary Society of the Protestant Episcopal Church in the United States of America 1899*, 188-189.

[59]A missionary district was a mission officially recognized by the General Convention of the Episcopal Church and placed under the oversight of a missionary bishop. In 1899 the three foreign missionary districts of the Episcopal Church were Cape Palmas and Parts Adjacent (Liberia), Shanghai (China) and Tokyo (Japan).

[60]William Reed Huntington, *Duties of War: A Sermon Preached in Grace Church New York, on the Sunday After the Breaking Out of Hostilities Between the United States and Spain, April 24, 1898* (New York: Thomas Whittaker, 1898), 5.

[61]*Annual Report of the Domestic and Foreign Missionary Society,* *1899,* 188.

[62]General Convention of the Protestant Episcopal Church, *Journal of the General Convention of the Protestant Episcopal Church: 1907* (New York: The Winthrop Press for The General Convention, 1907), 433.

[63]General Convention of the Protestant Episcopal Church, *Journal of the General Convention of the Protestant Episcopal Church: 1901* (Boston: Alfred Mudge and Son for The General Convention, 1902), 408-409. The Philippines and Puerto Rico were made missionary districts in 1901, Mexico and Cuba had to wait until the General Convention of 1904 before being granted the same status.

[64]The distinction between domestic and foreign mission fields of the Episcopal Church was based solely on the territorial sovereignty of the United States. Since 1835 the Episcopal Church had declared that the whole world is one mission field and that the separation between domestic and foreign was for administrative purposes only. The blurring of the lines between domestic and foreign missions that occurred in the "extra-continental missionary districts" attests to the unity of the mission field in Episcopal mission thought.

[65]Chapman and the mission at Anvik are remembered as the recipient of the first Woman's Auxiliary's "united offering" collected in 1889. The close connection between the Woman's Auxiliary and the Alaska mission led to the appointment of two female missionaries to Anvik in 1895: Bertha W. Sabine, who took charge of the school; and Dr. Mary V. Glenton, a medical missionary.

[66]Addison, 329.

[67]Julia C. Emery, *A Century of Endeavor 1821-1921. A Record of the First Hundred Years of the Domestic and Foreign Missionary Society of the Protestant Episcopal Church in the United States of America* (New York: The Department of Mission, Protestant Episcopal Church in the United States of America, 1921), 203.

[68]Ibid., 227.

[69]For example, upon ascending the throne, Kamehameha and Emma immediately founded a hospital, now known as Queen's Hospital after Queen Emma, to address the needs of those who were suffering from smallpox. For their Christian witness and their role in bringing the Anglican Church to Hawaii, Kamehameha and Emma are now commemorated in the Episcopal Church's calendar on November 28. See: *The Proper for the Lesser Feasts and Fasts*, 416-417.

[70]Ibid., 416.

[71]Addison, 346.

[72]During the first two decades of the twentieth century membership in the Episcopal Church grew by 400% while the population of the island increased by only 4%. Albright, 335.

[73]Forty-three of 103 foreign missionaries of the Episcopal Church were serving in the missionary district of Shanghai. The total valuation of mission property in the district was $275,350, over $40,000 more than the two districts in Japan combined. See: The Domestic and Foreign Missionary Society of the Protestant Episcopal Church in the United States of America, *Annual Report of the Domestic and Foreign Missionary Society of the Protestant Episcopal Church in the United States of America, 1900* (New York: The Domestic and Foreign Missionary Society of the Protestant Episcopal Church in the United States, 1900).

[74]Stephen Neill, *A History of Christian Missions* (New York: Penguin Books, 1964), 411.

[75]*Journal of the General Convention: 1901*, 409-410.

[76]*The Spirit of Missions*, 29: 177-178, quoted in Gray, 190.

[77]Ibid, 191.

[78]Nelson R. Burr, *Mission 1821-1971, An Essay to Commemorate the Sesquicentennial of the Domestic and Foreign Missionary Society of the Episcopal Church in the United States* (Hartford, Conn.: The Church Missions Publishing Company, 1971),32-33.

[79]Gray, 196-198.

[80]Ibid., 199.

[81]Forty-First Annual Report of the Executive Committee to the American Church Missionary Society in: *Annual Report of the Domestic and Foreign Missionary Society, 1900*, 276.

[82]Gray, 143.

[83]Ibid., 146.

[84]Ibid., 147.

[85]Burr, 36.

[86]The American Church Missionary Society existed in name only until 1930 when all of its remaining assets were transferred to the Domestic and Foreign Missionary Society and the corporation dissolved. Protestant Episcopal Church in the United States of America, National Council, *Annual Report of the National Council of the Protestant Episcopal Church in the United States: 1930* (New York: The Domestic and Foreign Missionary Society, 1930), 186.

[87]Gray, 214.

[88]Report of the Missionary District of Wuhu in: Protestant Episcopal Church in the United States of America, Board of Missions, *Annual Report of the Board of Missions of the Protestant Episcopal Church in the United States of America, 1910-1911* (New York: The Domestic and Foreign Missionary Society, 1911) 306. Pott was one of the foremost educators in China and argued that Western education in church-sponsored schools was the greatest gift of Christian missions to the emerging Chinese nation. See: F. L. Hawks Pott, *The Emergency in China* (New York: Missionary Education Movement of the United States and Canada, 1913).

[89]The Seventy-Sixth Annual Report on Foreign Missions, *Annual Report of the Board of Missions of the Protestant Episcopal Church in the United States of America, 1910-1911*, 273-274.

[90]Triennial Report of the Board of Missions, General Convention of the Protestant Episcopal Church, *Journal of the General Convention of the Protestant Episcopal Church: 1913* (New York: The Sherwood Press for The General Convention, 1914), 422.

[91]David M. Dean suggests that the lack of support for Holly resulted from the racist attitudes of the leadership of the Domestic and Foreign Missionary Society who did not want to support an independent-thinking African-American expatriate. See: David M. Dean, *Defender of the Race* (Boston: Lambeth Press, 1979).

[92]Gray, 165-166.

[93]William L. Wipfler, *James Theodore Holly in Haiti,* Builders for Christ Series, ed. Powel Mills Dawley, (New York: The National Council, 1956), 8-9.

[94]*The Spirit of Missions*, 29, "Report of the Board of Missions": 32, quoted in Gray, 168-169.

[95]The first bishop of African descent in the Anglican Communion was the Right Rev. Samuel Adjai Crowther, who at the initiation of Henry Venn and the Church Missionary Society was consecrated bishop of the Niger Mission at Canterbury Cathedral on June 24, 1865. J. Carleton Hayden, "James Theodore Holly: Pioneer Bishop," *Linkage*, March 1985, 11.

[96]Dean, 107-108.

[97]Triennial Report of the Board of Missions, *Journal of the General Convention of the Protestant Episcopal Church: 1913*, 424.

[98]Ibid., 98.

[99]Triennial Report of the Board of Missions, General Convention of the Protestant Episcopal Church, *Journal of the General Convention of the Protestant Episcopal Church: 1916* (New York: The Sherwood Press for The General Convention, 1917), 429.

[100]Addison, 347.

[101]Aspinwall was a great benefactor of the Episcopal Church and built the primary buildings at the Protestant Theological Seminary in Virginia. The main classroom and administration building at the seminary still bears his name. Prichard, 168-169.

[102]Potter's visit to Christ Church was the first visit of an Anglican bishop to Panama. In passing through the isthmus, Potter contracted "Panama fever" and died before reaching San Francisco. John L. Kater, Jr., "Beginnings of the Episcopal Church in Panama," *Anglican and Episcopal History* 57 (June 1988): 151.

[103]Ibid.

[104]The Triennial Report of the Board of Missions of the Protestant Episcopal Church in the United States, *Journal of the General Convention of the Protestant Episcopal Church: 1907*, 445.

[105]Gray, 122-123.

[106]Report of the Bishop of the Panama Canal Zone in: Protestant Episcopal Church in the United States of America, National Council, *Annual Report of the Presiding Bishop and Council for the Year 1920* (New York: The Domestic and Foreign Missionary Society, 1920), 63.

[107]Report of the Treasurer, Domestic and Foreign Missionary Society of the Protestant Episcopal Church in the United States of America, *Annual Report of the Domestic and Foreign Missionary Society of the Protestant Episcopal Church in the United States of America, 1901* (New York: The Domestic and Foreign Missionary Society, 1901), 46.

[108]Triennial Report of the Board of Managers to the Board of Missions, Domestic and Foreign Missionary Society of the Protestant Episcopal Church in the United States of America, *Annual Report of the Domestic and Foreign Missionary Society, 1901*, 415.

[109]DuBose Murphy, "From 'Churches' to Church," *Historical Magazine of the Protestant Episcopal Church* 15 (June 1956): 198.

[110]Triennial Report of the Board of Managers of the Domestic and

Foreign Missionary Society, General Convention of the Protestant Episcopal Church, *Journal of the General Convention of the Protestant Episcopal Church: 1904* (New York: The Winthrop Press for The General Convention, 1904), 439.

[111]Triennial Report of the Board of Missions of the Protestant Episcopal Church in the United States of America, *Journal of the General Convention of the Protestant Episcopal Church: 1907,* 448-449.

[112]These missionary districts would evolve over time into the provinces found in the Episcopal Church today.

[113]Emery, 257.

[114]Triennial Report of the Board of Managers of the Domestic and Foreign Missionary Society, *Journal of the General Convention of the Protestant Episcopal Church: 1904,* 439.

[115]Triennial Report of the Board of Missions of the Protestant Episcopal Church in the United States of America, *Journal of the General Convention of the Protestant Episcopal Church: 1907,* 449.

[116]Missionary numbers taken from: Protestant Episcopal Church in the United States of America, Board of Missions, *Annual Reports of the Board of Missions of the Protestant Episcopal Church in the United States of America, 1907-1908* (New York: The Domestic and Foreign Missionary Society of the Protestant Episcopal Church in the United States of America, 1908).

[117]Emery, 255-256.

[118]Ibid., 261.

[119]It was assumed that only men were gainfully employed and so the One Day's Income Plan was designed for the men of the Episcopal Church.

[120]Emery, 293-294.

[121]The beginning of the Episcopal Laymen's Forward Movement in 1904 predated, by two years to the day, the founding of the ecumenical Laymen's Missionary Movement. Both movements had a similar goal, the motivation of American men for foreign missions. There was often cooperation between the two programs with Episcopal men active in both the Forward Movement and the Laymen's Missionary Movement.

[122]Triennial Report of the Board of Missions of the Protestant Episcopal Church in the United States of America, *Journal of the General Convention 1907,* 447.

[123]Triennial Report of the Board of Missions, General Convention of the Protestant Episcopal Church, *Journal of the General Convention of the Protestant Episcopal Church: 1910* (New York: The Winthrop Press for The General Convention, 1910), 460.

[124]Emery, 288.

[125]This is the origin of the "duplex" offering envelope in the Episcopal Church. Duplex Envelope Company of Richmond Virginia continues to supply envelopes to Episcopal Churches throughout the United States although the two pocket system has long since been abandoned.

[126]Triennial Report of the Board of Missions, *Journal of the General Convention of the Protestant Episcopal Church: 1913,* 420.

[127]Emery, 312-319.

[128]William Langford in *The Spirit of Missions,* October 1888, quoted in Emery, 221.

[129]Emery, 223.

[130]William Reed Huntington, "The Machinery of Our Missions" (n.p.: reprinted from *The Church Standard,* [1904]), 2.

[131]Ibid., 1.

[132]Protestant Episcopal Church in the United States of America, Board of Missions, *Annual Report of the Board of Missions of the Protestant Episcopal Church in the United States of America, 1907-1908*, 2.

[133]Protestant Episcopal Church in the United States of America, Board of Missions, *Annual Report of the Board of Missions, 1910-1911*, 2.

[134]Emery, 271.

[135]William Joseph Barnds, "A Study in the Development of the Office of Presiding Bishop of the American Episcopal Church, 1794-1944," *Historical Magazine of the Protestant Episcopal Church* 27 (December, 1958): 269.

[136]Clark's address had to be read to the House of Bishops since he was not able to be present in San Francisco for the Convention. Roland Foster, *The Role of the Presiding Bishop* (Cincinnati, Ohio: Forward Movement Publications, 1982), 51.

[137]Ibid., 60.

[138]Barnds, 274.

CHAPTER THREE

OUR EXPANDING CHURCH
The Ideal and the National Council
1919 to 1946

The years between the two world wars were a tumultuous time in Protestant thought. The fundamentalist-modernist controversy pitted biblical literalists against those who were open to evolutionary science and biblical criticism. Mission theology in the early decades of the twentieth century was not immune to such theological wrestlings. Conservative mission theorists stressed the uniqueness of the Christian message. Evangelization and individual conversion were held up as the primary objective of missions. Liberals, however, followed a path of reconciliation with other faiths and emphasized the transformation of society as the goal for missionary efforts.

Missiological discussions between conservatives and liberals in Protestant mission agencies found a forum in the International Missionary Council (IMC). The IMC, established in 1921, carried forward the hope and enthusiasm for ecumenical cooperation begun at Edinburgh in 1910.[1] At major meetings of the International Missionary Council in Jerusalem in 1928 and Madras in 1938, Protestant foreign missions would address the challenges of secularism and non-Christian religions set before them.

Mission thinkers in the Episcopal Church were not affected significantly by the debates in Protestant mission thought. The fundamentalist-modernist controversy did not shake the foundation of the Episcopal Church as much as it did other American Protestant churches. By the second decade of the twentieth century most Episcopalians accepted Darwinism and the need for biblical criticism.[2] There was, however, a debate between conservative and liberal Episcopalians over the literal truth of passages in the Apostles and Nicene Creeds. Discussions were carried on both in seminary faculties and in the House of Bishops.[3] The disagreements over literalism in the creeds would dissipate with sweeping changes in liturgy and polity of the Episcopal Church in the mid-1920s.

The national church ideal that increasingly informed Episcopal missionary activities in the late nineteenth and early twentieth centuries found a new and vital expression in the 1920s. Canonical changes passed at the 1919 General Convention in Detroit placed the Episcopal Church under one central administrative structure with the provision of an elected Presiding Bishop as its head. The new structure, known at first as The Presiding Bishop and Council and soon thereafter as the National Council of the Protestant Episcopal Church, brought together the church's efforts in education, social service and missions. In addition to the canonical changes, the General Convention of 1919 instituted a nationwide campaign to provide financial support for the new council and its work. With a new centralized church structure under the leadership of an elected Presiding Bishop supported by a nationally planned fund-raising program, the Episcopal Church claimed its coming of age as the "national church."[4]

For the first time in its history the Episcopal Church saw itself as being a unified body with a unified mission. Drawing parallels between its new structure and the political organization of the United States, the Episcopal Church celebrated its close identification with the principles of American democracy. At the same time Christian religious education, social service and church extension were lifted up as the "threefold Mission of the Church."[5] The goal of Episcopal foreign missions was to export this threefold mission through good schools, good hospitals and right-ordered worship to overseas Episcopal churches. These churches were to have the same democratic polity and character as the parent church in the United States. Through them the vine of the national church ideal was to reach to the ends of the earth.

NEW DEBATES IN PROTESTANT MISSION THOUGHT

In the years immediately following the close of World War I, American Protestantism maintained a sense of excitement and optimism about its foreign missionary endeavors. Foreign missions played an important role in spreading worldwide democracy.[6] Mainline missionary efforts in schools and hospitals were celebrated as effective tools in Christianizing the new international order.

> The mission establishment could feel that a torn and confused political order needed its ministrations now at least as much as a ruthless imperialism had needed them before. Until about 1930, moreover, this sense of purpose, usefulness and toughened resolve seemed to be ratified by the numbers — by financial support especially, but also by steady growth in most of the other statistics that publicists called upon, in their tireless self-surveys, to certify the pulse and bloodcount of world evangelization.[7]

This spirit of optimism and growth in missionary commitments was reflected in the founding of the International Missionary Council in 1921. As the chair of the Continuation Committee, John R. Mott carried forward the hopes for ecumenical sharing in missionary activities first begun at the 1910 World Missionary Conference in Edinburgh. The years before the war saw the proliferation of national missionary councils in Asia and Europe. World War I, however, disrupted these efforts toward missionary cooperation and the Continuation Committee ceased to function. In its place was a newly formed Emergency Committee of Cooperating Missions organized to deal with the question of German missions left stranded by the war.[8] Oversight for the Emergency Committee was entrusted to Mott and under his careful eye, German missions as well as the freedom for missionaries to pursue their activities unencumbered by the political upheavals of the war were preserved. After the war, missionary societies that had cooperated in the efforts of the Continuation and Emergency committees were prepared to enter into a larger organization. With the founding of the International Missionary Council in 1921 at Lake Mohonk, New York, the hopes and dreams of Edinburgh 1910 for a worldwide consultative missionary body were realized. In the next decade the IMC would function primarily as a liaison between national Christian councils and mission agencies around the world.

The post-war optimism in American Protestant foreign missions was short-lived. Theological debates between fundamentalists and modernists began to have an effect on the theology and practice of missionaries. The fundamentalists wanted a return to a priority on personal evangelism rather than the increasingly popular emphasis on education and social service. Conservative scholars such as W. H. Griffith Thomas and Augustus Strong argued that the evils of modern science and biblical criticism had diluted the evangelistic motive in foreign missions.[9] Too much effort was being spent administering mission schools and hospitals instead of proclaiming Jesus Christ. What worried the fundamentalists the most, however, was the increasing openness of the liberals to consider the possibility of salvation outside of Christianity.

The liberals, on the other hand, were more concerned with the increase of secularism, materialism and militarism in the world than with the uniqueness of the Christian message. Mainline missionaries increasingly emphasized societal change rather than personal conversion. This emphasis on church and society was bolstered by the success of the Social Gospel movement in the United States. Where the missionary message of the nineteenth century had stressed salvation in the world to come, there was now more stress on salvation in the present world.[10] To address the world's social evils, missionaries committed their energies to educational activities and social service. The redoubling of missionary efforts in schools and hospitals widened the gulf between the liberals and the conservatives.

The growing emphasis on societal change as missionary motive was not limited to foreign fields. The death and destruction caused by Christian nations fighting each other in World War I shook the confidence of the West that it was the highest development of Christian society. American manifest destiny of the nineteenth century gave way to an acknowledgment that the United States was increasingly becoming a non-Christian land. Economic decline, racial bigotry and the demise of American moral standards were seen as examples of the decadence and despair of an increasingly urban America where the businessman ruled supreme. With Christianity faltering at home, liberal missionaries thought twice before preaching the American way of life overseas. Paralleling the acknowledgment of the evils of the West was a new appreciation of the cultures of the East and a recognition of the emerging churches in Asia and Africa. American missionaries such as E. Stanley Jones, a Methodist working in India, began to take seriously the contributions of cultures and religions beyond the Western world.[11]

In his life and scholarship Daniel Johnson Fleming (1871-1963) exemplified the new appreciation for non-Western cultures and religions. Fleming served two terms as a Presbyterian missionary teacher in India from 1898 to 1901 and again from 1903 to 1912. As a math and science teacher at Forman Christian College in Lahore, Fleming was exposed to the richness of Indian culture and religions. In 1915 he returned to the United States to become the director of the Department of Foreign Service at Union Theological Seminary in New York. Three years later he became professor of missions at Union, remaining in this position for twenty-six years until 1944. As a missiologist, Fleming believed in the superior revelation of Jesus Christ.[12] He stressed, however, a reconciliation of Christianity as it had been known in the West with the culture and religions of the East.

> He clearly believed that God was working through all religions and cultures and that all traces of a sense of Western superiority should be eliminated. We should respect and love what is of God in other religions and cultures.[13]

Fleming sought to break down the walls that separated Christians from non-Christians; those in the West from those in the East. His prolific writings on this theme included: *Marks of a World Christian* (1919), *Ways of Sharing with Other Faiths* (1929), *The World at One in Prayer* (1942) and *Bringing Our World Together* (1945).

The most important missiological work of Fleming's was his book *Whither Bound in Missions*, published in 1925. Like many of his predecessors, Fleming shared the opinion that the missionary should work to indigenize the church in the mission field. He stated that all too often the efforts of the missionary were self-serving rather than of service to the indigenous church. As a corrective Fleming emphasized that the missionary's job was to be "temporary, secondary and advisory."[14] Fleming's acknowledgment of the un-Christian aspects of American society led him to criticize the whole concept of missions from the "Christianized" West to the non-Christian East.

> Fleming questioned the entire vocabulary of foreign missions and of "mission fields." No area is "foreign" and none, more than any other, is a "field." Since we can no longer speak of Christian societies converting non-Christian ones (all societies being less than Christian) we must insist that "the whole world is the mission field; and if a person serves at all he serves in the mission field."[15]

For Fleming the mission field was not pagan beliefs but rather the social and political ills that plagued all people. He argued that the value of any religion would be demonstrated through its self-expression in social service.[16] The worlds that needed to be converted were not foreign continents but rather the realms of industrialization, materialism, racism, ignorance, militarism and poverty.[17] With this redefinition mission became the common struggle of all people, including all religions, to combat the evils of the secular world. Fleming's attempt to move from mission fields to the concept of a common mission set the stage for the concepts of *missio Dei* and partnership that became prevalent in mid-twentieth century missiology.

Sensitivity to indigenous Christian churches emerging in Asia and Africa as well as the concern for secularism were the dominant themes at the 1928 International Missionary Council meeting in Jerusalem. Under the leadership of John R. Mott, the planners of the meeting made sure that non-Western churches were better

represented at Jerusalem than they had been at Edinburgh eighteen years before. Of the 231 representatives at the 1928 meeting
of the IMC nearly one-fourth (52) came from the "younger"
churches.[18] Mott's opening address to the Council saluted the participation of these Christians and emphasized the importance of
equal participation of all churches in the global missionary task.
He reminded the delegates that

> "here representatives of the older and younger churches meet on a fifty-
> fifty basis, that is on parity as to numbers, status, participation, and inter-
> ests to be served."

Mott believed Jerusalem would help institute

> "the new and true conception of the Christian missionary undertaking as
> a shared enterprise. Then all churches will be regarded as sending church-
> es; and all churches will be regarded as receiving churches.[19]

The primary topic for consideration and discussion at the
1928 meeting of the IMC was "The Christian Life and Message in
relation to Non-Christian Systems of Thought and Life."[20] The
enemy at Jerusalem was not other religions but rather the growing evil of secularism in the world. In his preliminary study paper
for the meeting, Rufus Jones emphasized "that the greatest rival of
Christianity in the world today is not Mohammedanism,
Buddhism, or Hinduism, or Confucianism, but a world-wide secular way of life and interpretation of the nature of things."[21] The
need to Christianize social institutions was the primary concern
of the Jerusalem meeting of the IMC. Delegates maintained that
the social outreach of Christian missions in schools and hospitals
was a frontline force in the fight against secularism throughout
the world. Jerusalem 1928 thus sought unity in the common fight
against secularism rather than addressing the potentially divisive
issue of the relationship between Christianity and other faiths.[22]
Within two years, however, this issue could no longer be avoided.

The most significant event to focus the conflict in foreign mission thought in the first half of the twentieth century was the 1932
report of the Laymen's Foreign Mission Inquiry. A Commission of
Appraisal made up of fifteen lay people representing the major
American Protestant denominations but independent of their

official mission boards undertook a systematic study of foreign mission activities in the East. With the financial backing of John D. Rockefeller, Jr., in-depth studies were made of missions in India, Burma, Japan and China. A seven-volume final report containing data and recommendations on each of the fields was produced and a one-volume summary of the report, entitled *Re-Thinking Missions,* was released in 1932. The summary was produced by William Ernest Hocking, the chairman of the Commission of Appraisal.

Re-Thinking Missions, also known as the "Laymen's Inquiry" or the "Laymen's Report," was influenced greatly by Hocking's thoughts on the nature of the missionary enterprise. Hocking was an eminent professor of philosophy at Harvard University and a Congregationalist layman. His personal and professional interest "was to discover a 'world faith' capable of overcoming the heartless forces of modern secularism."[23] He believed that Christianity and the other religions of the world should grow together uniting all people in a final world faith.[24] Hocking's commitment to a world faith was bound to have an effect on the Inquiry's evaluation of the foreign missions.

Re-Thinking Missions did not question the continuance of missions but rather the methods and goals of foreign mission work. The Inquiry sought to advance humanistic activities as the aim of foreign missions. Hocking emphasized that the love of God as exemplified in the life and ministry of Jesus Christ should motivate the social outreach of missionaries. *Re-Thinking Missions* attempted to recast definitions of evangelism to include Christian social service.

> Ministry to the secular [everyday] needs of men in the spirit of Christ, moreover, *is* evangelism, in the right sense of the word;...We believe that the time has come to set the educational and other philanthropic aspects of mission work free from organized responsibility to the work of conscious and direct evangelism. We must work with greater faith in invisible successes, be willing to give largely without preaching, to cooperate wholeheartedly with non-Christian agencies for social improvement, and to foster the initiative of the Orient in defining the ways in which we shall be invited to help. (Italics in original)[25]

The Inquiry was controversial not because it emphasized

philanthropy and social service but because it allowed for collaboration with other religions in these activities. Critics argued that such cooperation implied equality between Christianity and other religions. For Hocking and his Committee, Christianity needed to work side by side with non-Christian traditions for the transformation of the world.

> It is clearly not the duty of the Christian missionary to attack the non-Christian systems of religion — it is his primary duty to present in positive form his conception of the way of life and let it speak for itself....The Christian will therefore regard himself as a co-worker with the forces within each such religious system which are making for righteousness.[26]

Hocking and his colleagues further stated that a new kind of missionary was needed. They believed that the missionary of the future should be a kind of Christian ambassador who would work alongside people of other faiths rather than in opposition to them.[27] The report insisted that such missionaries must be better trained and better equipped intellectually and spiritually than the majority of the individuals currently working in the East. This backhanded critique of the quality of missionaries supported by American mainline denominations infuriated mission boards as much as Hocking's liberal acceptance of collaboration with other world religions. Such opinions brought swift criticism to *Re-Thinking Missions* and the Laymen's Inquiry.

Discussion of the Laymen's Inquiry representing a wide variety of opinions was found in both the religious and the secular press. One of the most outspoken supporters of Hocking and his committee was Pearl Buck. As a daughter of missionaries to China, the wife of a Presbyterian missionary and a celebrated author, Buck was in a good position to evaluate *Re-Thinking Missions*. In a glowing article published in the *Christian Century*, Buck praised the work as "the only book I have ever read which seems to me literally true in its every observation and right in its every conclusion."[28] Other views were not as positive. Robert E. Speer wrote an extensive review of Hocking's report in his 1933 book entitled: *Re-Thinking Missions Examined*. Speer acknowledged a need for high-quality missionaries who would work collegially with indigenous Christians in the East. But Speer was unwilling to accept Hocking's liberal position advocating cooperation with other religions. Speer criticized the report because it did not hold up the uniqueness of the Christian Gospel or recognize that the divine revelation of Jesus Christ made the Christian religion distinctly different from other world faiths.[29] Speer spoke for many of his colleagues in American Protestant missions who dissented from the Laymen's Inquiry because of its flawed theology.

Concern over the liberal theology found in *Re-Thinking Missions* was also voiced in continental Europe. Dr. Hendrick Kraemer, former missionary in the Dutch East Indies and professor of history of religions at Leiden University in the Netherlands, led the charge. Kraemer was greatly influenced by the writings of Karl Barth and was a leading voice in neo-orthodox theology. In 1936 the International Missionary Council commissioned Kraemer to write a theological and biblical study for the next meeting of the IMC. The study was to focus on evangelism in the modern world and the attitude that Christians should take toward other faiths.[30] What resulted was Kraemer's book *The Christian Message in a Non-Christian World,* published in 1938. In this work, Kraemer argued for the uniqueness of the Gospel and the radical discontinuity between Christian revelation and other religions of the world. Kraemer thus maintained that proclamation of Jesus Christ as Lord and Savior of the whole world was the only true aim of missions.

> The starting-point of missions is the divine commission to proclaim the Lordship of Christ over all life; and therefore a return to the pristine enthusiasm for evangelism and a new vision of what this implies in word and deed in the present complicated world are needed.[31]

With Hocking on one side and Kraemer on the other, the 1938 meeting of the International Missionary Council was forced to consider the question of the relationship of Christianity to other world religions.

Late in 1938, 471 men and women from sixty-nine countries gathered at the Madras Christian College in Tambaram, India, for a world conference of the International Missionary Council. At the Madras meeting of the IMC, the number of delegates from the "younger churches" outnumbered, for the first time, the number of official representatives from the "older churches."[32] For two and a half weeks, Christians from all over the worked, worshiped and lived together as true equals. The shared experience of the unity of the worldwide Christian church became the dominant theme of meeting. The spirit of the church's oneness that pervaded the Madras IMC meeting was reflected in the conference's report entitled: *The World Mission of the Church*.

In the question of Christianity and other religions, Madras tried to steer a center course. The majority of delegates at the 1938 IMC conference did not agree with Hocking and his belief that there is truth outside the Gospel. On the other hand, few individuals at the Madras meeting could wholeheartedly agree with Kraemer's insistence on the radical discontinuity of the Christian message. In general the delegates seemed to have a sympathy for the best in other faiths while remaining strong in their determination to witness for Christ among all people.[33] As is the case with most meetings representing a wide variety of opinion, Madras could only conclude that Christians were not in agreement as to whether non-Christian religions manifested God's revelation or not.[34] The conference agreed, however, that there were rival forces in the world that were at odds with the truth of the Christian message and the unity of the church. Nationalism, as experienced in Japanese Shinto, socialist and fascist movements in Europe, and communism in Russia and China were seen as the emerging enemies of the worldwide church. "These new pagan religions not only challenged Christianity's right to universality but also sought to subjugate it or to eradicate it altogether."[35] There was good reason for the IMC delegates to be concerned — within a year Hitler's army would march into Poland and the world would be plunged into a second global conflict.

In the next decade the International Missionary Council stood as a beacon of hope in a world divided by war. The IMC program for "orphaned missions" was a unique expression of Christian unity during World War II. At first German missions and then later the whole missionary endeavor of European Protestantism were left stranded as their home bases were plunged into war. To their rescue came the International Missionary Council. Soliciting contributions from member churches and denominational mission boards, the IMC served as a conduit to fund the missions cut off from their usual means of support. From 1940 to 1949 over eight million dollars was sent to the "orphaned missions" although this did not meet the vast needs of the stranded missions. The majority of these funds came from Protestant churches in the United States.[36] The orphaned missions program of the IMC, however, marked the beginning of a new era. It signaled a new level of collegiality between the older and younger churches in a common world mission enterprise. In particular, it initiated the sending of significant financial grants instead of missionary personnel as a viable vehicle for foreign mission work.

THE FOREIGN MISSION OF THE EPISCOPAL CHURCH AND THE NATIONAL COUNCIL

The foreign mission work of the Episcopal Church in the years between the two world wars was not affected greatly by the debates in Protestant mission theology. While the International Missionary Council sought new forms of cooperation between younger and older churches, the Episcopal Church maintained a colonialistic stance to its foreign missionary districts.

In the first two decades of the twentieth century, leaders of the Domestic and Foreign Missionary Society sought to bring together the Episcopal Church's outreach in education, social service and missions under one central coordinating body. The centralization process culminated in the founding of the National Council in 1919. Episcopalians now had a national church structure that would match its national church ideal. Episcopal foreign mission activities from the 1920s through the 1940s sought to export the model of mission envisioned by the National Council. During these "golden years" Episcopal missionaries were less concerned with planting indigenous churches than with extending the programmatic reach of the National Council to "our overseas Episcopal Church."

Realization of the National Church Ideal

Unlike other American Protestant churches, the Episcopal Church's confidence in its missionary outreach was not shaken by World War I. The United States military victory in the "war to end all wars" was consistent with the national church ideal. The triumph of democratic freedoms excited the Episcopal Church's missionary calling. The time seemed right for the church to take new and inventive steps to advance its work at home and around the world. This new energy for the mission work of the Episcopal Church, sometimes referred to as the "Nation-wide Movement," would lead to a radical overhaul of the organization of Episcopal mission work and an institutionalization of the national church ideal.[37]

The General Convention of 1919, held in Detroit, revolutionized the Episcopal Church. Foreseeing the impending changes in the church, the president of the Board of Missions, Arthur Selden Lloyd wrote in *The Spirit of Missions*:

> This Convention will probably be a turning point in the history of the American Church.[38]

In his sermon at the opening service, the Right Rev. Charles Henry Brent set the tone for General Convention. Brent had been the first Episcopal missionary bishop to the Philippines and during World War I had served as senior chaplain of the American Forces. Brent's sermon, entitled "Liberty through Discipleship," challenged Episcopalians to pursue their national church ideal in the post-war world.

> The new era is upon us. It began in international affairs and its spirit must be given cordial hospitality in domestic affairs. The truth and justice and honor and liberty which the war has hewn free cannot be allowed to rest until they have found permanent lodging in every department of human life, at home and abroad.[39]

Inspired by Brent, delegates to the convention affirmed that the Episcopal Church should emulate the American values that had triumphed in war.

We have seen since the last Convention our great people mobilized in a great war. We have seen them become, with all sectionalism vanished, a whole nation, thoroughly American, thoroughly devoted to the achievement of victory. No less than the nation, the Church must mobilize its resources,...and give to the world that insight which the nations of the world have had into the courage and sacrifice of the United States of America.[40]

The first contribution of the 1919 General Convention to the realization of the national church ideal was the ratification of an elected Presiding Bishop. Since 1901, legislation had been introduced in each General Convention attempting to change the office of Presiding Bishop from the senior member of the House of Bishops to an elected position. Since the matter involved a change in the constitution of the church, it required identical action by both the House of Deputies and the House of Bishops in two consecutive General Conventions. It was not until the convention of 1916 that a constitutional amendment was ratified approving for an elected Presiding Bishop. Three years later, at the Convention of 1919, the amendment received its final approval by both houses and became part of the constitution of the Episcopal Church. Upon the resignation or death of the current Presiding Bishop, the Right Rev. Daniel Sylvester Tuttle, Bishop of Missouri, a new Presiding Bishop would be elected by the House of Bishops. The specific term and duties of the prime bishop were left to a later convention to define.

The consolidation of the Episcopal Church's mission, education, social service and mission boards by the General Convention of 1919 was as significant as the elected Presiding Bishop for the realization of the national church ideal. The primary advocate for a more centralized organization of Episcopal mission activities was the Right Rev. Arthur Selden Lloyd (1857-1936). Lloyd was a son of Virginia, born just outside of Alexandria. Both of his parents came from prominent families who traced their roots to Virginia before the Revolutionary War. Brought up in a faithful Episcopal home, the Lloyds counted leading Virginia Episcopalians, including Robert E. Lee, as family friends. Lloyd was educated at the Virginia Polytechnic Institute and the University of Virginia in Charlottesville before entering the

Episcopal Seminary in Alexandria in 1877.[41] After graduating from seminary, Lloyd was ordained and served parishes in Farmville and Norfolk, Virginia. During his tenure at St. Luke's in Norfolk, the parish became a vital center for the support of mission work, contributing between one quarter and one-third of its receipts to missions through the Domestic and Foreign Missionary Society.[42] Lloyd became known for his commitment to missions and in October, 1899, was elected general secretary of the Board of Managers of the Domestic and Foreign Missionary Society.

Lloyd arrived in New York in December of 1899 to take up his position as general secretary in the new Church Missions House. Lloyd's administrative powers rose with the increasing consolidation and centralization of the missionary apparatus of the Episcopal Church. When the General Convention of 1904 replaced the Board of Managers with a more efficient Board of Missions, Lloyd was elected its general secretary. Lloyd served as the general secretary of the Board of Missions for six years until June of 1909 when he was elected bishop coadjutor of Virginia. He was bishop of his home diocese for only a year, though. In 1910, the General Convention raised the office of general secretary for the Board of Missions to president of the Board with increased power and responsibility over the missionary work of the church. On the first anniversary of his consecration, Bishop Lloyd was called by the General Convention to be the new President of the Board of Missions. Sensing this to be a genuine call, Lloyd left his beloved Virginia to return to the work of the whole church.

As president of the Board of Missions, Lloyd worked to promote and advance the missionary cause of the Episcopal Church. A chief concern of Lloyd's was the need for a more effective, and centralized, missionary structure that would encourage greater participation of all Episcopalians in the church's mission work. Lloyd believed strongly that the total mission of the Episcopal Church was represented in the three boards: Missions, Christian Education and Social Service.

> The work involved in the Church's Mission can be clearly separated into three factors. First is the Church's duty to bring to men the knowledge of

Christ in order that they may possess the life He has given them and know the truth that will make them free. Following upon this is the obligation to inform the minds which have been awakened to teach men how to use the wonderful gifts of which they find themselves possessed; and then follows the third factor which must successfully be accomplished before there can be a civilization that is worthy of those made able to become the sons of God. Those made alive again and educated must be showed how to surround themselves with such conditions as are fit for the children of free men to grow in.[43]

Lloyd further believed that a combined witness of the three boards could best represent the unity of the mission of the Episcopal Church. At Lloyd's initiative, a plan was put in place to unite the Board of Missions, the Board of Religious Education and the Commission on Social Service into one national committee.[44]

With Lloyd's guidance, a committee was appointed to develop a proposal for the consolidation of the separate boards under one administrative structure. The proposal was presented to the 1919 General Convention and was promptly adopted by both houses. A new canon, "Canon 60: Of the Presiding Bishop and Council," outlined the new administrative structure. Canon 60 provided for a new council "to administer and carry on the Missionary, Educational, and Social work of the Church, of which the Presiding Bishop shall be the executive head."[45] "The Presiding Bishop and Council" took over all of the responsibilities of the previous boards of mission, education and social service. Although the three boards were dissolved, the constitution of the Domestic and Foreign Missionary Society was maintained for legal purposes and the Missionary Society became the incorporated title of the new council.[46]

Canon 60 also provided specific organizational details for the Presiding Bishop and Council. The council was to be composed of twenty-four members: four bishops, four presbyters, eight laymen to be elected by the General Convention, and eight additional laymen to be elected one from each province of the church.[47] The work of the council was to be divided into five departments. The three departments of Religious Education, Christian Social Service, and Missions and Church Extension took over the work of the previous boards. In addition, a Department of Finance and a Department of Publicity were added to support the other three bureaus.

The final contribution of the 1919 General Convention to the Episcopal Church's national church ideal was the official sanctioning and promotion of the Nation-wide Campaign. The Nation-wide Campaign was initially begun early in 1919 by the Board of Missions. At the board's February meeting, the Rev. Dr. Alexander Mann of Boston, Massachusetts, proposed: "That a nationwide campaign of missionary education and inspiration should be begun at the earliest possible moment."[48] The campaign was initially conceived of as a fund-raising event to overcome the Board of Missions financial shortfall at the close of 1918. The board, however, felt that the time was right to begin a significant campaign that would go beyond meeting existing deficits. It envisioned a true nationwide effort designed to challenge every man, woman and child, every organization, parochial and diocesan, to cooperate in supporting the missionary work of the Episcopal Church. Responsibility for the Nation-wide Campaign was entrusted to the existing committee commissioned to pursue Bishop Lloyd's plan for the unification of the three boards of education, social work and missions.[49] As a result the Nation-wide Campaign was linked inextricably to the centralization process leading to the founding of the Presiding Bishop and Council.

The new campaign was to build on the earlier efforts of the Forward Movement. Following a comprehensive survey of the church's needs at home and abroad, every Episcopalian would be challenged to contribute to the Episcopal Church's work through an annual every-member canvass. Recognizing that the Nation-wide Campaign continued the work of the Forward Movement campaign begun in 1916, the Forward Movement threw its whole effort into the new venture. In March of 1919, the Rev. Dr. Robert W. Patton, secretary for the Province of Sewanee, was appointed director of the Campaign.[50] Under Patton's leadership,

a survey of the entire field of Church work was undertaken, largely by questionnaires and correspondence, during the summer of 1919. Even though this preliminary work was hastily done, and the answers reflected pious hopes and vague ideals more often than sober and attainable possibilities, yet it was made abundantly clear that the Church was facing rich opportunities everywhere. All that was needed was well organized support.[51]

The organization and support were achieved at the General Convention of 1919.

At the General Convention, Patton reported on the preliminary efforts of the Nation-wide Campaign and the early findings of the survey. Mann's original vision for the campaign had grown since he had suggested it to the Board of Missions. As president of the House of Deputies, Mann emphasized that the Nation-wide Campaign was of national importance.

> The report of the Nation-wide Campaign as thus far carried on seems to me of primary importance. It is an effort to lift us all out of our comparative isolation to give us consciousness of the national life of the Church and consciousness of her responsibility to the nation.[52]

Eloquent speeches in support of the campaign were made in joint sessions of the General Convention; both the House of Bishops and the House of Deputies wholeheartedly endorsed the Nation-wide Campaign.

The campaign immediately became the vehicle by which the newly instituted Presiding Bishop and Council would secure funds for its combined work in education, social service and missions. Building on the earlier apportionment plan of the Domestic and Foreign Missionary Society, the Nation-wide Campaign was given responsibility for allocating to each diocese its share in the work of the Presiding Bishop and Council. Each diocese was expected to parcel out its quota to each of its parishes, adding an additional figure to pay for diocesan needs. On the last Sunday of the liturgical year (the Sunday prior to the beginning of Advent), each Episcopalian was to be canvassed as to his or her commitment of "time, talents and treasure" to the church. Through this annual every-member canvass, the Nation-wide Campaign sought to involve each Episcopalian in the support of the "whole work of the whole church."[53]

Finally, Canon 60 adopted by the 1919 General Convention provided for an interim president for the new council until a duly elected Presiding Bishop could assume responsibility as its chief executive officer. Since Lloyd's term of office as president of the Board of Missions still had three years to run and since he was the inspiration behind the National Council, he was expected to assume the interim presidency. Lloyd, however, resigned his position so that the General Convention would have complete freedom to elect the person of their choice. Much to the surprise of many at the convention, the Right Rev. Thomas Frank Gailor, bishop of Tennessee and chairman of the House of Bishops, was elected interim president of the council. Lloyd's biographer, Alexander C. Zabriskie, reports that Lloyd accepted the loss with dignity.

> Though he never said anything about it, some of his close friends were positive that Lloyd hoped to be elected President. He more than any one man was responsible for the evolution of the Council and for the new day of forward movement which the Nation-wide Campaign had promised. It was wholly natural that he should desire a chance to lead the perfected machinery on to greater efforts. But if he desired the post, he was disappointed.[54]

After the convention, Lloyd returned to "281" and presided over the last meeting of the Board of Missions in December 1919. The Presiding Bishop and Council was installed early in 1920, and Lloyd returned to parish ministry as the rector of St. Bartholomew's Church in White Plains, New York.[55]

Just as Lloyd had predicted, the General Convention of 1919 was a turning point in the history of the Episcopal Church. The ratification of an elected Presiding Bishop combined with a unified organizational structure in the Presiding Bishop and Council gave the Episcopal Church a common national identity. In addition, the Nation-wide Campaign guaranteed that the new national structure would have a source of funding for its work. At the 1919 General Convention the Episcopal Church emerged from a nineteenth-century federation of Episcopal churches to a truly national Anglican church in the United States. In its new organization and national identity the Episcopal Church realized fully its national church ideal. The Rev. Dr. George P. Atwater, chairman of the Ohio delegation to the General Convention, summed up the accomplishments of the 1919 General Convention.

> We have become a national Church in organization, and what is better, in spirit and determination....A national consciousness has dawned. We are

now the Church in the United States, and not a Church scattered through various geographical areas. National thinking, national action, and national cooperation will result in glorious national achievement. (Italics in original)[56]

At the 1922 General Convention, the name of the council was changed from the Presiding Bishop and Council to The National Council, further emphasizing the national church ideal implicit in the new structure.

> Thus was accomplished a veritable revolution in the government of the American Episcopal Church. From being the least centralized of any part of the Anglican Communion, she had now become the most. It is important to bear in mind that nothing comparable to the National Council existed, or ever had existed, in Anglicanism. The American Church now had a body capable of long range planning, of effective strategy. It had a Curia.[57]

The Mission of the National Church[58]

With the founding of the National Council, the Episcopal Church began to articulate a missiology in keeping with its national church ideal. The emerging Episcopal missiology blended a catholic theology of mission with an American commitment to the social gospel. This "national church missiology" saw the Episcopal Church as the inheritor of God's mission to give life more abundantly in the physical, mental and spiritual dimensions of the world.

The individual who first outlined a theology of mission consistent with the Episcopal Church's national church ideal was William Codman Sturgis. Sturgis was not a professional theologian but an Episcopal layman trained in philosophy at Harvard University. In 1907 Sturgis became a member of the Board of Missions and ten years later was appointed educational secretary for the Board. With the founding of the National Council, Sturgis continued his work as educational secretary under the auspices of the Department of Missions. While in this position Sturgis wrote extensively about the nature of mission as understood by the National Council of the Episcopal Church. Sturgis's books, *The Church's Life: A Study in the Fundamentals of the Church's Mission* published by the Domestic and Foreign Missionary Society in 1920, and *The Church Awake: A Study of the Vital*

Elements in the Gospel published by the National Council in 1927, best represent the "national church missiology" of the Episcopal Church.

Sturgis believed strongly that God's mission and the church's mission were one and the same. He defined God's mission as a desire to make God known in the world. Drawing on Hebrew Scripture, Sturgis saw God's election of Israel as a vehicle for the fulfillment of God's mission on earth. God's

> plan has been to reveal Himself first to one carefully selected man of spiritual capacity to receive the revelation; then from him, to build up a people chosen, isolated, disciplined, instructed, blessed; in order that through them the message might be carried everywhere. The man was Abraham, the people, Israel, God's ancient Church.[59]

Sturgis further emphasized that although God revealed himself through his chosen people Israel, God's fullest revelation was to be found in the incarnation of Jesus Christ.

For Sturgis, God's mission as realized in Jesus was to "give life 'more abundantly' to every man, woman and child on earth; and to apply that principle to the whole of life — body, mind and soul."[60] Sturgis stressed that the church was the Body of Christ and as such was the new Israel, the new purveyor of God's mission in the world.

> To [Jesus, God] entrusts the perfect revelation of Himself; to Him He gives the task of begetting a new race — a new Israel — a new Church...So the Christian Church arises as God's messenger like the Jewish Church of old, but having this supreme advantage, that she is born of One divinely human and humanly divine, able perfectly to receive and perfectly to impart the complete revelation of God, and able further to make His Church a trustworthy witness, proclaiming God's message to all men everywhere, and thus fulfilling her mission.[61]

Sturgis believed strongly that the mission of the church was coequal with God's mission as realized in the incarnation of Jesus Christ. For him the mission of the church was universal (catholic) and singular.

Because of Sturgis' high priority on the unity of the church's mission as God's mission in the world, he took issue with the word "missions." For him the word "missions" grew out of an inadequate theology that did not represent the oneness of the calling of the church.

The word "Missions" also gives the unfortunate impression that there are all kinds of missions, and therefore all sorts of messages. Consequently the average layman has come to speak of "foreign missions" and "domestic missions" and "diocesan missions" and "parochial missions"; and worse still, he even picks and chooses among these and states, sometimes, as though he were perfectly reasonable, that he believes in one kind and not in another. Of course this is stupid, and could have been largely avoided if only we Churchmen had all been taught, from childhood up, that the one church has one mission, which is to carry a message received from God and to deliver it to every man, woman, and child within reach — to John Smith around the corner in my town, quite as much as to John Chinaman in Hankow, and *vice versa*. (Italics in original)[62]

Sturgis thus built on the teaching of the Episcopal Church, first stated in 1835 by the Domestic and Foreign Missionary Society, that there is no theological distinction between the church's work in domestic and foreign fields.

Although Sturgis emphasized that the church's mission was one, he maintained that the church pursued its mission in three different spheres: the physical, the mental and the spiritual. Following the example of Jesus, the church is called to heal, to teach, and to lead people to God.

The Church, as the living Body of Christ, has a three-fold mission on earth. Her privilege and her duty are to provide every man, woman and child with an opportunity to become a sharer in a more abundant form of life, incidentally for the body and the mind, but primarily and supremely for the soul, whereby man is raised above the plane of mere humanity into membership in the Family of God, and eternal life is imparted and maintained here and now. This three-fold mission of the Church is expressed in the terms Social Service, Religious Education and Evangelism or Church Extension.[63]

Sturgis saw the National Council as the embodiment of the church's three-fold mission.

The Episcopal Church has, of recent years, recognized the fact that her mission on earth, like that of Jesus Christ, is of a three fold nature — the ministry to the physical, the intellectual, and the spiritual needs of all mankind. This essential principle she has now placed officially in the very structure of her organization, so that her interest and activity must of necessity be expressed in terms of Christian social service and religious education, coordinately with evangelization. In this respect her official organization is almost unique, among the Churches of Christendom, and it lays upon every one of her members a definite responsibility toward the physical, the intellectual, and the spiritual building of our nation.[64]

The National Council thus represented the unity of the Episcopal Church's efforts to make Christ known at home and overseas. Its three departments of Religious Education, Social Service and Church Extension were consistent with the three-fold nature of the church's mission.

> If the Church represents the projection of Christ's life in the world, and the continuation of His ministry to the world; and if, further, He is our supreme example in connection with our mission, it would appear that that mission should always and everywhere include hospitals, homes for the poor and the neglected, asylums, orphanages, playgrounds and other agencies for ministering to bodily needs; schools, colleges, seminaries and other means of mental and industrial training; and, above all, church buildings and an adequate supply of workers, ordained and lay, to preach the Word, to administer the sacraments, to provide opportunity for worship, and to minister effectively to the spiritual needs of the community. Evidently these three forms of missionary activity are expressed today by the terms, *Social Service, Religious Education* and *Church Extension*. These, together, constitute the full round of the Church's mission, and those Christians who engage in them are properly "missionaries." (Italics in original)[65]

Sturgis believed that every Episcopalian was given the opportunity to engage in the Episcopal Church's mission through the work of the National Council. He maintained that the power of the Holy Spirit propelling the church's mission was expressed in three forms of energy: prayer, service and money.[66] The Nationwide Campaign sought to release these three forms of missionary energy. Each and every Episcopalian who participated in the work of the National Council and contributed to it through his/her parish and diocesan quota system was thus seen as a missionary. The fact that every Episcopalian was considered a missionary by virtue of his/her baptism and participation in the work of the National Council was consistent with the catholic mission theology of the Episcopal Church. Sturgis's position was consistent with the Episcopal Church's affirmation of 1835 that it is baptism that makes one a member in the church's missionary society, not one's voluntary contribution.

Sturgis was thus a significant voice in the emerging missiology of the national church ideal as it was realized in the National Council. His definition of evangelism as "church extension" reflected his high regard for the church as a universal (catholic) institution. For Sturgis the ultimate goal of the church's mission was to bring people into the "one holy catholic and apostolic, Church" where the historic sacraments were "rightly and duly administered." He believed that the Episcopal Church's work in hospitals and schools should contribute to the spread of the one, true, church around the world. Sturgis emphasized that the Episcopal Church, and the National Council in particular, represented a unique expression of God's universal church. He gave a voice to the unstated assumption that good schools and good hospitals combined with right-ordered sacramental worship would lead people in the United States and around the world into the "abundant life" as Episcopalians knew it.

Blinded by the national church ideal, Episcopalians were unable to see the cultural limitations of a church organization that was, in fact, a creation of her people and not fore-ordained by God. The catholic theology implicit in the national church ideal deliberately and steadily ran against Protestant voluntarism. The Episcopal Church thus rejected the dominant ethos of American Protestant missions and its handmaid, evangelism. Thus when the International Missionary Council and other American Protestants began to be more critical of American values and the exportation of them in their foreign mission ventures, the Episcopal Church did not participate in the critique. Instead Episcopalians pushed forward with the triumphalism of American culture.

The Episcopal Church's self-assurance as a national church grew in the decade following the founding of the National Council. With new confidence the Episcopal Church expanded the pursuit of its three-fold mission beyond the geographic boundaries of the United States. In 1924 and 1925 the National Council published three books that related the work of the national church to the larger world. "*My Father's Business:*" *World Problems and Personal Responsibility,* prepared by J. M. B. Gill, and *The World and I,* by Alfred Newbury were both promotional and educational works outlining the responsibilities of the National Council in addressing general world problems such as industrialism, war, race prejudice and international interdependence.[67] *That Freedom: A*

Study of Democracy in the Americas, written by the National Council's Secretary of Latin America, Arthur R. Gray, placed the work of the Episcopal Church in Brazil, Central America, Mexico and the Caribbean within the context of American political interests in Latin America.

"My Father's Business" was an attempt by the National Council, speaking for a uniquely American Episcopal Church, to define the church's response to world problems. The book states unabashedly that the history and organization of the Episcopal Church embody the American democratic spirit. It suggests that the church's foreign mission work should be evaluated in light of its contribution to the building of American democracy around the world.

> The more carefully we study the organization of the Church the more deeply we are impressed by its essentially American character and its absolutely democratic spirit. Intelligent study of and loyal adherence to the Church is good training for citizenship. Domestic and parochial missionary work is a valuable adjunct to any program of Americanization. It might be profitable to consider the value of [foreign] missions from this point of view.[68]

The book pointed out that the creation of the National Council was "the capstone which completed the organization and brought it fully in line with the democratic organization of the State."[69] It presented the following comparison of the United States government and the Episcopal Church in order to show "how completely they parallel each other."[70]

STATE	CHURCH
I. CITY, TOWN VILLAGE	I. THE PARISH
a. Mayor	a. Rector
b. Aldermen or Councilmen	b. Vestry; Parish Council
c. Citizens	c. Congregation
II. STATE	II. THE DIOCESE
a. Governor	a. Bishop
b. State Offices	b. Standing Committee; Diocesan Counci;
c. Legislature	c. Diocesan Convention
1. Senate	1. Clergy
2. Assembly	2. Laity

STATE	CHURCH
III. UNITED STATES	III. NATIONAL CHURCH
a. President	a. Presiding Bishop
b. Cabinet	b. National Council
c. Congress	c. General Convention
1. Senate	1. House of Bishops
2. House of Representatives	2. House of Deputies

The comparison between the state and the church was offered as proof of the Episcopal Church's unique embodiment of the American democratic spirit. It concluded:

This comparison shows how completely our Church is in harmony with the spirit of America. In organization and government she is the creation of her people just as our secular government is the creation of her citizens.[71]

The Episcopal Church celebrated its American spirit and sought to export it around the world.

"My Father's Business" sought to apply the unique combination of American democracy and Christian truth found in the Episcopal Church to world problems in the 1920s. The evils of materialism, industrialism, racism and war were expected to melt away as the church pursued its three-fold mission of social service, education, and church extension around the world. The foreign missionary was to be the purveyor of the national church ideal and the American democratic spirit.

A nation should be judged by its ideals and standards, for these alone keep a nation from being dragged down to the low plane of absolute materialism. To interpret these ideals to alien races is a somewhat specialized work, in which the real uplift and advantage of our educational, economic and political institutions and methods are, as it were, isolated from their material envelope and set forth for examination and appreciation. This is the work of the missionary. This is the Church working toward the realization of a warless world, an international brotherhood.[72]

"My Father's Business" applauded the efforts of the Episcopal Church in Japan and China. Mission schools were praised as the most important means for imparting American democratic values in the "orient."

Throughout the mission schools of secondary and primary grade, patriotism, service, and social responsibility are emphasized and all strengthened and inspired by Christian principles. Washington, Lincoln and Roosevelt are as well known as their own national heroes. It is our aim to show the real meaning of the Chinese proverb "All under heaven are one family."[73]

In Latin America, the Episcopal Church's mission of social regeneration through Christian moral truths and American democracy was interpreted as "Christianize the Monroe Doctrine." The Episcopal Church believed that the Monroe Doctrine presented a vehicle by which republics in North and South America could "advance hand in hand in the appreciation and development of all that pertains to true democracy in government and national life."[74] The history of the Monroe Doctrine, however, represented a different scenario. Instead of mutual cooperation between republics it became the means by which the rich United States exploited its southern neighbors. What was needed was a curative that would return the Monroe Doctrine to its true democratic ideals of "freedom and justice for all." This was the mission of the church.

The only agency whose policy can be wholly altruistic and disinterested is the Christian Church. She, and she alone, exhibits the spirit of America, American ideals untainted by commercialism and greed. The Church comes to give and not to get. The great responsibility of being an interpreter of Christian America to Latin-Americans; of revealing the sound principles of human brotherhood upon which our civilization is built; of removing suspicion and distrust from the relations of countries having a common purpose and goal; of promoting international fellowship and peace — this is our responsibility viewed solely in its secular aspect. It is an unparalleled opportunity to serve the countries involved and also the larger cause of peace. We can Christianize the Monroe Doctrine.[75]

The particular role of the Episcopal Church in "Christianizing the Monroe Doctrine" was articulated in Arthur R. Gray's book, *That Freedom: A Study of Democracy in the Americas*, published by the National Council in 1925. Gray stated that there are two kinds of freedom: This Freedom and That Freedom. "This Freedom" is a false freedom of individual caprice and greed. "That Freedom" is "a perfect freedom, based on the service of a God of Law and Order, nourished by self-sacrifice, and bearing its proper fruit at last in harmony and peace, righteousness and justice."[76]

Gray maintained that the Monroe Doctrine needed to be grounded in "That Freedom," which respects the dignity of each person. He believed the Episcopal Church's work in education, social service and church extension was the best means for the realization of "That Freedom." His book concludes with a review of the work of the Episcopal Church in each of its Latin American missionary districts. The Episcopal Church's three-fold mission in education, health and the building of churches is offered as the vehicle by which the Monroe Doctrine will be Christianized.

Motivated by a *noblesse oblige*, Episcopalians set out to share the wealths of their Anglican tradition and American way throughout the world. *The World and I*, published by the National Council in 1925, outlined the responsibilities of Episcopalians in meeting the needs of the "less fortunate" at home and abroad. It emphasized that God was using the American Episcopal Church to realize God's kingdom in the world.

> If in any respect we really desire to see the Kingdom of righteousness and peace and justice and love established throughout the world, it is because the Kingdom of God has come to be, more or less, within us. It is the value which each one of us individually places upon Jesus Christ and His Gospel that determines the speed and extent of the whole three-fold Mission of the Church, to the minds, bodies and souls of men throughout the whole world.[77]

The World and I celebrated the accomplishments of the three-fold mission of the Episcopal Church.

> [The American Episcopal Church] is busied with her Mission. She bears in her hands ten-thousand Indian members of one single tribe; a thousand of her congregations are organized to meet the problems of the Foreign-born; her schools for Negroes empty the jails in their vicinity; her hospitals minister to the desperate needs of the frozen North; she planted the Church in Liberia; and to her efforts are due the Holy Catholic Churches of China and Japan.[78]

The mission of the "national church" for Episcopalians was to give life "'more abundantly" to every man, woman and child on earth. The Episcopal Church emphasized that the abundant life was actualized in good hospitals, good schools and right-ordered sacramental worship, all coupled with American democratic freedoms. With the development of the National Council, the Episcopal Church realized its resources and identity as a "national church" and its three-fold mission in the United States and around the world.

The National Church Moves Forward

The vision and enthusiasm of the early years of the National Council would meet with financial and administrative ambiguities. Fiscal hardships caused by the Depression and questions over the role and responsibilities of the Presiding Bishop threatened the work of the National Council. Despite these ups and downs, the National Council supported more foreign missionaries during the years between the world wars than in any other period in the church's history. On average more than 400 American Episcopal missionaries served outside of the United States at any one time.[79] In general more women than men served overseas as Episcopal missionaries. Because women were excluded from the ordained ministry, most women missionaries worked as teachers, doctors and nurses. The majority of men serving overseas were clerics assigned to parochial ministries. As a result, in the three-fold mission of the Episcopal Church, spiritual affairs were reserved for the ordained men while women ministered to the body and mind.

In these first few decades of the National Council, the Episcopal Church would not add any new foreign district to its missionary portfolio.[80] Instead the church sought to build on its existing overseas work. Although the need to build up indigenous, self-governing, self-supporting and self-extending churches was mentioned from time to time, Episcopal foreign mission work from 1919 to 1946 sought to expand the influence and programs of the National Council around the world.

The Nation-wide Campaign was hailed as a breakthrough in the support of the mission work of the Episcopal Church. The publication of the financial needs of the Episcopal Church, in a unified national program under the Presiding Bishop and Council (National Council), combined with a well-organized every-member canvass, had tremendous results.[81] The campaign was credited with increasing both the spiritual well-being and the financial resources of the Episcopal Church during the triennium 1919-1922.

> The Nation-Wide Campaign has accomplished one of the most stupendous tasks that has ever confronted the Church in establishing principles and practice of Christian stewardship among our people. The whole Church has a wide vision of her chief purpose and responsibility.

One hundred and eighty-seven new missionaries have been sent into the field so far during the last three years. There has been a decided increase in Baptisms and Confirmations. Church Sunday Schools show an increased enrollment of twenty-four-thousand pupils. Teachers have increased in numbers seventeen hundred. There was an increase of one hundred and seventeen percent in the General Church revenues and about three hundred percent in Diocesan revenues.[82]

The work of the Nation-wide Campaign was so successful that following its first year the Presiding Bishop and Council (National Council) formally organized the Campaign as one of its six departments. The new department was to work in conjunction with the Departments of Finance and Promotion providing support for the work of the Departments of Religious Education, Christian Social Service, and Missions and Church Extension. At the 1922 General Convention in Portland, Oregon, the canon for the National Council was changed so that the Department of the Nation-wide Campaign became known as the Field Department. The role of the Field Department was to educate all Episcopalians as to their stewardship responsibilities in the "whole work of the whole Church."

The function of the Field Department is the prosecution of the Forward Movement which the Church has come to know as the Nation-wide Campaign for the Church's Mission. Its special responsibility is the education of the Church on the Church's official program, unanimously adopted by the General Convention, and the training of leaders in methods for fulfilling that program.[83]

Following each General Convention, an extensive review of the "General Church Program" for the coming triennium was published by the National Council. These overviews of the budget and activities of the National Council sought to educate all Episcopalians about their responsibilities to the mission work of the national church.

Excitement over the accomplishments of the Nation-wide Campaign, which had realized a 59% jump in income for the national church from $2,069,550 in 1919 to $3,483,125 in 1920, was carried forward into the planning of the National Council's program for the next triennium. The "General Church Program" for the years 1923-1925 anticipated the same growth in giving experienced during the years 1919-1922. To both maintain and advance the work of the Council, the Program recommended annual budgets of: $5.5 million in 1923, $6.5 million in 1924, and $7.5 million in 1925.[84] The fatal flaw of the General Church Program, as adopted by the National Council for its second triennium, was that proposed expenditures were based upon perceived needs in the domestic and foreign mission fields rather than the amount of income actually provided via the diocesan quota system. By the end of the triennium, it was clear that the National Council's income would in no way meet the planned expenditures. Instead of the $7.5 million the Council hoped to receive in 1925, its actual receipts totaled only $3,466,550. The National Council bemoaned the fact that its ambitions for expanded mission activities had to be curtailed. Even with a narrowing of its program, the National Council had a deficit budget of over $1.5 million at the end of the 1923-1925 triennium.

Recognizing the defect in the existing quota system, the 1925 General Convention instructed the National Council to implement a "Pay-As-You-Go" policy. The "Pay-As-You-Go" policy was a "balanced budget amendment" to the missionary canon that sought to do away with the unbridled spending of the National Council. The policy requested dioceses to certify to the National Council by January 15 of each year the amount they expected to pay toward the General Church Program. The Council then adjusted its appropriations to an amount not to exceed the total income expected. The goal of the new fiscal plan was to tie the Council's spending to real income and thus avoid future deficits. The "Pay-As-You-Go" policy did bring about a balanced budget, but it severely limited the National Council's ability to initiate new mission work at home and overseas.

> The 1925 General Convention [thus] brought the system to administrative perfection by directing the National Council to adjust its missionary enterprise, not to each diocese's fair share or quota of the current task, but to what each diocese "expected" to pay on its quota without an opportunity to be converted by, or even to hear about, the concrete needs and opportunities of the church's mission which its quota was to finance.[85]

Following the "Pay-As-You-Go" policy, expenditures for the National Council remained at approximately $3,850,000 for the next five years and by 1929 the deficit of $1.5 million was erased. Another source of significant support for the mission work of the Episcopal Church during the early decades of the National Council was the Church School Lenten Offering. The Lenten Offering of the children of the Episcopal Church was begun by two laymen of the Diocese of Pennsylvania. In 1877, John W. Marston, Superintendent of the Sunday School at Lower Merion, Pennsylvania, collected nearly $200 in nickels and dimes from the schoolchildren as part of their Lenten observance. This money was then given to support missions within the diocese as well as around the world. George C. Thomas, Superintendent of the Sunday School of the Church of the Holy Apostles in Philadelphia as well as Treasurer of the Domestic and Foreign Missionary Society from 1896-1909, capitalized on Marston's idea and promoted the Lenten Offering nationally. Under Thomas's leadership, church school students collected their nickels and dimes in mite boxes each Lent and gave it to the work of the Foreign and Domestic Missionary Society. At the fiftieth anniversary of the Church School Lenten Offering in 1927, the change collected by the young people in their mite boxes totaled an all-time high of $553,253.[86] Although this sum was never achieved again, the Church School Lenten Offerings continued to be a major source of support for the work of the National Council. The Department of Missions and Church Extension acknowledged this fact in its annual report of 1929.

> The Church schools are steadily pushing their Lenten Offerings toward the high goal attained in 1927, the fiftieth anniversary of the first offering. For 1929 the total was $532,821.47. This one gift was more than enough to pay all the appropriations for either China or Japan and almost enough to pay for the appropriations in all continental domestic districts. Its influence was felt in every field in which the Church works.[87]

The National Council, however, never had access to the full amount collected by the children. Since 1920, the Church School Lenten Offering was split between dioceses and the national church. The division of the offering was criticized by the National Council, which felt that the total sum of the children's offerings should go to the general mission work of the Episcopal Church.

The Department [of Missions and Church Extension] shares with the Department of Religious Education the hope that in the near future it may be possible, in consultation with the dioceses, to work out some plan under which the entire amount of the Easter offering of the Church schools may come into the treasury of the National Church, as was the case prior to 1920, and be used exclusively for the general mission work of the Church at home and abroad, instead of being used in part, as is the case at present, for diocesan purposes.[88]

The National Council saw the sharing of the Church School Lenten Offering with the dioceses as standing in opposition to the national church ideal of a centralized and unified mission of the Episcopal Church.

The depression of the United States economy in the late 1920s and early 1930s resulted in a dramatic decline in giving to the mission work of the Episcopal Church. Freed from debt in 1929, the National Council's budget began to grow again. In 1930 the income for the council broke the $4 million mark and in 1931 the budget increased to $4,101,767.[89] In the same year, feeling the pinch of the Depression, only five dioceses paid their full apportionment quota and only thirty-seven of ninety-eight paid their expected pledge in full. The resulting shortfall of over $250,000 was made up through undesignated legacies to the National Council given in 1931.[90] Anticipating declining income, the National Council down-scaled its work each year, decreasing its expenditures from $4,101,767 in 1931 to $3,342,658 in 1932 and $2,786,304 in 1933. Despite these attempts to keep expenditures in line with income, the National Council had unavoidable cost over-runs of over $529,000 in 1933 and close to $329,000 in 1934. The result was another deficit for the National Council, this time in the amount of $852,740.[91]

For the next two decades the National Council would struggle to overcome this debt.[92] Annual income for the Council would remain below the $2.5 million mark until after World War II. As a result, the vision of the Nation-wide Campaign, where the national church pursued its three-fold mission as one strong, collective body, suffered. Diocesan contributions to the National Council never met expectations and its mission work was constrained by the balanced budget mandate and ongoing debt payments.

Each Presiding Bishop elected to serve as the head of the Episcopal Church and the President of the National Council, from 1919 to 1946, left his mark on the development of the national church. The General Convention of 1919 had mandated that following the death of the incumbent Presiding Bishop, the Right Rev. Daniel Sylvester Tuttle, the Episcopal Church would choose its first elected Presiding Bishop. The first election of a Presiding Bishop took place at the 1925 General Convention in New Orleans.[93] Anticipating the election, the General Convention of 1925 articulated the expectations of the office. A Committee to Consider the Election of a Presiding Bishop carefully combed all the canons to draw together the many duties of the Presiding Bishop. The committee stressed that the Presiding Bishop was to be the executive and administrative head of the educational, social and missionary work of the church. The elected Presiding Bishop, however, was expected to retain his diocesan jurisdiction. The committee concluded by emphasizing the symbolic responsibilities of the Presiding Bishop as the spiritual head of the Episcopal Church.

> However great the demand may be for administrative and executive capacity in the office, its supreme opportunity is spiritual. To interpret the Church's growing consciousness of her unity and of her mission to the world, to interpret it to both the Church and the world, to lead and inspire, to carry confidence and faith and develop devotion and loyalty, your Committee believes that such is the chief responsibility which will rest upon the Presiding Bishop.[94]

On the fourteenth ballot, the Right Rev. John Gardner Murray, bishop of Maryland, was chosen as the first elected Presiding Bishop of the Episcopal Church.

On January 1, 1926 Murray took office and immediately assumed responsibility as the president of the National Council, replacing the Right Rev. Thomas F. Gailor who had served as interim president since 1919. The combination of a Presiding Bishop and the president of the National Council was celebrated as tying "up even more closely than before the National Council and its departments to the whole work of the Church."[95] Gardiner served for almost four years as Presiding Bishop and president of the Council while traveling widely throughout the Episcopal Church as its chief missionary and pastor.

Bishop Murray died in office on October 3, 1929. The following month the House of Bishops met in special session to elect a successor to fill the remainder of Bishop Murray's term. The Right Rev. Charles Palmerson Anderson, bishop of Chicago, was chosen for the position. Bishop Anderson served for less than three months; he suffered a heart attack and died on January 30, 1930. Again the bishops met in special session to elect a Presiding Bishop to complete an unexpired term. On March 26, 1930, the Right Rev. James DeWolf Perry, bishop of Rhode Island, was elected. When the General Convention met in September 1931 in Denver, Colorado, Perry was reelected to serve a regular six-year term as Presiding Bishop.[96] Bishop Perry would be the first elected Presiding Bishop to complete a full term in office.

In addition to reelecting Bishop Perry, the General Convention of 1931 made changes to the Missionary Canon that would alter the way the Episcopal Church went about its mission work. Since the founding of the National Council, the three-fold mission of the Episcopal Church was represented by the three departments of religious education, Christian social service, and missions and church extension. The Department of Missions and Church Extension continued the work of the earlier Domestic and Foreign Missionary Society and was the largest department of the National Council.[97] Recognizing that the bulk of the Council's energy was occupied with the domestic and foreign missions of the Episcopal Church, the General Convention accepted a proposal to divide the Department of Missions and Church Extension into the Department of Foreign Missions and the Department of Domestic Missions.[98] The separation of the foreign and domestic missionary work of the Episcopal Church into two distinct divisions represented an administrative decision rather than a theological position. The parceling out of the Episcopal Church's work at home and abroad, however, was contrary to the Episcopal Church's historic affirmation that the mission of the church throughout the world was one. In addition, the 1931 General Convention made provision for the appointment of a first vice-president to oversee the work of the Departments of Foreign Missions, Domestic Missions, Religious Education and Christian

Social Service and a Second Vice-President to supervise the Field Department and the Departments of Publicity and Finance. It was hoped that these structural adjustments would facilitate the administration of the National Council. This administrative fine-tuning, however, did little to prepare the Council for the program reduction it would experience in the next few years.

During 1933 and 1934 the Depression took its toll on the financial support of the National Council. The Council's financial difficulties profoundly affected the church's capacity to fulfill its mission. From February to June 1933, Presiding Bishop Perry visited the Episcopal Church's missions in the Philippines, China, Japan and Honolulu. The reason for his trip was to observe personally the "problems caused by financial and other administrative matters" in the foreign fields.[99] Bishop Perry concluded that there needed to be a gradual reduction in the number of evangelistic workers appointed in the foreign fields as well as a limitation on the number of teachers supported by the National Council. Hospitals and medical missionaries, however, were spared the immediate cuts in appropriations. As a result of Bishop Perry's recommendations, the number of foreign missionaries supported by the Episcopal Church fell from an all-time high of 486 in 1933 to 407 in 1934.

The 1934 General Convention in Atlantic City, New Jersey, sought to address the financial and administrative difficulties of the national church. The report of the Joint Committee on Budget and Program documented the declining income and resulting deficit of the National Council from 1932-1934. The committee closed its report with a recommendation that a new Forward Movement be inaugurated "to reinvigorate the life of the Church and to rehabilitate its General, Diocesan and Parochial work."[100] The convention appointed a Commission on a Forward Movement made up of five bishops, five presbyters and five lay people to carry out the ambitious mandate of the Budget and Program Committee. This Joint Commission on the Forward Movement was chaired by the Right Rev. Henry Wise Hobson, bishop of Southern Ohio. Under Bishop Hobson's leadership, the commission sought first to underscore the fact that the Episcopal

Church was a united body moving forward in a common mission. Second, the commission hoped to serve as a coordinating body that would "bring together the suggestions and ideas which are born in the minds and hearts of many of the clergy and lay people, and make these available to the whole Church."[101] In the fall of 1935, the Commission on the Forward Movement began publishing a short manual of daily Bible readings and meditations entitled *Forward — Day by Day*. It was hoped that the meditations in the manuals would inspire Episcopalians to new discipleship and commitment to the mission of the Episcopal Church. Writing in 1935, Bishop Hobson summarized the work of the Forward Movement.

> The Forward Movement appeals to the whole membership of the Church. First it calls each individual to face the demands of Discipleship, and as a loyal Disciple to go forward with Christ in every relationship of life. Second, it calls individual members of the Church to *unite* in forwarding the *whole program* which God has entrusted to His Church. It says definitely: there is a Disciple's Way founded on Christ's own life and the claim He has ever made on His Disciples, and it calls us to follow the steps of that Way: *Turn - Follow - Learn - Pray - Serve - Worship - Share*. It affirms that as the individual sincerely tries to take these steps, using the manual *Forward — Day by Day* as a guide to the study of the Bible and the practice of prayer, he will discover the program which the Forward Movement expects him to follow both in his personal relationship to God, and in his *corporate* relationships in the Church, in his family, his country, and in every area and experience of his life. (Italics in original)[102]

It was hoped that the Forward Movement would initiate a spiritual renewal in the Episcopal Church. A religious renewal, however, cannot be legislated into being by a General Convention Joint Committee on Budget and Program. The Forward Movement failed "to re-invigorate the life of the Church and to rehabilitate its work." *Forward — Day by Day*, however, did prove to be a useful tool for daily Bible study and continued to be published.

The General Convention of 1934 also addressed administrative difficulties of the national church. A continuing problem for the office of the Presiding Bishop was how to fulfill his responsibilities as the head of the national church while remaining a diocesan bishop. In order to ease the administrative duties on Bishop Perry, the General Convention backtracked and separated the office of the Presiding Bishop from that of the president of the National Council. The Right Rev. Philip Cook, bishop of Delaware and First Vice-President of the National Council, was elected president of the Council. Cook helped Perry with the administrative burden of the national church such that in 1935 Perry was able to move permanently back to Rhode Island from New York.[103] It soon became clear, however, that this compromise of splitting the two offices of the Presiding Bishop and president of the National Council was not working well. "A bishop of Rhode Island who was Presiding Bishop and a bishop of Delaware who was President of the National Council hardly provided the kind of energetic central leadership envisaged since 1919."[104] What was needed was a strong Presiding Bishop who had an unqualified commitment to the three-fold mission of the Episcopal Church as it was embodied in the work of the National Council.

Forward in Service

The 1937 General Convention in Cincinnati, Ohio, had to select a new Presiding Bishop as Perry's six-year term was to end on the last day of December. On the second ballot, the House of Bishops elected the Right Rev. Henry St. George Tucker, bishop of Virginia, to be the next Presiding Bishop. The election was confirmed by the House of Deputies and Bishop Tucker took office on January 1, 1938. None was better qualified to lead the Episcopal Church forward in its mission than Bishop Tucker. Following in the footsteps of Arthur Selden Lloyd, Tucker maintained the tradition of a loyal son of Virginia who was deeply committed to the national church ideal.

Tucker had been born in Warsaw, Virginia, on July 16, 1874. He came from a long line of Virginian Episcopalians and his father, Beverly Dandridge Tucker, served as bishop of Southern Virginia from 1918-1930. Like Lloyd, Tucker received his education at venerable Virginia institutions including Norfolk Academy, the University of Virginia and Virginia Theological Seminary. Following in the footsteps of many graduates of the Virginia Seminary, Tucker left for foreign missionary service shortly after his graduation in 1899. From 1901 until 1903 he served as mission-ary-in-charge of the Episcopal parish in Sendai, Hirosaki, Japan. In 1903 he was called to be the president of St. Paul's College in Tokyo. Tucker served as president of St. Paul's until 1912 when he was elect-ed the second missionary bishop of Kyoto. As a teacher and bishop, Tucker worked unceasingly to promote the educational outreach of the mission in Japan. In 1923 Tucker left his missionary episcopate and returned to full-time teaching at his alma mater, Virginia Theological Seminary. Three years later he left teaching, once again returning to the episcopate as bishop coadjutor of Virginia. The fol-lowing year Tucker became the eighth diocesan bishop of Virginia. When he was elected Presiding Bishop, Tucker had served as dioce-san bishop of Virginia for over ten years and had been a bishop of the church for over twenty-six years.

Tucker's election as Presiding Bishop signaled a return to the original vision of the Presiding Bishop as the chief missionary of the Episcopal Church. His experience in the Japan mission was applauded as fundamental to the promotion of the church's mis-sion work. An editorial in *The Living Church,* shortly after his election, stated the expectation that Tucker would lead the church's missionary affairs.

> Bishop Tucker's primacy will inaugurate a new era of missionary advance...The New Presiding Bishop...will have greatly increased power in the administration of the Church's missionary affairs...[and] a new place of leadership in the formation of the policies of the Church.[105]

Unlike Perry, Tucker planned to be a full-time Presiding Bishop. Although he maintained his position as titular head of the diocese of Virginia, ongoing episcopal oversight for the diocese was entrusted to the Right Rev. Frederick C. Goodwin, who was elected coadjutor in 1937.[106] Canonical changes at the 1937 General Convention returned the Presiding Bishop to the presidency of the National Council. The Cincinnati convention also provided, once again, for two vice-presidents of the National Council, one of the positions having been dropped under Philip Cook's leader-ship. Tucker seized the opportunity to bolster the administration of the National Council.

Part of the genius of Tucker's leadership was his ability to attract thoughtful and skilled colleagues to share in the work of the National Council. To begin with, he called the Rev. Charles W. Sheerin to the post of second vice-president and entrusted him with oversight of the National Council's promotional concerns. He then called John Wilson Wood to be first vice-president. The first vice-president was to serve as technical expert in the management of domestic, foreign and extra-continental missionary districts. Wood had been associated with the work of the Domestic and Foreign Missionary Society since early in the century and had served as executive secretary of the National Council's Department of Missions and Church Extension, and Department of Foreign Missions. No one, except perhaps Tucker himself, was better qualified to oversee the missionary activities of the Episcopal Church.[107] Wood, however, was advanced in age and served for only three years before retiring in 1940. Upon Wood's retirement, Tucker turned to the Rev. Dr. James Thayer Addison to fill the position. As the new vice-president for administration, Addison would work closely with Tucker to see the National Council through changes in missionary polices during World War II. Writing in 1946, Charles W. Sheerin acknowledged the accomplishments of the Tucker-Addison team.

> I would say that the newer missionary policies that have been adopted are a greater change than the promotional work, but by reason of Dr. Addison's personality and Bishop Tucker's strong but gentle manner, few in the Church have realized the fact. Beginning with the selection and appointment of missionaries, through the many details of material arrangements, great advancement in more efficient work has been made; and yet all of this has been accomplished during World War II, when the Japanese and Chinese situations were anything but easy to handle and when closer cooperation with the Church of England had to be arranged under the handicap of great difficulty of communication.[108]

The team of Tucker and Addison brought together the church in Virginia (Tucker) with the church in New England (Addison). This combination of the two centers of the Episcopal Church in the eastern United States helped to reinvigorate the national church ideal.

James Thayer Addison was one of the most important Episcopal mission thinkers in the period between the two world wars. As a missionary, academic and administrator, Addison was committed first and foremost to the three-fold mission of the Episcopal Church. Like Tucker, Addison was born into a prominent Episcopal family. At the time of his birth in 1887 his father, the Rev. Charles Morris Addison, was rector of Christ Church, Fitchburg, a cardinal parish in central Massachusetts. Addison attended Harvard University, receiving his bachelor of arts in 1909. Upon his graduation from Harvard, he went to China under the auspices of the Episcopal Church where he taught at St. John's University, Shanghai. After a year of teaching in China, Addison returned to Massachusetts to pursue the study of theology at the Episcopal Theological School (ETS) in Cambridge. In 1913 he finished seminary and was ordained to the diaconate in June by Bishop Lawrence of Massachusetts and priested in December of the same year. Returning to missionary service, this time in the domestic field, Addison served as missionary in charge of St. Mark's Church, Nowata, and St. Paul's Church, Claremore, in the missionary district of Oklahoma from 1913-1915.

Addison's experience as both a foreign and domestic missionary provided invaluable insights for his future ministry as a teacher and mission administrator. In 1915 Addison returned to Cambridge, Massachusetts, as a lecturer in history and missions at ETS. While teaching at ETS, he pursued graduate work in church history at Harvard Divinity School and received a master of sacred theology in 1917. Addison's teaching at ETS was interrupted with military service from 1918-1919, when he served as chaplain to the First Gas Regiment of the American Expeditionary Forces.[109] Following the war, Addison returned to ETS where he was named full professor of the history of religion and missions. He remained in this position until 1940 when he was called to be vice-president of the National Council by Presiding Bishop Tucker.

Addison was trained as a historian but his writings reflect a wide-ranging mind interested in many subjects. He wrote extensively on world religions. Articles and short books traced the history of religions in India and Japan.[110] Addison's encounter with ancestor worship in China led him to study the question of life beyond death in other cultures. In 1924 he published a brief investigation into the question of ancestor worship in Africa; he followed this with a longer book on Chinese ancestor worship in 1925.[111] Seven years latter Addison published *Life Beyond Death in the Beliefs of Mankind*. This study was an attempt to "present a brief survey of all the important beliefs about the future life among uncivilized peoples and the great religions of the world."[112] Although it did present the views of other world religions, the book held out Christ's resurrection as the most advanced belief about life after death. As a scholar of world religions, Addison's most extensive research was in the relationship between Christianity and Islam. An article in the *Harvard Theological Review* traced the growth of the Ahmadiya movement in Islam.[113] In addition, Addison produced a short introduction to the beliefs of Islam for American Episcopalians, *The World of Islam*, published by the National Council.[114] Addison's most significant contribution to the study of Islam and Christianity, however, was *The Christian Approach to the Moslem*, published in 1942. This book presented a general historical survey of missionary efforts to Muslims and argued for an increased effort on the part of Christians in the conversion of Muslims.[115] Other histories of Christian mission produced by Addison included a biography of Francis Xavier and a history of the conversion of northern Europe.[116] In addition to these missiological studies, Addison produced a series of short devotional books.[117] He is best remembered not for his study of world religions or his devotional titles but rather for his history of the Episcopal Church, *The Episcopal Church in the United States 1889-1931*, published in 1951.

As a missiologist Addison was unapologetic about the superiority of the Christian faith. His belief in the "unique supremacy" of Jesus Christ as the one true revelation of God led Addison to take issue with the Laymen's Foreign Mission Inquiry.[118] At first, both the National Council and the Woman's Auxiliary applauded the efforts of the Layman's Inquiry. Official organizations of the

Episcopal Church endorsed the role of Mr. and Mrs. Harper Sibley as Episcopalians on the Inquiry's Appraisal Commission.

> Two years ago Mrs. Sibley outlined the plans of the Inquiry both to the Executive Board of the Woman's Auxiliary, and by special invitation, to the National Council. Both bodies recognized the significance of the project and the National Council adopted formal resolutions bidding Mr. and Mrs. Sibley godspeed.[119]

When the full report of the Laymen's Inquiry was published in 1932, the National Council distanced itself from the study. The Council agreed that humanistic endeavors should be central to the work of the missionary; However, it took exception to both the theological and programmatic conclusions of William Ernest Hocking's report. In particular the Council disagreed with the Inquiry's

> unfortunate theological basis, which seems to regard the Christian religion as simply one of the world's religious philosophies and which regards our Lord as merely one of the world's religious teachers.[120]

In addition, the National Council defended the quality of Episcopal missionaries from criticisms of the Laymen's Inquiry and argued for the continued commitment to evangelism in the work of Christian schools and hospitals.

A neo-orthodox, Addison was sympathetic to Dr. Hendrick Kraemer's critique of the Laymen's Inquiry and Hocking's theological position. Addison admitted that elements of God's revelation could be found in other world religions but at the same time he emphasized that only in Jesus Christ was God's fullest truth to be found. In his "Missionary Sermon" preached before the 1934 graduating class of Virginia Theological Seminary, Addison emphasized the superiority of the Christian faith.

> However ready we may be to adapt ourselves to the growing knowledge of our day as to what is noble and worthy in these other religions, we still remain rooted and grounded in the faith that only in Christ has God fully and once revealed Himself, that only in Christ is God Himself incarnate. Secure in that central conviction, we see the relation between Christianity and the non-Christian religions not as a contrast between black and white or between truth and falsehood but rather as a contrast between the complete and the partial, between the perfect and the imperfect. And the crying need that God moves us to meet is not so much the need to save the

lost from hell as the need to answer the unspoken desires for something better, the unrealized longing for something deeper and more satisfying, the dumb yearning of unnumbered hearts for all that Christ can give in abundance.[121]

Addison's book *Our Expanding Church*, first published in 1930, presented an overview of the theology and achievements of Episcopal missionary endeavors. Addison's missiology, presented in *Our Expanding Church* and his other writings, began with the affirmations of faith found in the historic creeds of the Christian church.[122] He argued that the missionary imperative resulted from the profession of belief in a Trinitarian God and a catholic and apostolic Church.

> Whenever these central truths [of the Creed] are warmly alive in the hearts of believers, the outcome is a victorious Christianity and an expanding Church. But whenever they are ignored or doubted or denied, the advance of Christ's cause falters or slackens or ceases. When our God is less than the Almighty Creator of all men, our religion becomes merely national or racial....When Jesus Christ is someone less than 'God of God,' when He is simply a very good man who uttered noble sayings many years ago, our religion becomes only one among others, no longer absolute, but purely a matter of preference with no eternal validity. And when our Church is something less than Catholic and Apostolic, when it is little better than a local club, it ceases to have expansive power. It becomes no more than a museum for preserving ancient traditions or a society for mutual improvement.[123]

For Addison, then, mission was at the heart of the church. The aim of Christian missions, "the manifestation of Christ, the unfolding of His nature, the demonstration of His power, the revelation of His glory," was synonymous with the life of the church.[124] It was the church's mission to make Christ known throughout the world and it was the responsibility of every baptized Christian to participate in this mission. In this position, Addison was in keeping with the established mission theology of the Episcopal Church. Addison's articulate presentation of the mission of the church made explicit the church-centered mission theology of the American Episcopal Church. His defense of the missionary activities of the Episcopal Church provided an apologetic for the *missio ecclesia* of the national church ideal.[125]

Henry St. George Tucker agreed with Addison's conviction that the church's mission and Christ's mission were one and the same.

He saw the church as continuing Christ's work in the world as it had been handed down through the apostles.

> Christ communicated His own sense of a mission to His friends. If He had not done so we should not be in the company of those who hear again his words and seek communion with His Spirit and the fuller penetration of our lives by His life. The Mission of the Church is at bottom simply Christ's Mission carried on through the lives He draws into His service.[126]

Like Addison, Tucker believed that there was no room for questioning the church's work in missions. The church was given Christ's mission in the world and it was the church's primary responsibility to carry forward the mission both near and far.

> To ask whether missions should go on is to ask whether the Mission of Christ should go on; whether the Church should go on. It is like asking whether good will should go on. How far should good will reach? It is the glory of Christ that He stretched the imaginations of His people to look beyond the reach of their own families, their own race and nation, to the needs of the outcasts in India and of Chinese farmers in remote villages and of brown men in the hills of the Philippines. It is the glory of the Church that with all its tawdriness and failures it has had the vitality to be a light to the Gentiles and to those who sit in darkness.[127]

As Presiding Bishop, Tucker believed that his primary duty was to motivate Episcopalians to support the mission of the church, the mission of Christ.

Under Tucker's leadership the official publication of the Episcopal Church, known since 1835 as *The Spirit of Missions,* changed its name to *Forth*. The new name was chosen to promote more engagement by Episcopalians in the mission of the church. The January 1940 issue of *Forth* presented a new format with modern graphics. More important, this new issue followed a different editorial policy. The magazine no longer concentrated on the work of the departments of Domestic and Foreign Missions of the National Council but rather was enlarged to include the work of parishes and dioceses in the United States. It was hoped that the new policy would make *Forth* "the magazine of the whole Church devoted to the whole Mission of the Church."[128] Charles W. Sheerin, Vice-President of the National Council, explained the new publication's policy in the opening editorial of the first issue of *Forth*.

Now the name is changed. Why? Because of the new editorial policy whereby the Mission of the Church is the magazine's prime concern. Because the old name was adopted in the days when missions were thought of as separate and distinct from the work of parishes and the Church at home. (Fortunately we have gotten away from that idea.) Because we felt the need of a title which bears the imprimatur of the Church at the same time being short and signalizing Christian action. (Parentheses in original.)[129]

It was hoped that the call to all Episcopalians to action in the world was reflected in the new name.

The [name] finally chosen — FORTH — was selected for one primary reason; it has the stamp of approval of Christ. He charged His followers to "*Go Forth*". His marching orders were: "*I send ye FORTH!*" "*Forth*" is one of the most moving and commanding terms He ever employed. It has the ring of sincerity about it. It signifies *action*. It is a direct command to Christians that they *do something* about their religion. It embraces the heart of the Church's missionary cause: "*Go ye into all the world.*" (Italics in original)[130]

Exciting Episcopalians to an active engagement with their faith and with the world was the primary agenda for the episcopacy of Presiding Bishop Tucker.

At the 1940 General Convention in Kansas City, Presiding Bishop Tucker issued to the Episcopal Church a call to action. He challenged the church to respond to the present problems of the world through a recommitment to Christian service at home and abroad. Addressing the convention on the eve of the Second World War, Tucker saw the conflict in Europe as providing an opportunity for the American Episcopal Church. He believed that God would use the war to advance God's reign, and he called the Episcopal Church to participate in God's redemptive actions.

Man's extremity is God's opportunity. Should we not then expect Him at such a time to issue a call to His Church to cooperate with Him in a great redemptive effort? And if, as is usually the case in times of crisis, God selects some particular portion of the Church to render service, have we not reason to believe that His choice will fall upon us as Christians in America? This is not because of our superior merit, but rather because we are particularly the only considerable body of Christians in the world today whose hands are untied. If we have been spared the horrors of war; if we are enjoying comparative prosperity; if we are able to maintain our democratic way of life, it does not mean that we are heaven's favorites or that we have earned these blessings by our own virtues. "Unto whomsoever much is given, of him shall much be required." "We that are strong ought to bear the infirmities of the weak." If we interpret the signs of the times in accordance with these principles, we cannot but conclude that God's call for sacrificial service in a demoralized world is addressed to us.[131]

Tucker saw the fortunate position of the United States as providing a unique opportunity for American Christians. Echoing the national church ideal, Tucker emphasized, the responsibility of the Episcopal Church to respond to God's call.

> If my interpretation of these signals [of the war] is correct, God is saying to us, as representatives of a great branch of the American Church, "Go forward in service."[132]

Tucker proclaimed before the General Convention that the mission of the Episcopal Church was to go forward in service to heal a broken world.

Tucker's challenge to the 1940 General Convention initiated a new ten-year program of the National Council, Forward in Service. Forward in Service was designed to pick up where the previous Forward Movement program had left off. Whereas the earlier Forward Movement, initiated by the 1934 General Convention, hoped to strengthen the personal prayer and devotional life of Episcopalians, Forward in Service sought to motivate Episcopalians to a new level of action and involvement with their faith and their church. The continuity between Forward Movement and Forward in Service was acknowledged in the promotional materials of the new program.

> A forward movement, to be known as Forward in Service has been initiated by the Presiding Bishop and endorsed with enthusiasm by the General Convention. Its characteristic note is to be an expression of our loyalty and devotion to Christ and His Church through practical service in parish, in diocese, in nation and in the world. Continuous with the preceding stage of the Forward Movement, and taking advantage of the spiritual fruits of that movement throughout the Church, the new program aims to "go forward in service."[133]

Forward in Service was charged with stimulating the whole life of the church. Each year the program would emphasize one particular aspect of the Episcopal Church's work. A theme was chosen annually and a "Plan of Action" outlining the Forward in Service program for the year was developed.[134] This information was disseminated through a series of provincial and diocesan conferences to every diocese and parish in the Episcopal Church.

Forward in Service fell far short of Bishop Tucker's vision. As with the earlier Forward Movement, the National Council was unable to initiate a spiritual renewal from the top down. In addition, the time was not right for a nationally planned program of the National Council. The specter of World War II overshadowed any attempt at renewal in the church. By 1946 Forward in Service had all but ceased to exist. Writing in the same year, the Rev. Charles W. Sheerin commented on the downfall of the program.

> By far the biggest handicap [to Forward in Service] was the fact that already America had become the "arsenal of democracy"; the draft had set in, and every day we came nearer and nearer to war. Rectors could hardly be expected to carry out programs of renewal, whether spiritual or material, when their youth were leaving every day for military service — no one knew just where. Bishops could hardly be expected to give their full time to an essential Church program when, overnight, huge cantonments and war plants were springing up in their dioceses, bringing all sorts of Church problems caused by moving millions of persons.[135]

Two aspects of the Forward in Service program were successful, however. These were the beginning of a formal relief agency in the Episcopal Church and aid to English missions.

In his opening sermon to the 1940 General Convention, Tucker outlined the responsibilities of American Episcopalians to work for the relief of those who were suffering because of the war in Europe.

> There is, however, one problem created by the war for which we have a more direct responsibility, namely the relief of those to whom it has brought suffering.
>
> I trust that this General Convention will call upon our people to take their full part in relief activities, wherever they are practical under the conditions of war, not only as an obligation but still more as a Christian privilege.[136]

On the fifth day of the convention, Bishop Bertrand W. Stevens of Los Angeles moved a resolution calling for the Department of Christian Social Relations of the National Council "to keep in touch with developing [relief] needs, to advise the Church about responsible agencies giving relief to sufferers from war, and to request the Presiding Bishop to issue calls to our Church people for their support."[137] The resolution was passed by the House of Deputies the following day. Following the lead of Episcopalians in the diocese of Southern Ohio, who had helped German refugees fleeing Nazi oppression since 1938, the National Council embraced a full-scale refugee assistance program.[138]

At the next meeting of the National Council in December of 1940, the Council took an additional step in its war relief efforts and established the Presiding Bishop's Fund for World Relief (PBFWR). The fund was organized to receive contributions for the aid of human suffering created by the war and to distribute such funds through the Department of Christian Social Relations. Appeal letters were prepared and sent to every parish and diocese in the Episcopal Church. These letters named the following range of "war sufferers":

–the millions in China who need our help
–the refugees from Europe and elsewhere who have been forced from their homelands
–orphaned missions cut off from normal support
–eight or ten million prisoners of war
–the needs of people through this war-torn world.[139]

In its first year the Fund received $36,502. At the 1943 General Convention, the Presiding Bishop's Fund for World Relief was officially endorsed by the governing synod of the Episcopal Church. By the end of the year contributions to the fund topped $116,000.[140] In addition, the 1943 General Convention called for a Reconstruction and Advance Fund to assist with the reconstruction needs caused by the war in the Far East, Near East, Europe and Britain.[141]

Bishop Tucker's call for relief for those who were suffering from the war was followed by a petition on behalf of Christian missions cut off from their traditional sources of support. He emphasized that the American Episcopal Church had a particular responsibility to come to the aid of missions of the Church of England.

> Another problem created by the war which can be met only by the cooperation of American Christians is the maintenance of the missionary activities that have been carried on by the Churches of the belligerent nations. Without our help this work would have to be greatly curtailed and in some instances entirely stopped, because of the inability of the home Churches to furnish support. Many of the Churches in the United States have already

undertaken to give generous help. I am confident that our own Church will do likewise. Because of our relationship to the Church of England and in view of the fact that in many of the American colonies our Church owes its origin to the work of one of the English missionary societies, we should feel a peculiar interest in aiding them to maintain similar work in various parts of the world.[142]

In response to Tucker's charge, the General Convention pledged to assist the mission work of European and Continental churches devastated by the war. To facilitate cooperation with other Christian denominations in this worldwide mission assistance, the 1940 General Convention agreed to become a member of the Federal Council of Churches of Christ in America and to cooperate in the plans for a World Council of Churches. The convention also authorized $300,000 to be made available "for mission fields of the Anglican Communion whose support has been seriously affected by war conditions."[143] This "Aid to British Missions" marked a new level of involvement in the historic mission fields of the Church of England by the Episcopal Church in the United States.

With the end of the war, the original committee designated to supervise the distribution of monies given to the Presiding Bishop's Fund for World Relief was expanded in 1945 to serve as a Committee on Aid to Sister Churches. Eventually this committee would become known as the Committee on World Relief and Inter-Church Cooperation. Its primary responsibility was to disburse funds given to the Presiding Bishop's Fund for World Relief through voluntary gifts, the National Council budget, and other monies given for mission and reconstruction in Europe and Asia.[144] At Bishop Tucker's last General Convention, held in Philadelphia in 1946, he challenged the Episcopal Church to engage in a greatly expanded relief and rehabilitation program. The convention responded by empowering the National Council to sponsor a $1,000,000 appeal for each year of the triennium. The convention's resolution read:

that such funds be raised in the name of the Presiding Bishop's Fund for World Relief, to be allocated by the Presiding Bishop and the National Council for the relief of interchurch aid programs coordinated by Church World Service through the World Council of Churches in Europe and through the National Christian Councils in Eastern Asia.[145]

The new Presiding Bishop elected at the 1946 General Convention, the Right Rev. Henry Knox Sherrill, would commit himself completely to the "Million Dollar Fund" and the work of the Presiding Bishop's Fund for World Relief.

The Woman's Auxiliary to the National Council

Through the ups and downs of the National Council, from its founding in 1919 to the end of Tucker's episcopacy as Presiding Bishop, one segment of the Episcopal Church remained constant in its support of mission. The women of the Episcopal Church, through the Woman's Auxiliary to the National Council, could always be counted on for financial and spiritual support for the mission of the Episcopal Church. Because the Woman's Auxiliary linked local women's groups under a national umbrella, the Auxiliary was able to excite its constituency to give and participate in mission activities while at the same time remaining firmly within the program of the national church. No other organization in the Episcopal Church was able to combine a voluntary ethic with the national church ideal as was the Woman's Auxiliary to the National Council.

By the time of the founding of the National Council, Episcopal churchwomen had demonstrated that they were major players in the mission work of the Episcopal Church. The Woman's Auxiliary to the Board of Missions, established by the General Convention of 1871, had grown under the direction of the Emery sisters to become a broad-based grass-roots women's mission movement. The women's Supply Box Program provided a constant and significant source of material support for the many Episcopal missionaries in the United States and overseas. The United Offering, or United Thank Offering (UTO) as it came to be known in 1919, had grown to almost a half million dollars. The monies collected by the United Thank Offering were used to meet material needs in the domestic and foreign mission fields as well as provide direct support for Episcopal women missionaries. These missionaries were designated as United Offering Workers. In 1919, 91 of the 181 Episcopal women missionaries working in the foreign and extra-continental mission fields of the Episcopal Church were funded by the United Offering.[146]

With the advent of the National Council following the 1919 General Convention, the question of women's participation in the new structures of the church was raised. Since the Woman's Auxiliary had been an auxiliary to the Board of Missions of the Domestic and Foreign Missionary Society and since the Board was to be superseded by the new church structure, the issue of how the Auxiliary would relate to the National Council remained. There were two possible options. One side maintained that since women were to be included in the membership of the Department of Missions and Church Extension of the National Council, there was no longer a need for a separate woman's auxiliary. The other option was to expand the work of the Auxiliary in the areas of religious education and social service and thus become auxiliary to the whole National Council in the three-fold mission of the Episcopal Church. Since the Woman's Auxiliary had been involved historically, and often stimulated many of the church's initiatives into religious education and social service, it seemed appropriate to expand the Auxiliary to match the new, broad agenda of the National Council.[147]

In 1916 Julia Emery resigned as general secretary of the Woman's Auxiliary. Emery's assistant of eight years, Grace Lindley, was appointed to serve until the next Triennial Meeting in 1919. Lindley was well versed in the work of the Auxiliary, having worked with Episcopal churchwomen at the parish, diocesan and national levels for many years.

> She had "come up through the ranks" serving as an officer of her local parish auxiliary and then as secretary of "junior work" in the dioceses of Newark and New York. When Julia Emery left the New York office to attend the Pan-Anglican Congress in London in 1908 and then to continue around the world, visiting mission stations all along the way, Grace Lindley was asked to help in the national office and was later hired as full-time assistant secretary.[148]

Lindley's appointment as acting general secretary of the Woman's Auxiliary at a time when the whole missionary structure of the Episcopal Church was in flux reflected an earnest desire on the part of the women to maintain continuity with the Auxiliary's past method of operations.

Having served in the national offices of the Board of Missions since 1908, Lindley was well aware of the canonical changes coming before the General Convention of 1919 and what effect they would have on the Woman's Auxiliary. She believed that the incorporation of the Woman's Auxiliary into the Department of Missions would seriously curtail the work of Episcopal churchwomen. She thus argued that the Auxiliary must be reconstituted as an auxiliary to the National Council in the same manner that it had been auxiliary to the Board of Missions. Under Miss Lindley's leadership the 1919 Triennial Meeting requested that when the National Council was established, the Woman's Auxiliary should be asked to become auxiliary to the National Council.[149]

The request of the women was accepted by the General Convention and when the National Council began its work on January 1, 1920, the Woman's Auxiliary to the Board of Missions became the Woman's Auxiliary to the National Council. Emulating the new National Council's work in the three-fold mission of the Episcopal Church, the new Auxiliary expanded its portfolio to include the work of Episcopal women in religious education and social service.

> The enlargement of the work of the Auxiliary...was met by resolving to become Auxiliary to the Presiding Bishop and Council...thereby adding religious education and social service to the accustomed work for missions; by undertaking larger educational policies; re-organizing the box work on Red Cross lines; planning to make the United Offering a contribution from all the women of the Church, and giving it the title of the *United Thank Offering*, and by replacing the general secretary by an executive secretary to be nominated triennially by the Auxiliary to the Board or Council, who should have an executive board to aid her in the direction of the work, and other such secretaries as might be needed.[150]

The Triennial of 1919 immediately chose Grace Lindley as the first executive secretary of the Woman's Auxiliary to the National Council. This was no surprise since Lindley had served so well as the interim general secretary and had originally suggested the idea of a National Executive Board.[151]

The establishment of the new Woman's Auxiliary guaranteed that the voice of women would be heard, strong and distinct, in all aspects of the Episcopal Church's new structure and program.

At the Triennial of 1919, the Woman's Auxiliary was also augmented by a new Church Service League. The League was to serve as
a federation of all national organizations of Episcopal women
such as the Girl's Friendly Society, the Daughters of the King, and
the Church Periodical Club. As head of the Auxiliary, and thus a
spokesperson for the League, Lindley hoped that the new federation might develop into a great lay organization where Episcopal
women could come together in service to both the church and
the world. Lindley commented on the ground-breaking events of
the 1919 Triennial in the last annual report of the Woman's
Auxiliary to the Board of Missions.

> So the last year of the Woman's Auxiliary to the Board of Missions was
> marked by preparation for important changes, and at the beginning of its
> work as an Auxiliary to the Presiding Bishop and Council the Woman's
> Auxiliary faces its tasks in a spirit of eager anticipation, induced not by
> changes in its machinery, but by the realization of those great facts repre-
> sented in the words "responsibility," "opportunity," "a wonderful future"!
> For we are facing these, created not only by conditions in the Woman's
> Auxiliary, not only by the new outlook for women's work, not even alone
> by conditions in the Church, but also by reason of the age in which we live.
> Today we are called upon to take our place in the great reconstruction time
> of the world, and as surely as we believe that the new civilization must be
> built upon Rock, so surely will we do our part to see that the women of
> the Church accept their responsibility. For the Woman's Auxiliary of today
> has it in its power to be a tremendous influence. Surely the Church is going
> to save civilization.[152]

Under Lindley's leadership the expanded Woman's Auxiliary
embraced wholeheartedly the three-fold mission of the national
church ideal.

Although the Woman's Auxiliary was subject to the economic
instability of the Depression years, the contributions of Episcopal
women to the mission of the Episcopal Church suffered less than
general contributions to the National Council. The crucial role of
the Woman's Auxiliary and the United Thank Offering in the mission work of the church was no secret. Each year the annual
reports of the National Council expressed deep gratitude for the
work of the women. The Department of Missions and Church
Extension was particularly thankful for the contributions of
Episcopal women and in 1921 celebrated with the Woman's

Auxiliary their fifty years of service to the mission work of the Episcopal Church.

> The Department of Missions congratulates the Woman's Auxiliary upon the completion of its first fifty years of service. During every one of those years, the Church's mission work has been blessed and bettered by the cooperation of the Auxiliary membership. The Auxiliary is responsible for the inauguration of mission study, for the beginnings of the present wide-spread summer conference plan, for the wonderful United Thank Offering, for better methods of recruiting and training women missionaries, until at present time, in the foreign fields of the Church, the number of unmarried women workers exceeds the number of men. During the past fifty years the Woman's Auxiliary has given $14,000,000 for the Church's Mission. Of this total $2,014,300.18 has been given through the United Offering.[153]

The total number of Episcopal women missionaries serving in the foreign and extra-continental missionary districts of the Episcopal Church in 1920 was 203 — of whom 96 were sponsored with funds provided by the United Thank Offering.[154] The number of women missionaries supported by the Episcopal Church in the overseas fields continued to grow through the 1920s reaching a high of more than 240 women in 1927. In the same year only 196 men were working overseas. When the economic strains brought on by the Depression caused a cutback in the number of mission-aries sent out by the National Council, women continued to out-number men in the overseas mission fields.

The significant presence of women in the mission fields of the Episcopal Church was guaranteed by the contributions of the United Thank Offering. The Offering continued to grow through-out the 1920s and, in 1928, broke the million-dollar mark for the first time.[155] Of this sum, one-tenth was set aside for the Pension Fund for retired United Thank Offering workers, $100,000 for building pro-jects in the United States, $25,000 for St. Catherine's School in San Juan, Puerto Rico, and $50,000 for a chapel at St. Margaret's School in Tokyo, Japan. The remainder — more than $800,000 — was used for the direct support of women missionaries.[156]

Because of the Depression, the United Thank Offering of 1931 showed a decrease in giving for the first time in its forty-two year history. The drop was very modest (from $1,101,450 in 1928 to $1,059,575 in 1931, a decrease of $41,875) but the downward trend in giving would continue throughout the decade. The Offering reached its lowest point in 1934 with a total of $789,561. In 1937 and 1940 the United Thank Offering increased and by 1943 it was back over the million-dollar mark with a total of $1,119,879 given.[157] Although the United Thank Offering decreased during the 1930s, the commitment to funding women missionaries remained strong. The 1931 offering totaled $1,059,575, one-tenth of which was put into the trust fund for retired women missionaries. An additional $678,000 was used to support more than 200 women United Thank Offering missionaries in the foreign and domestic missions of the Episcopal Church during the years 1931 to 1933.[158]

The 1920s and 1930s proved to be the golden era of Episcopal women's foreign missionary work. The two decades, however, were not without their problems. The question of whether the work of Episcopal churchwomen should be coordinated through the Woman's Auxiliary or through the existing departments of the National Council was never resolved fully. In 1927, the Department of Religious Education recommended that the educational work of the Woman's Auxiliary be consolidated in that department. There was much discussion over this proposed merger both in the Executive Committee of the Woman's Auxiliary and in the National Council itself, for it called into question the role of a separate woman's organization within the national church program. Finally the Department of Missions asked the National Council to define the status of the Auxiliary's relationship to the Council. After extensive review, the National Council reaffirmed the decision of 1920 to constitute the Woman's Auxiliary as auxiliary to the National Council in all its departments.[159]

By 1934 the important role of the Woman's Auxiliary in all three aspects of the national church's mission, religious education, social service and church extension, could not be denied. Recognizing this fact, the General Convention of 1934 amended Canon 60 so that four women would serve as members of the National Council. The four women were to be nominated by the leadership of the Woman's Auxiliary and elected by the Triennial Meeting. Those who favored the incorporation of the Woman's Auxiliary into the National Council saw the inclusion of women on the National Council as a necessary first step. They argued that with women's representation guaranteed at the highest level of the national church, there was no longer any need for a semi-autonomous women's organization for women.

At the 1940 Triennial Meeting in Kansas City, Grace Lindley retired as the executive secretary of the Woman's Auxiliary. Margaret I. Marston, the educational secretary of the Auxiliary, was nominated by the Triennial and then appointed by the Presiding Bishop to succeed Lindley. Concomitant with this leadership transition was the question, once again, of the Auxiliary's relationship to the National Council. Many women at the Triennial Meeting believed that the name and structure of the Woman's Auxiliary should be changed in order to facilitate the incorporation of women and women's work into the established departments of the National Council. It was proposed that the secretaries of the Woman's Auxiliary be combined with the secretaries of the departments of the National Council, thus eliminating a separate staff of and for women in the Episcopal Church. This proposal was more radical than the suggestion in 1927 that only the educational work of the women be transferred to the Department of Religious Education. Upon the advice of Presiding Bishop Tucker, who recognized the important role of the Woman's Auxiliary in his planned Forward in Service program, the proposal was dropped.[160]

The winds of change, however, were blowing over the Woman's Auxiliary and in the next three decades the work of this semi-autonomous women's organization would become increasingly incorporated into the other departments of the National Council. In the 1940s, two important programs of the Woman's Auxiliary were slowly done away with: the Supply Box Program and the United Thank Offering Missionary Worker. The demise of these two forms of outreach seriously limited the connection between women in the United States and women missionaries overseas. The Woman's Auxiliary, as a semi-autonomous women's organization supporting the mission of the Episcopal Church, would decline in the post-war era.

NOTES

[1]Other missionary bodies, such as the Interdenominational Foreign Mission Association (IFMA), were organized around a particular theological position. The IFMA, founded in 1917, stressed a conservative theology of mission based on the "fundamental doctrines of the historic Christian faith." Gerald Anderson, "American Protestants in Pursuit of Mission: 1886-1986," *International Bulletin of Missionary Research* 12 (July 1988): 105.

[2]David L. Holmes, "The Anglican Tradition and the Episcopal Church," in *Encyclopedia of American Religious Experience*, ed. C. Lippy and P. Williams (New York: Scribners, 1987), 410.

[3]Robert W. Prichard, *A History of the Episcopal Church* (Harrisburg, Va.: Morehouse Publishing, 1991), 206-211.

[4] DuBose Murphy maintains that the founding of the National Council marked the beginning of the Episcopal Church as a unified American Anglican church. See: DuBose Murphy, "From 'Churches' to Church," *Historical Magazine of the Protestant Episcopal Church* 15 (June 1956).

[5]Isabel. Y. Douglas, *The Story of the Program, 1923-1925: A Brief Survey of the Work of the Episcopal Church at Home and Abroad* (New York: National Council of the Protestant Episcopal Church, 1925), 7.

[6]Charles W. Forman, "A History of Foreign Mission Theory in America," in *American Missions in Bicentennial Perspective*, ed. R. Pierce Beaver (South Pasadena, Calif.: William Carey Library, 1976), 95.

[7]William R. Hutchison, *Errand to the World: American Protestant Thought and Foreign Missions* (Chicago: The University of Chicago Press, 1987), 146.

[8]William Richey Hogg, *Ecumenical Foundations: A History of the International Missionary Council and Its Nineteenth-Century Background* (New York: Harper and Brothers, 1952), 183.

[9]Hutchison, 139-141.

[10]Gerald Anderson documents this change of missionary emphasis by examining two articles by functionaries of the American Board of Commissioners for Foreign Missions in the January 1915 issue of the *Harvard Theological Review*. See: Gerald Anderson, "The Theology of Missions: 1928-1958" (Ph.D. diss., Boston University, 1960), 19-20 and "American Protestants in Pursuit of Mission: 1886-1986," *International Bulletin of Missionary Research* 12 (July 1988): 105.

[11]Forman, 97-99

[12]Lydia Huffman Hoyle, "The Legacy of Daniel Johnson Fleming," *International Bulletin of Missionary Research* 14 (April 1990): 68-70.

[13]Forman, 100.

[14]Daniel Johnson Fleming, *Whither Bound in Missions* (New York: Association Press, 1925), 143, quoted in Hutchison, 151.

[15]Hutchison, 152.

[16]Hoyle, 69.

[17]Hutchison, 52.

[18]Hogg, 245.

[19]Rodger C. Bassham, *Mission Theology, 1948-1975: Years of Worldwide Creative Tensions; Ecumenical, Evangelical, and Roman Catholic* (Pasadena, Calif.: William Carey Library, 1979), 21.

[20]Anderson, "The Theology of Missions, 1928-1958," 42.

[21]Rufus Jones, "Secular Civilization and the Christian Task," *The Christian Message in Relation to Non-Christian Systems*, vol. 1 of *The Jerusalem Meeting of the International Missionary Council* (8 vols., London: International Missionary Council, 1928), 284, quoted in Anderson, "The Theology of Missions, 1928-1958," 44.

[22]Bassham, 23.

[23]Hutchison, 159.

[24]Forman, 102.

[25]William Ernest Hocking, *Re-thinking Missions* (New York: Harper and Brothers, 1932), 326.

[26]Ibid. 327.

[27]Hutchison, 162.

[28]Ibid., 166-167.

[29]Forman, 103.

[30]Bassham, 25.

[31]Hendrick Kraemer, *The Christian Message in a Non-Christian World,* Studies in the World Mission of Christianity, 2nd. edition (New York & London: International Missionary Council, 1947), 60.

[32]Of the 377 delegates 191 were from the younger churches and 186 from the older churches. In addition 58 of the 377 delegates were women. Anderson, "The Theology of Missions," 122.

[33]Bassham, 25.

[34]Hogg, 296.

[35]Ibid.

[36]On average more than 90% of the funding provided for the "orphaned missions" came from the United States. Hogg, 316.

[37]Julia C. Emery, *A Century of Endeavor, 1821-1921: A Record of the First Hundred Years of the Domestic and Foreign Missionary Society of the Protestant Episcopal Church in the United States of America* (New York: The Department of Missions, Protestant Episcopal Church in the United States of America, 1921), 319.

[38]Arthur Selden Lloyd, "Editorial: The Progress of the Kingdom," *The Spirit of Missions* 84 (October 1919): 637, quoted in C. Rankin Barnes, "General Convention of 1919," *Historical Magazine of the Protestant Episcopal Church* 21 (June 1952): 224.

[39]Full text of the sermon found in *The Living Church* 61 (October 11, 1919): 840-842, quoted in Barnes, 226. It is interesting to note that for the first time in the history of the General Convention, the sessions of the House of Bishops were open to the public. This opening of the governing bodies of the Episcopal Church emulated the freedom of the American democratic process and had a significant effect on the legislative atmosphere of the Convention. Roland Foster, *The Role of the Presiding Bishop* (Cincinnati, Ohio: Forward Movement Publications, 1982), 63.

[40]Address by the Rev. Ernest M. Stires to the Joint-Session on the Nation-wide Campaign of the General Convention, Wednesday, October 15, 1919. *The Living Church* 61 (October 25, 1919): 914.

[41]Alexander C. Zabriskie, *Arthur Selden Lloyd: Missionary Statesman and Pastor* (New York: Morehouse-Gorham Co., 1942), 3-11.

[42]Ibid., 37.

[43]Arthur Selden Lloyd, "Editorial: The Progress of the Kingdom," *The Spirit of Missions* 84 (January 1919): 7.

[44]Barnes, 233.

[45]*Constitution and Canons for the Government of the Protestant Episcopal Church in the United States of America* in General Convention of the Protestant Episcopal Church, *Journal of the General Convention of the Protestant Episcopal Church 1919* (New York: The Abbott Press for The General Convention, 1919) 154-155.

[46]Today the legal name for the national offices of the Episcopal Church is: The Domestic and Foreign Missionary Society of the Protestant Episcopal Church in the United States of America.

[47]Women were not allowed to serve on The Presiding Bishop and Council.

[48]Emery, 319.

[49]Barnes, 233-234.

[50]Emery, 319.

[51]Murphy, 199.

[52]Barnes, 236.

[53]G. Maclaren Brydon, "Concerning the Financial Support of the Church, 1066-1960," *Historical Magazine of the Protestant Episcopal Church* 29 (December 1960): 311-312.

[54]Zabriskie, 218.

[55]Ibid., 236-238.

[56]*The Living Church* 62 (November 1, 1919):11, quoted in Barnes, 241-20-241.

[57]George E. DeMille, *The Episcopal Church Since 1900* (New York: Morehouse-Gorham Co., 1955), 28.

[58]The term "national church" refers to the offices and program of the National Council. It does not presuppose the Episcopal Church as an established church for the United States although the Episcopal Church's establishmentarian tradition informed the national church ideal as demonstrated above.

[59]William C. Sturgis, *The Church's Life: A Study of the Fundamentals of the Church's Mission* (New York: Domestic and Foreign Missionary Society of the Protestant Episcopal Church, 1920), 25.

[60]William C. Sturgis, *The Church's Mission Today,* Faith and Life Series (Boston: Irving P. Fox, n.d.), 7. A further exposition of John 10:10 ("I am come that they might have life, and that they might have it more abundantly.") and the mission of the church is found in chapter five of Sturgis's book *A Church Awake.* See: William C. Sturgis, *A Church Awake: A Study in the Vital Elements of the Gospel* (New York: The National Council of the Protestant Episcopal Church, 1927), 96-118.

[61]Sturgis, *The Church's Life*, 26-27.

[62]Ibid., 30. In *A Church Awake*, Sturgis made the same point that "the Church has only one mission, and it is merely a matter of comparative need and urgency which determines whether she shall expend her efforts in New York or Hankow." See: *A Church Awake: A Study in the Vital Elements of the Gospel*, 94.

[63]Sturgis, *The Church's Life*, 79-80.

[64]William Codman Sturgis, "Epilogue," in *Building a Christian Nation*, Thomas Burgess and others (New York: The National Council of the Protestant Episcopal Church, 1932), 152.

[65]Ibid., 60-61.

[66]Sturgis, *A Church Awake*, 121.

[67]J. M. B. Gill, *"My Father's Business" World Problems and Personal Responsibility* (New York: The National Council of the Protestant Episcopal Church, 1924), iii from Introduction.

[68]Ibid., 3.

[69]Ibid., 6.

[70]Ibid., 7.

[71]Ibid.

[72]Ibid., 45.

[73]Ibid., 50.

[74]Ibid., 52.

[75]Ibid., 54-55.

[76]Arthur Romeyn Gray, *That Freedom: A Study of Democracy in the Americas* (New York: The National Council, 1925), Introduction/Editorial Note.

[77]Alfred Newbery, *The World and I* (New York: The National Council of the Protestant Episcopal Church, 1925), 72.

[78]Ibid., 73.

[79]This number does not include wives of male missionaries who often served side-by side with their spouses in the foreign and extra-continental missionary districts. It also does not include the more than 2,000 indigenous church-workers ("nationals") who were supported by the National Council.

[80]The Episcopal Church did attempt to begin work in the Middle East and India during the years 1919-1946. These efforts were very modest and did not result in new missionary districts.

[81]Financial goals for the Campaign and an overview of the "General Church Program" of the National Council is found in: Isabel Y. Douglas, *Program Presented* (New York: National Council of the Protestant Episcopal Church, n.d.) and Isabel. Y. Douglas, *The Story of the Program, 1923-1925.* (New York: National Council of the Protestant Episcopal Church, 1925).

[82]"Report of the Committee on the States of the Church," General Convention of the Protestant Episcopal Church, *Journal of the General Convention of the Protestant Episcopal Church: 1922* (New York: The Abbott Press for The General Convention, 1923), 551.

[83]"Annual Cyclopedic of the Church," in *The Living Church Annual 1924* (Milwaukee. Wis.: Morehouse Publishing Co., 1923), 101.

[84]Protestant Episcopal Church, The National Council, *General Church Program for 1923-1925* (New York: The National Council, 1923), 7.

[85]Allen J. Green, "Episcopal Missionary Giving, 1920-1955," *Overseas Mission Review* 1 (Whitsunday 1956): 8.

[86]Report of the Department of Missions and Church Extension in: Protestant Episcopal Church in the United States of America, National Council, *Annual Report of the National Council of the Protestant Episcopal Church in the United States: 1927* (New

York: National Council of the Protestant Episcopal Church, [1928]), 14.

[87]Report of the Department of Missions and Church Extension in: Protestant Episcopal Church in the United States of America, National Council, *Annual Report of the National Council of the Protestant Episcopal Church in the United States: 1929* (New York: National Council of the Protestant Episcopal Church, [1930]), 19.

[88]Ibid.

[89]Protestant Episcopal Church in the United States of America, National Council, *Annual Report of the National Council of the Protestant Episcopal Church in the United States: 1931* (New York: National Council of the Protestant Episcopal Church, 1931), 214.

[90]Ibid., 210.

[91]"Annual Cyclopedic of the Church," in *The Living Church Annual 1936* (Milwaukee, Wis.: Morehouse Publishing Co., 1935), 449.

[92]Each year income from undesignated legacies would be used to pay down the debt after the National Council's budget had been balanced. Using this process the deficit was retired in 1946.

[93]Bishop Tuttle died in April of 1923. Since the next General Convention would not meet until 1925 the senior bishop of the House of Bishops continued to serve as Presiding Bishop until the convention. Alexander C. Garrett, bishop of Delaware, thus held the position of Presiding Bishop from April 17, 1923 until February 18, 1924. He was followed by Ethelbert Talbot, bishop of Bethlehem, who served as Presiding Bishop from February 18, 1924 to January 1, 1926.

[94]General Convention of the Protestant Episcopal Church, *Journal of the General Convention of the Protestant Episcopal Church: 1925* (New York: The Abbott Press for The General Convention, 1926), 29, quoted in Foster, 76.

[95]Protestant Episcopal Church in the United States of America, National Council, *Annual Report of the National Council of the Protestant Episcopal Church in the United States: 1925* (New York: National Council of the Protestant Episcopal Church, 1926) 7.

[96]Foster, 77-79.

[97]In the year 1930, 73% of the total expenditures for the National Council was allocated to the Department of Missions and Church Extension ($2,862,119 of the total $3,906,190). In addition, 180 pages of the *Annual Report for the Council* were dedicated to the work of the Department of Missions and Church Extension while the reports on the remaining five departments totaled only 50 pages. See: Protestant Episcopal Church in the United States of America, National Council, *Annual Report of the National Council of the Protestant Episcopal Church in the United States: 1930* (New York: National Council of the Protestant Episcopal Church, n.d.).

[98]Responsibility for the extra-continental missionary districts was placed in the Department of Foreign Missions.

[99]Protestant Episcopal Church in the United States of America, National Council, *Annual Report of the National Council of the Protestant Episcopal Church in the United States: 1933* (New York: National Council of the Protestant Episcopal Church, n.d.) 8.

[100]General Convention of the Protestant Episcopal Church, *Journal of the General Convention of the Protestant Episcopal Church: 1934* (Hammond, Ind.: W. B. Conkey Company for the General Convention, 1934), 447.

[101]Henry Wise Hobson, *The Forward Movement in the Episcopal Church*, The Twenty-fourth Annual Hale Memorial Sermon, delivered March 9, 1938 (Evanston, Ill.: Seabury-Western Theological Seminary, [1938]), 11.

[102]Henry Wise Hobson, "The Forward Movement — Thus Far," in *The Living Church Annual, 1936* (Milwaukee, Wis.: Morehouse Publishing Co., 1935), 14.

[103]Foster, 81.

[104]Ibid., 83.

[105]*The Living Church*, 23 October 1937, 501, quoted in Foster, 88.

[106]Foster, 89.

[107]Charles W. Sheerin, "Profile of a Presiding Bishop," *Historical Magazine of the Protestant Episcopal Church* 15 (March 1946): 82.

[108]Ibid., 85-86.

[109]Addison later wrote an extensive history of this World War I fighting battalion. James Thayer Addison, *The Story of the First Gas Regiment* (Boston and New York: Houghton Mifflin Company, 1919).

[110]James Thayer Addison, *Religion in India* (New York: The National Council of the Protestant Episcopal Church, 1930), and James Thayer Addison, "Religious Life in Japan," *Harvard Theological Review* 18 (October 1925): 321-356.

[111]James Thayer Addison, "Ancestor Worship in Africa," *Harvard Theological Review* 17 (April 1924): 155-171, and James Thayer Addison, *Chinese Ancestor Worship* (London: Society for the Promotion of Christian Knowledge, 1925).

[112]James Thayer Addison, *Life Beyond Death in the Beliefs of Mankind* (Boston and New York: Houghton Mifflin Company, 1932), Preface.

[113]James Thayer Addison, "The Ahmadiya Movement and its Western Movement," *Harvard Theological Review* 22 (January 1929): 1-32.

[114]James Thayer Addison, *The World of Islam* (New York: The National Council of the Protestant Episcopal Church, 1937).

[115]James Thayer Addison, *The Christian Approach to the Moslem* (New York: Columbia University Press, 1942).

[116]James Thayer Addison, *Francis Xavier* (Hartford, Conn.: Church Missions Publishing Company, 1929), and James Thayer Addison, *The Medieval Missionary: A Study in the Conversion of Northern Europe, AD 500-1300* (New York: The International Missionary Council, 1936).

[117]Addison's devotional books, usually prepared for Lenten study programs, include: *Our Father's Business* (New York: George H. Dorin, [1927]); *The Way of Christ* (Boston and New York: Houghton Mifflin Co., 1934); *The Lord's Prayer* (New York and Milwaukee, Wis.: Morehouse, 1937); *Parables of Our Lord* (New York: Morehouse-Gorham, 1940); and *The Completeness of Christ* (New York: Morehouse-Gorham, 1947).

[118]James Thayer Addison, "The Missionary Sermon," delivered at the Virginia Theological Seminary, Alexandria, Virginia, June 6, 1934, in *Seminary Bulletin*, Virginia Theological Seminary (October 1934): 13-20.

[119]G. Warfield Hobbs, "Laymen's Missions Inquiry Presents Report," *The Spirit of Missions* 97 (December 1932): 741-742.

[120]Report of the Department of Missions and Church Extension in: Protestant Episcopal Church in the United States of America, National Council, *Annual Report of the National Council of the Protestant Episcopal Church in the United States: 1932* (New York: National Council of the Protestant Episcopal Church, 1932), 86.

[121]Addison, "The Missionary Sermon," 16.

[122]James Thayer Addison, *Our Expanding Church*, 3rd ed., (New York: National Council of the Protestant Episcopal Church, 1944), and James Thayer Addison, *Why Missions* (New Brunswick, N.J.: Joint Commission of General Convention on Strategy and Policy, 1940).

[123]Addison, *Our Expanding Church*, 5.

[124]Ibid., 14.

[125]Addison's short pamphlet entitled *Why Missions* reiterated the *missio ecclesia* theology of *Our Expanding Church*.

[126]Protestant Episcopal Church in the United States of America, National Council, Forward in Service, *The Source of Power: The Presiding Bishop's Booklet for Clergy on His Ten-year Program"* (New York: National Council of the Protestant Episcopal Church, [1940]), 19-20.

[127]Ibid., 20.

[128]Charles W. Sheerin, "Behold, I Send Ye Forth," *Forth: The Spirit of Missions* 105 (January 1940): 5.

[129]Ibid.

[130]Ibid.

[131]Henry St. George Tucker, *Go Forward in Service: A Call to the Church to Meet Present Problems* (New York: The National Council of the Protestant Episcopal Church, 1940), 9-10.

[132]Ibid., 10.

[133]Protestant Episcopal Church in the United States of America, National Council, Forward in Service, *Forward in Service: Plan of Action of Presiding Bishop's Ten Year Forward Movement* (New York: National Council of the Protestant Episcopal Church, [1940]), 1.

[134]Themes of the Forward in Service program included: 1941-42, "Worship and Prayer" with an emphasis on parish programs; 1942-43, "Freedom through Christ" with an emphasis on evangelism and stewardship; 1943-44, "The Kingdom of God and His Righteousness" with an emphasis on Christian community service; and 1944-45, "The Christian Fellowship" emphasizing international and interracial understanding.

[135]Sheerin, *Profile of a Presiding Bishop*, 87.

[136]Tucker, 5-6.

[137]General Convention of the Protestant Episcopal Church, *Journal of the General Convention of the Protestant Episcopal Church: 1940* (Hammond, Ind.: W. B. Conkey Company for the General Convention, 1940), 390.

[138]Edith M. Denison, *In the Name of Refugees: Fifteen Years of Episcopal World Relief and Refugee Work, 1938-1953* (New York: The National Council, [1954]), 1-2.

[139]Samir J. Habiby, ed., "An Analysis of the Evolution of the Fund and its Ministry — Part I, June 15, 1986" The Presiding Bishop's Fund for World Relief, New York, 9.

[140]Ibid., 5-6.

[141]Ibid., 9.

[142]Tucker, 6.

[143]*Journal of the General Convention: 1940*, 160.

[144]Habiby, 10.

[145]General Convention of the Protestant Episcopal Church, *Journal of the General Convention of the Protestant Episcopal Church: 1946* (Hammond, Ind.: W. B. Conkey Company for the General Convention, 1947), 332.

[146]The number of United Offering missionaries was arrived at by counting women so designated in the Alphabetical List of Episcopal missionaries. See: Protestant Episcopal Church in the United States of America, Board of Missions, *Annual Report of the Board of Missions of the Protestant Episcopal Church for the Fiscal Year 1919* (New York: The Domestic and Foreign Missionary Society of the Protestant Episcopal Church in the United States of America, [1920]), 226-235.

[147]Margaret M. Sherman, *True to Their Heritage: A Brief History of the Woman's Auxiliary, 1871-1958* (New York: National Council of the Protestant Episcopal Church, 1958), 16.

[148]Mary Sudman Donovan, *A Different Call: Women's Ministries in the Episcopal Church, 1850-1920* (Wilton, Conn.: Morehouse-Barlow, 1986), 143.

[149]Avis E. Harvey, *Every Three Years: The Triennial Meetings, 1874-1967* (New York: Executive Council of the Episcopal Church, n.d.), 10.

[150]Grace Lindley, "Forty-Eighth Annual Report of the Woman's Auxiliary to the Board of Missions," in *Annual Report of the Board of Missions 1919*, 238.

[151]Sherman, 16.

[152]Lindley, 239.

[153]Report of the Department of Missions and Church Extension in: Protestant Episcopal Church in the United States of America, National Council, *Annual Report of the National Council of the Protestant Episcopal Church in the United States: 1921* (New York: National Council of the Protestant Episcopal Church, [1922]), 13-14.

[154]Protestant Episcopal Church in the United States of America, National Council, *Annual Report of the Presiding Bishop and Council for the Year 1920* (New York: The Domestic and Foreign Missionary Society, [1920]), 142-269, 274-279.

[155]The offering collected at the Triennial Meeting in 1928 totaled $1,101,450.40. Francis M. Young, *Thankfulness Unites: The History of the United Thank Offering, 1889-1979* (Cincinnati, Ohio: Forward Movement, 1979), 85.

[156]Ibid., 31.

[157]Ibid., 85.

[158]Ibid., 35.

[159]Sherman, 19.

[160]Ibid., 24-25.

CHAPTER FOUR

AMERICAN SUPREMACY
The Ideal and the Emerging Anglican Communion, 1946 to 1963

Following World War II the United States and the Soviet Union became the undisputed political and economic powers of the world. Paralleling the increasing affluence of the United States was a resurgence of popular piety in all corners of American society. An enlivened civil religion equating love of God with love of country grasped the minds and hearts of Americans returning from war. Personal religious faith and patriotic commitment became two sides of the same coin. In 1954 the phrase "under God" was added to the Pledge of Allegiance and two years later the statement "In God We Trust" was elevated from its ceremonial place on the country's currency to the official motto of the United States. As a symbol of American civil religion, President Dwight D. Eisenhower summarized American religiosity when he said in 1954: "Our government makes no sense unless it is founded on a deep religious faith — and I don't care what it is."[1]

Americans affiliated themselves with institutional religion in record numbers as an outgrowth of the blossoming civil religion. American religious communities of all types (Protestant, Catholic and Jewish) experienced a dramatic increase in membership, monetary support and building construction.[2] The Episcopal

Church, in particular, showed a marked rise in membership and all other "worldly" criteria. It seemed as if more Americans than ever sought to express their civil religiosity in the one denomination that seemed to embody the ideals of a national church.[3] The ascendancy of the Episcopal Church both at home and in the emerging Anglican Communion paralleled the American economic and political supremacy of the new world.

The post-war years also saw an increasing commitment to global Christian ecumenical councils. In 1948 the Faith and Order and Life and Work movements, initiated by the 1910 World Missionary Conference in Edinburgh, came together culminating in the First Assembly of the World Council of Churches (WCC), in Amsterdam. The International Missionary Council (IMC), also begun at Edinburgh, held world missionary conferences in Whitby (1947), Willigen (1952) and Accra (1958). At the Third Assembly of the WCC in New Delhi in 1961, the IMC was integrated into the World Council of Churches. This integration completed the merging of the three streams of ecumenical thought begun at Edinburgh and marked the peak of the modern ecumenical movement.

The period of the late 1940s to the early 1960s was considered a first stage in the development of ecumenical, or conciliar, missionary thought and was characterized by an emphasis on the church as the agent of God's mission in the world.[4] Although a few thinkers in this period challenged the primacy of the church in God's mission, the bulk of conciliar ecumenical thought promoted a missiology where the church equaled mission.[5]

The high regard for the church as mission and the calling of all baptized persons to participate in mission signaled an agreement of thought between Episcopal and ecumenical missiology never before realized. The congruence of Episcopal and ecumenical mission theology combined with the preeminence of the United States in world affairs placed the American Episcopal Church in a powerful position as it promoted its national church ideal in the emerging Anglican Communion.

TOWARDS A CONCILIAR THEOLOGY OF WORLD MISSION

The mission theology promoted by both the World Council of Churches and the International Missionary Council in the years after World War II began to recognize the universal call of all Christians to participate in one worldwide missionary endeavor. Ever since Edinburgh, individuals such as Daniel Fleming had argued for a "Christian World-mindedness" based upon mutuality and partnership between all churches, young and old. It was not until after World War II, however, that an appreciation of a unified global mission in which all Christians participate as equal partners emerged as a dominant theme in ecumenical conversations. By the end of the colonial era it was acknowledged widely that Christians in the West could no longer speak of their "foreign missions," but rather all churches, young and old, were called to participate in one mission: the mission of the church universal. Writing in 1963 Bishop Stephen Neill, the Anglican missionary to South India and mission scholar, summarized the new missiological reality. He stated: "The age of missions is at an end; the age of mission has begun."[6]

With the decline of the nineteenth century missionary model and the increasing acceptance of one world mission, issues relating to partnership among Christians increasingly set the agenda for most ecumenical missionary gatherings. The 1947 meeting of the International Missionary Council in Whitby, Canada, underscored the importance of partnership between Christians from the "older" and "younger" churches. As first envisioned, Whitby did not pretend to stand in the tradition of Edinburgh, Jerusalem and Madras. Whereas the earlier gatherings had been meetings of the full International Missionary Council, Whitby was planned as an enlarged meeting of the Committee of the Council. As such, fewer individuals attended the Whitby IMC meeting (112 as compared with 471 in Madras). Although the number of participants at Whitby was small, over forty countries were represented. The diversity of the gathering, combined with the fact that Whitby

was the first real post-war reunion of the worldwide Christian
family, ensured that the meeting would be an important event.[7]

Whitby did not stand out immediately as a landmark in the history of ecumenical mission thought. Unlike the two earlier meetings of the IMC, Whitby saw no significant debates over theology.
Instead Whitby witnessed a new spirit of cooperation and desire
to move forward with the missionary task in the post-war era.

> Whitby made no unusually provocative or explosive proposals that fired
> intense theological debate. It did not, for example generate anything like the
> widespread and lengthy debate about the "continuity" or "discontinuity" of
> the Gospel with the world that Madras provoked. There was, in fact, a basi-
> cally conciliatory and pragmatic tone to its proposals:...[the meeting] was
> more geared towards providing some of the practical considerations that
> could lead to a "plan of action" and to the next steps which the missionary
> movement and the churches involved in it could take in the coming years[8]

To encourage ongoing conversations and cooperation among the
many missionary agencies collected at Whitby, the meeting initiated a study of the theology of mission. This seemingly small step to
study the missionary obligation of the church would have major
significance for the theology of missions in the next two decades.[9]

According to historian William Richey Hogg, the Whitby meeting is best remembered for three things: its determination to place
evangelism at the center of the modern missionary movement, its
revelation of the new equality between older and younger churches, and its demonstration of the unity of the Protestant world
Christian community.[10] Following in the tradition of the Student
Volunteer Movement, those gathered at Whitby gave a high priority to the urgent need to preach the Gospel to the ends of the earth.
Responsibility for preaching the Gospel to the ends of the earth,
however, was no longer the exclusive domain of Western missionaries but rather the duty of the emerging global church. The statement "Christian Witness in a Revolutionary World," issued by the
Committee of the International Missionary Council meeting in
Whitby, stressed the universal call to evangelism of all churches,
young and old. It stated:

> The task of world evangelism starts to-day from the vantage ground of a
> Church which, as never before, is really world-wide. This universal fellow-
> ship is, in the oft quoted words of William Temple, the great new fact of our

> era. It is working itself out today in the real partnership between older and
> younger churches....Yet when we consider the present extension of the
> Church, and the divine and human resources available, we dare to believe
> it possible that, before the present generation has passed away, the Gospel
> should be preached to almost all the inhabitants of the world in such a way
> as to make clear to them the issue of faith or disbelief in Jesus Christ. If this
> is possible, it is the task of the Church to see that it is done.[11]

Whitby envisioned new models of cooperation among all churches in making Christ known in the world.

The 1947 gathering of the IMC was the first to emphasize partnership as a central theme in missionary endeavors. The statement, "Partnership in Obedience," issued by Whitby, presented a
bold vision for collaboration between churches young and old. In
particular it stressed the need for partnership in four areas of mission activity: personnel, finance, policy and administration. In
terms of personnel, "Partnership in Obedience" emphasized the
necessity to develop indigenous leadership in the younger
churches. It also suggested that the missionary movement should
be ecumenical and multi-directional with equal exchange
between younger and older churches. With regard to finance,
"Partnership in Obedience" stressed the importance of stewardship in all churches and the urgent need to end the dependency
of any church upon another. In terms of policy and administration, the Whitby statement reaffirmed "the supernationality of
missions." "Partnership in Obedience," however, went on to state
that the responsibility for mission in any one location is primarily the obligation of the church in that place. Other Christians are
called to support the local church in its mission activity, but the
burden of responsibility belongs to the indigenous church.
Whitby thus emphasized that

> churches as the bearers of the missionary obligation are in a missionary sit-
> uation wherever they are. And while different situations demand different
> duties and engender different needs, all and each are called to the same
> missionary obligation by their One Lord. The equality of all churches
> implies the equal sharing in the responsibility to unite in the fulfillment of
> their common missionary task — wherever they are, wherever the needs
> are greatest, and with whatever contribution they are able to make.[12]

This vision of partnership heralded by Whitby was a radically
new understanding of the world Christian community. It would

take years for churches to fully comprehend the changes in mission implied by "Partnership in Obedience." Almost two and a half decades after Whitby, the Anglican Communion would begin a program of "Partners in Mission" that resembled closely the prophetic call of those individuals gathered in Canada in the summer of 1947.

The study of the theology of Christian mission begun at Whitby was to have a direct impact on the next meeting of the International Missionary Council. From 1947 until the summer of 1952, study papers from eminent missiologists such as Walter Freytag, A. G. Herbert, Max A. C. Warren, Johannes C. Hoekendijk and John A. Mackay, along with reports from the Dutch Missionary Council and the American National Council of Churches wrestled with theological questions about the nature of Christian mission.[13]

From July 5 to 17, 1952, 190 delegates and consultants from fifty countries, of whom some forty were "nationals from the younger churches," met in Willingen, Germany, to take up the question of "The Missionary Obligation of the Church."[14] The Willingen meeting of the IMC reflected a unity of opinion about the church's call to mission while significant dissenting voices raised questions about the increasing ecclesio-centric emphasis in mission theology.

Those attending the IMC Conference in Willigen were divided into five major theme groups: the missionary obligation of the church, the indigenous church, the role of the missionary society in the present situation, vocation and training, and reviewing the pattern of missionary activity. The reports of four of the five theme groups were presented to the collected body and adopted. The report of the group on the missionary obligation of the church, however, was not accepted. Instead the conference adopted two statements, one on the missionary calling of the church and the second on missions and unity.[15] In the "Statement on the Missionary Calling of the Church" the Willigen Conference outlined its basic affirmations of the church's call to mission. It stated in part:

> The missionary movement of which we are a part has its source in the Triune God Himself. Out of the depths of His love for us, the Father has sent forth His own beloved Son to reconcile all things to Himself, that we and all men might, through the Spirit, be made one in Him with the Father in that perfect love which is the very nature of God.

> We who have been chosen in Christ, reconciled to God through Him, made members of His Body, sharers in His Spirit, and heirs through the hope of His Kingdom, are by the very facts committed to full participation in His redeeming mission, There is no participation in Christ without participation in His mission to the world. That by which the Church receives its existence is that by which it is also given world-mission. "As the Father hath sent Me, even so I send you."[16]

The centrality of the church as the bearer of God's mission in the world and the responsibility of every Christian to participate in this mission was attested to by the conference's adoption of the report presented by Missionary Vocation and Training Group. It affirmed:

> The Call to Mission is always a call to the Church. The manner of response to the call in commitment of life and resources is, under God's guidance, the responsibility of the Church...It is the duty of the Church to remind men and women that the call of God comes to all to serve Him as Christian witnesses wherever they may be. It is in the setting of this general Christian vocation that the Church should help young people, in deciding their life work, to make their choice on the basis of God's will for them as participants in the mission of the Church.[17]

Willingen's commitment to the church as the focal point for mission and its emphasis on the universal call of all Christians to participate in the church's mission signaled a convergence of opinion between conciliar mission thought and the missiology espoused by the Episcopal Church in the United States.

Charles Long, one of the last Episcopalian missionaries appointed to China and a member of the North American delegation to Willigen, contributed significantly to the convergence of mission theology between the IMC and the Episcopal Church. In his article "Christian Vocation and the Missionary Call" published in the *International Review of Missions* in 1950, Long articulated the concerns of the Willingen report on missionary vocation and training two years in advance of the IMC meeting in Germany. As an Episcopalian, Long subscribed to his church's century-old missiological premise that all Christians are called to participate in the church's mission. He emphasized this position in his article.

> We are all called to be missionaries. The Holy Spirit is seeking to bear witness through the life of every baptized person... Moreover, every Christian, through the gift of the Holy Spirit is "sent" to proclaim the Gospel to non-Christians, whether under his own roof or at the ends of the earth. We believe the Holy Spirit will guide every man to discover to whom he is specially sent.[18]

Although Long emphasized that all Christians are sent to proclaim the Gospel, he maintained that there is still a need for professional missionaries who are specially called to a service of social and cultural martyrdom.[19] The difference between the work of the professional missionary and the calling of all baptized Christians to witness to Christ is not one of kind but of degree.

> We have tried to suggest that for those who choose to be professional missionaries, the difference between this and any other form of Christian vocation lies primarily in the consequences and not in the merit of the choice itself.[20]

Long's article was one of eight published in the *International Review of Missions* in preparation for the Willingen Conference. Long recalls that he was invited to Willingen on the merits of the article and that he, Keith Bridston and Johannes Hoekendijk "were the young Turks" at the conference.[21]

Whereas Long's position on the universal call of all Christians to participate in God's mission was affirmed by the Willingen Conference, Johannes Hoekendijk's challenge to the increasingly church-centered missiology of the IMC fell on less sympathetic ears. Hoekendijk had been active in student and mission work in the Netherlands, his home country. He had served as the secretary of the Student Christian Movement in the Netherlands and then with the Netherlands Missionary Council. At the time of the Willingen Conference, Hoekendijk was secretary for evangelism at the World Council of Churches. He later went on to become professor of theology at Utrecht and was professor of missions at Union Theological Seminary in New York from 1965 to 1975.[22]

In the article "The Call to Evangelism" printed in the *International Review of Missions* in 1950, Hoekendijk challenged the emerging emphasis on the church as the locus for mission. Hoekendijk criticized church-centered evangelism.

> To put it bluntly: the call to evangelism is often little else than a call to restore "Christendom," the *Corpus Christianum*, as a solid, well-integrated cultural complex, directed and dominated by the Church. And the sense of urgency is often nothing but a nervous feeling of insecurity, with the established Church endangered; a flurried activity to save the remnants of a time now irrevocably past.[23]

Hoekendijk cautioned that the discussions of the church as mission that had emerged since Whitby were misdirected.

> But we should be aware of a temptation to take the Church itself too seriously, to invite the Church to see itself as well established, as God's secure bridgehead in the world, to think of itself as a *beatus possidens* which, having what others do not have, distributes its possession to others, until a new company of *possidentes* is formed.[24]

In short: "Evangelization and *churchification* are not identical, and very often they are each other's bitterest enemies." (Italics in original)[25]

Instead of a church-centered evangelism, Hoekendijk argued for an eschatological-centered evangelism. The goal of evangelism was not to establish the church as the *Corpus Christianum* but rather to participate with God in God's new creation, to work for God's shalom.

> The aim of evangelism can be nothing less than what Israel expected the Messiah to do, i.e. He will establish shalom. And shalom is much more than personal salvation. It is at once peace, integrity, community, harmony and justice. Its rich content can be felt in Psalm LXXXV, where we read that shalom is there, where "mercy and truth are met together; righteousness and peace have kissed each other. Truth shall spring out of the earth; and righteousness shall look down from heaven."[26]

Hoekendijk's emphasis on the eschatological vision of God's shalom shifted the missiological terrain from that of the *missio ecclesia* to the *missio Dei*. He was the first of his generation to suggest that it was God's mission in the world to bring about God's shalom, God's kingdom, God's reign. The church was called to participate in God's mission in all of creation and not be the exclusive purveyor of it. Hoekendijk's vision of the *missio Dei*, however, was premature. It would be two decades before "Kingdom-centered" mission would come to the forefront in conciliar missiological discussions. Protestant churches, especially the Episcopal Church in the United States, in the post-war era were unwilling to accept a theology of mission that did not place them at the center.

The final meeting of the International Missionary Council, as such, was held from December 28, 1957 to January 8, 1958 on the campus of University College in Legon, Ghana, eight miles from the capital city of Accra. The general theme of the assembly to which about 200 delegates and consultants addressed themselves was "The Christian Mission at This Hour."[27] On first investigation it appeared that the majority of the discussions at the Ghana IMC meeting were not concerned with missionary strategy and theology but rather with administrative questions about the integration of the International Missionary Council with the World Council of Churches. Lying behind the administrative questions, however, was a deeper theological query. If the Church as a whole, as compared to the missionary councils and voluntary societies, had a missionary obligation, then the missiological agenda belonged to the larger body of the collected churches (the WCC) rather than those who have a special interest in missions (the IMC). Put another way, the increasing commitment to an understanding of the church as the focal point for mission and the concomitant call of all Christians to participate in the church's mission, emphasized in the Willigen meeting of the IMC, moved the responsibility for mission beyond the domain of the International Missionary Council into the portfolio of the wider World Council of Churches.

Concerns over the increasingly ecclesio-centric view of mission were addressed by the 1958 meeting of the IMC. In the statement "The Christian Mission at This Hour" those gathered at the Ghana assembly sought to outline the theological tenets behind the integration of the IMC and the WCC. The statement opened by emphasizing that mission belonged to Christ first and not to any particular individual or Christian body. Christians, however, were called to be both fellow-workers with Christ in His mission to the world as well as accountable to each other as members of one body, the church.

> So we are responsible. Each of us in his own place, each local company of Christ's people, each church in its organized life cannot be Christ's without being His missionary servant. A vague and generalized acceptance of the world mission is no substitute for responsible action in the discharge of missionary obedience.
>
> But we are responsible to one another in Christ. We are called in Him to recognize with gladness that our fellow Christians, our neighboring congregations,

our sister denominations in our own and other lands are called by the same
missionary Lord, and need the same freedom as we ourselves do to respond
to His calling. [28]

On the eve of the integration of the IMC and the WCC, the Ghana
assembly acknowledged the tensions inherent in the merging of
the missionary and ecumenical agendas.

> There is a tension which can easily become a contradiction — the tension
> between missionary passion and a due regard for the claims of the
> Christian fellowship. It has shown itself at many points in our discussions,
> as we have talked together about the place and function of the missionary,
> the structure and tasks of the Christian Councils, and especially in our dis-
> cussion of the proposal that the I.M.C. and the W.C.C. should become one
> body. We have not seen how the contradiction can be removed. It may well
> be that the tension is one that is inherent in the Christian life.[29]

The question that the Ghana IMC meeting was unable to
answer and the one that would continue to haunt the World
Council of Churches for the next decade was: if the whole church
was called to participate in Christ's mission, then what in particular constituted missionary activity and who was responsible for it?

One of the final acts of the International Missionary Council
before integration with the WCC was the publication of a document summarizing its missiological position at the time. *One
Body, One Gospel, One World*, written by Lesslie Newbigin, then
general secretary of the IMC and later the first director of the
WCC's Division of World Mission and Evangelism, was both a
defense of the continuing need for missionaries in the post-war
world as well as an attempt to define the mission agenda for the
churches on the eve of the IMC-WCC integration.[30] Newbigin
began by summarizing the affirmation that all who called themselves Christians, the church, were called to participate in Christ's
mission locally and in the larger world. Newbigin emphasized
that the primary responsibility for evangelism in any one area
belonged to the local church. He added, however, that all churches were called to be in partnership with each other as they shared
their local mission with sisters and brothers in Christ around the
world. Although Newbigin concluded that the mission in Christ's
way embodied the church's call to both witness and service, he
was unwilling to compromise the missionary's unique vocation to

cross the boundary between faith in Jesus Christ and unbelief.[31] Newbigin's articulation of the church as embodying Christ's mission, local responsibility for evangelism, and worldwide partnership in mission would be echoed by Anglicans attempting to enunciate new methods for mission in the post-colonial world.

In November 1961, at the Third Assembly of the World Council of Churches in New Delhi, the International Missionary Council and the World Council of Churches formally merged. The merger of the IMC and WCC marked the final coming together of the three streams of the modern ecumenical movement (faith and order, life and work, and mission) begun at the World Missionary Conference in Edinburgh, 1910. The rationale for the integration of the IMC and the WCC was the then-accepted affirmation that both mission and unity were central to the life of the church.

> A basic and long forgotten truth is being rediscovered in our time, which might be stated thus: the *unity* of the Church and the *mission* of the Church both belong, in equal degree, to the *essence* of the Church. If Christian churches would be in very truth the Church, they must carry the Gospel into all the world. They must also strive to achieve the unity of all those throughout the world for whom Jesus Christ is Lord. This truth has already become manifest in the life of both the world bodies. It has led them into association with each other and now obliges them to go further. They exist to help the churches to witness to the wholeness of the Gospel and must, therefore, seek to express that wholeness in their own life.[32]

To represent the voice of the International Missionary Council, a new Commission on World Mission and Evangelism (CWME) was created in the WCC. The stated aim of the CWME and its programmatic offices in the WCC, the Division of World Mission and Evangelism, was "to further the effective proclamation to all men of the Gospel of Jesus Christ."[33]

One of the first agenda items for the new Commission on World Mission and Evangelism was to examine church structures to see if they represented, in reality, the affirmation that all churches were called to participate in the one mission of Jesus Christ. The study program established by the CWME to look into the missiological foundations of the member churches of the WCC was given the title: "The Missionary Structure of the

Church." This study would investigate both how present church structures affected mission as well as how mission should shape the structures of the church.[34] This latter issue raised the question of the church's openness to the world as it pursued Christ's mission. Criticism of church-centric mission, first raised by Hoekendijk ten years earlier, gained a wider audience. "The Missionary Structure of the Church" challenged conciliar Protestants to look beyond the church to the world for their mission agenda. Reflecting on "The Missionary Structure of the Church," James Scherer believes that the CWME departed from its original mandate.

> This study ["The Missionary Structure of the Church"] was to have an unexpectedly heavy influence on the development of ecumenical mission theology in the post–New Delhi period. Based mainly on Western theological trends and sociological analysis, and reflecting the troubled cultural milieu of this period, this study would decisively divert the attention of the churches from the practice of church-mission integration toward a world-oriented understanding of mission.[35]

This new "world-oriented" understanding of mission would become the primary agenda of the Commission on World Mission and Evangelism for the next two decades.

Although mission thinkers and ecumenical councils heralded a new era of mission partnership, the idea that all churches suddenly were to participate equally in the one missionary task of the church was not easily put into practice. The fact that American churches in the post-war years enjoyed a new level of economic prosperity and popularity while the younger churches struggled to throw off the mantle of colonialism perpetuated an unequal relationship between the churches of the haves and have-nots. As the economic and political power of the United States grew, so too did the American foreign mission force. Whereas in the first decade of the twentieth century two-thirds of all Western Protestant foreign missionaries came from outside of North America, by the mid-1950s the tables had turned and two-thirds of the foreign mission force were Americans.[36] The Episcopal Church, following its ideal as a national church, made great strides in the post-war years.

Bolstered by the popular religiosity and economic prosperity of the United States in the decades after World War II, the Episcopal Church would come to play a central role in the emerging Anglican Communion. The foreign mission policies of the Episcopal Church, however, did not seriously consider the realities and challenges of the new Anglican Communion but chose instead to follow old missionary methods.

ASCENDANCY OF THE EPISCOPAL CHURCH IN THE POST-WAR ANGLICAN COMMUNION

In the two decades following World War II, the Episcopal Church in the United States came the closest to realizing its ideal as a national church. Under the leadership of Presiding Bishop Henry Knox Sherrill, the National Council broadened its institutional reach in Christian education, social service and church extension. When missionaries were expelled from China following the Revolution of 1949, the Episcopal Church increased its missionary efforts in Latin America. Bolstered by the American affluence of the 1950s, the Episcopal Church increased financial grants to emerging autonomous churches in the Anglican Communion. Under the leadership of Bishops Walter H. Gray and Stephen Bayne, the Episcopal Church emerged as a significant leader in inter-Anglican conversations. With new mission fields, new money and new leadership, the Episcopal Church in the United States saw itself increasingly as the preeminent church in the Anglican Communion.

Henry Knox Sherrill: Chief Executive Officer

As Presiding Bishop of the Episcopal Church from January of 1947 until November of 1958, Henry Knox Sherrill embodied the vision and programmatic reach of the national church ideal. His leadership in Anglican and ecumenical councils reflected the position of the Episcopal Church as an increasingly significant player in inter-church affairs. Sherrill's gifts for raising money and developing national and international church programs fortified the Episcopal Church's three-fold mission. The visibility and power of Henry Knox Sherrill as Presiding Bishop in the post-war years represented the fullest flowering of the Episcopal Church's image of itself as a national church.

Sherrill was born in Brooklyn, New York, on November 6, 1890 to an upper middle class family. His childhood was spent in Brooklyn with summers at a family farm in western Massachusetts. Sherrill was educated at the Polytechnic Preparatory School in Brooklyn and later attended Hotchkiss School in Lakeville, Connecticut. Raised an Episcopalian, Sherrill's religious life was deepened during his Hotchkiss years as he encountered great Christian leaders such as Robert E. Speer and Lyman Abbott. In his autobiography, *Among Friends*, Sherrill remembered the impact of Hotchkiss on his ministerial vocation.

> At Hotchkiss in a more personal way than ever before I felt the appeal of Christian service. I had been confirmed by Bishop Burgess at St. Paul's Church, Flatbush, four years before at my own desire, but that came, I should say, under the head of Christian nurture rather than deep personal experience. Now in long walks along the lakeshore on Sunday afternoons, without saying anything to anyone I began to think of the ministry as a possibility.[37]

After graduation from Hotchkiss, Sherrill attended Yale University. The strong missionary presence at Yale, strengthened by the visits of notable Christian leaders such as John R. Mott, broadened Sherrill's vision of world Christianity and the relevance of the Gospel to contemporary society.[38] Immediately after graduating from Yale Sherrill pursued theological studies at Episcopal Theological School (ETS) in Cambridge, Massachusetts, entering in the fall of 1911. At ETS Sherrill made many lifelong friends, one of whom was James Thayer Addison. The school's historic commitment to the study of the relationship between church and society, as found in the writings of F. D. Maurice, was formative for Sherrill and deepened his growing commitment to the church at home and around the world.

> The School gave me a deepened sense of the church. The study of church history, of theology, especially the course in which we read all the books of F. D. Maurice, made me conscious of the great tradition which was ours in the continuing life and thought of the generations of Christians. My experience of the church had been largely parochial. Many missionary bishops and others visited the School: John Magee, a graduate of Hotchkiss and Yale,

had graduated from the seminary the year before I entered, but he was still in the United States before going to China. No one of us escaped walking with him around Fresh Pond as he brought us the challenge of Christian missions. My fellow students were of varying backgrounds: Thayer Addison had taught in China after graduation from Harvard; Norman Nash had been on the staff of George Foster Peabody; Malcolm Peabody had taught in the Philippines. My horizons were constantly being enlarged.[39]

Upon his graduation from the Episcopal Theological School, Sherrill first considered missionary work in Utah under Bishop Franklin S. Spaulding, a well-known Christian Socialist. He was persuaded, however, to remain in the East and accepted a position in the summer of 1914 as assistant minister at Boston's Trinity Church, Copley Square. After ordination to the diaconate in his home diocese of Long Island by Bishop Frederick Burgess, Sherrill returned to Boston, transferring his canonical residence to Massachusetts. In May of 1915 he was ordained to the priesthood by the Right Rev. William Lawrence, bishop of Massachusetts.

For the next thirty-two years Sherrill pursued an active and successful ministry in the Diocese of Massachusetts. His tenure in the diocese would be interrupted from 1917 to 1919 when he served as an American Expeditionary Force chaplain at a war hospital in Talence, France.[40] Returning to Massachusetts, Sherrill became rector of the Church of Our Savior in Brookline. Five years later in 1923, he once again took up the pulpit at Trinity Copley, this time as rector. Trinity would be Sherrill's final parish position; in 1930 he was elected bishop of Massachusetts, becoming the spiritual and administrative head of the largest diocese in the Episcopal Church.

Occupying one of the preeminent diocesan seats in the Episcopal Church for over seventeen years, Sherrill played a significant role in the national affairs of the church. In 1930, shortly after his consecration as bishop of Massachusetts, Sherrill was elected to the National Council as the representative of Province One.[41] For four years he was intimately involved in the governance of the Episcopal Church in the United States and overseas and helped steer the national church through lean economic times during the Depression. The exposure to the inner workings of the

Episcopal Church at the national level gained during his years on the National Council would serve Sherrill well in the future.

> This experience on the National Council, demanding as it was, with the constant budgetary difficulties, was a great experience for me. I learned much of the world-wide work of the church, an education which was to prove invaluable in the years to come.[42]

While serving on the National Council, Sherrill made many good and lasting friendships. In particular his association with Henry St. George Tucker helped to mold Sherrill's vision of the national church.

> One of the best rewards I received from membership on the National Council was the opportunity to know Bishop Henry St. George Tucker...When the Council was not in session I had many a delightful hour with Bishop Tucker when we talked about everything under the sun. We saw Church affairs from the same point of view.[43]

The close association between Tucker and Sherrill ensured that the national church ideal, which had come to the fore during Tucker's regime, would continue to motivate the outreach of the Episcopal Church under Sherrill's leadership.

The 1943 General Convention in Philadelphia enacted a canonical change that required the Presiding Bishop to resign from his diocesan position in order to dedicate himself solely to the pastoral and administrative responsibilities of the church at the national level. Thus when Henry Knox Sherrill was elected Presiding Bishop to succeed Tucker, he became the first full-time Presiding Bishop elected specifically to that office. The ideal of a full-time chief executive officer to direct the affairs of the national church, just as the president leads the government of the United States, was finally realized in Henry Knox Sherrill.[44]

Sherrill was Presiding Bishop of the Episcopal Church from the first day of January 1947 until November 14, 1958. Scholars and contemporary church leaders alike acknowledge that Sherrill embodied the Episcopal ideal of a national church. David E. Sumner emphasizes that "Sherrill's leadership, particularly his ecumenical leadership; brought the Episcopal Church into the national and international arena in a new way."[45] He quotes Arthur Walmsley, bishop of Connecticut, as saying:

> Up until the time of Henry Sherrill, we did not have a national identity. We were still very much a collection of dioceses; we had a low profile...[46]

Sumner emphasizes that Roger Blanchard, former bishop of Southern Ohio, shared this opinion.

> Henry St. George Tucker was a transitional person from the old to the new. But when Henry Sherrill was elected, he gave up his diocese, knowing that when he was elected that he would give up his diocese. He enabled the church to become a national church in a way it was never before. It took its place in the Anglican Communion in a way that it never had before because he brought a sense of unity, of wholeness, of a national church rather than a collection of ninety-plus dioceses.[47]

And Roland Foster, in his study *The Role of the Presiding Bishop*, celebrates Sherrill's leadership as the first full-time Presiding Bishop.

> Although no person ever fits completely within one image, my impression is that he came closest to fulfilling the idea set forth in 1919 and 1925 as a chief executive officer who is primarily concerned for the mission of this church and its vigorous prosecution. He was devoted to Bishop Tucker (and in fact, worked for Tucker's election in 1937). Like Tucker, he was a "witness-in-chief to Christ, missionary of missionaries, first in every forward movement, and Father-in-God to all Bishops."[48]

Sherrill compared the office of Presiding Bishop to that of an administrative head of a multi-national corporation.

> The duties of the Presiding Bishop are varied. He is responsible for the consecration of bishops when elected and certified; he is chairman of the House of Bishops, the executive head of the "Missionary, Educational, and Social Work of the Church." As Presiding Bishop he deals with many affairs involving the entire Anglican Communion as well as the cooperative work of the churches in the United States. The planning is difficult in that it must be so long-range. Just as I missed the parish contacts when I became Bishop, so now I missed the confirmation and ordination services....But there were great compensations, particularly in the wide national and international outreach.[49]

As chief executive officer of the Episcopal Church, Sherrill instituted new programs that fortified the national church ideal of the Episcopal Church. At the outset of his episcopacy, Sherrill moved to establish a national conference center for the Episcopal Church and residence for the Presiding Bishop. With the authorization of the General Convention and the financial backing of many well-heeled Episcopalians, Sherrill purchased a hundred-acre estate in

Greenwich, Connecticut. The conference center and episcopal residence was named Seabury House after the first American Episcopal bishop, Samuel Seabury. With its close proximity to the Church Missions House in New York City, Seabury House became a vital resource for the national headquarters of the Episcopal Church. Gatherings of Episcopal churchwomen, conferences for out-going missionaries and retreats for various national groups within the Episcopal Church were held at Seabury House. At the Presiding Bishop's residence, Sherrill and his wife, Barbara, hosted many visiting church and state dignitaries and even granted a nationally televised interview with Edward R. Murrow on its grounds.[50] Like the White House, Seabury House stood as a symbol, a focal point, of the national and international reach of the executive office.

To support the growing work of the national church, Sherrill conceived and established the Episcopal Church Foundation. With the exception of the Presiding Bishop, the foundation was composed of lay people who had significant financial resources. Sherrill believed that such a foundation could open up new opportunities for giving to the three-fold mission of the national church beyond the diocesan assessment.

> This foundation could present the program of the church in terms of necessary millions of dollars and act as a support to the entire work of the church without reference to the smaller essential budgets. The purpose of the foundation was to present the need and opportunity of the church in the largest and broadest and most challenging terms.[51]

The Board of Directors of the Episcopal Church Foundation was composed of individuals of national prominence in church, business and state. Prescott Bush, United States senator from Connecticut, was a prominent player in the establishment of the foundation. His son, George Herbert Walker Bush, would follow him in service on the foundation's board.[52] When Sherrill suggested that members of the Board of Directors make significant contributions to the foundation, Walter Teagle asked: "Bishop, what you are saying is that we ought to buy stock in our own corporation."[53] Sherrill agreed with this corporate description of the church and half a million dollars was contributed at the opening meeting of the Board.

The resources from the Episcopal Church Foundation were used to build up the Episcopal Church's infrastructure. It established a revolving loan fund that assisted with the construction of hundreds of Episcopal churches in the United States and abroad. In addition, through its Fellowship Program, the foundation has supported students in doctoral programs who plan to teach in seminaries of the Episcopal Church. Sherrill's vision for the Episcopal Church Foundation lives on; the foundation continues to be a financial resource for important programs of the Episcopal Church that otherwise would go unfunded.

As leader of the Episcopal Church, Sherrill played a key role in the development of major ecumenical bodies during his tenure. His experiences with Christians of various traditions at Hotchkiss, Yale, and in the Student Christian Movement prepared Sherrill for his ecumenical work. Following the 1948 Lambeth meeting, Bishop and Mrs. Sherrill attended the First General Assembly of the World Council of Churches in Amsterdam in September. There he was appointed to the Nominating Committee and helped to determine the first group of presidents of the WCC. Returning to the United States, Sherrill became involved in the planning conversations for the National Council of Churches of Christ in the United States of America (NCC). He assisted in drawing up the constitution of the new NCC. At the Constituting Convention in Cleveland, Ohio, in December, 1950, he was elected first president of the National Council of Churches. In Sherrill's presidential address to the convention, he echoed the historic calling of the Episcopal Church's national ideal and appropriated it as the agenda for the new National Council of Churches.

> My friends, a nation, a world, or a church under God rests upon dedicated men and women. If we here and our brethren in the churches we represent can at this time experience the gift of God's grace, then we can make the words of another our own, "We shall this day light a candle by God's grace that I trust shall never be put out." Together we shall move forward with renewed resolve and great hope in the building of a Christian America in a Christian world.[54]

Sherrill believed that the National Council of Churches had a prophetic role to play in national and international politics. When

President Truman proposed an ambassador to the Vatican, the NCC called on Sherrill to present its dissenting position to the president. At the Second General Assembly of the World Council of Churches held in Evanston, Illinois, in 1954, Sherrill was elected one of its six presidents. The following year he and nine other leaders of the National Council of Churches were invited to visit Moscow by the Russian Orthodox Church. Sherrill remembered this visit in 1956 as a high point in his Christian life and a symbol of the ecumenical movement's commitment to world peace and understanding.

New Developments in Foreign Mission, 1947-1958

During Henry Knox Sherrill's tenure as Presiding Bishop, the foreign mission work of the Episcopal Church moved forward in new and significant directions. Post-war realities, the decline of Western colonialism and revolution in China affected the way the Episcopal Church went about its business outside the United States. Latin America became a fertile field for new missionary districts. Fortified by the affluence of the United States, the financial grants to younger churches became a primary strategy in the church's foreign mission work. Although the number of foreign missionaries, especially women, supported by the Episcopal Church would drop during these years, the growing ecclesial and economic reach of the Episcopal Church propelled the church into a preeminent position in the emerging Anglican Communion.

Even before the close of China to Western missionaries, the Episcopal Church recognized the great missionary opportunities south of the United States borders. Reviewing the growth of the Episcopal Church at home and abroad from 1930-1940, Walter Herbert Stowe concluded that the presence of the Episcopal Church in American territories outside of the United States would become increasingly central in the post-war years.

Our extra-continental missionary districts — Alaska, Honolulu, Panama Canal Zone, Philippine Islands, and Puerto Rico — will become increasingly important to the Church after the war as they already are to the nation. Their strategic importance to the United States is starkly patent to every American...What is true of our extra-continental districts is true of the Western Hemisphere as a whole and of our foreign missionary districts therein. The war has only made more visible its enlarged stature in world affairs. The whole Caribbean area, Central and South America, will find their golden age in the future and not in the past. The Church cannot be indifferent to its opportunity in those regions. The rich spiritual harvest to be garnered has been brilliantly foreshadowed in the recent decade 1930-1940.[55]

The victory of Mao Tse-Tung in 1949 resulted in the departure of Episcopal missionaries from China in 1950, effectively closing the most prominent foreign mission field in the history of the Episcopal Church.[56] The closing of China coincided with the graduation of the first generation of post-World War II seminarians. A good number of these graduates, who had been abroad during the war, were excited about returning overseas as foreign missionaries for the Episcopal Church.[57] This new manpower, and it was manpower since women were excluded from seminaries at the time, enabled the Episcopal Church to continue its work in its historic missionary districts as well as initiate a new mission in Okinawa in 1951.[58]

To assist with its administration of foreign missions, the Overseas Department of the National Council in 1949 divided its foreign missions into two geographic areas: the Atlantic Division and the Pacific Division. The Pacific Division was comprised of the missionary districts of Alaska, Honolulu and the Philippine Islands. It also included the Episcopal Church's continuing interests in China and Japan and its modest support for a missionary in Dornakal in the Church of South India. During the 1949-1952 triennium the Pacific Division focused its energies on Japan and the Philippines. Both were considered essential to the Episcopal Church's presence in the East.

Japan and the Philippines stand as outposts and bastions of the Christian faith and of democratic institutions in the Far East. The future of the Christian missionary enterprise in all East Asia will depend in a large measure upon the success of the Church's Mission in Japan and the Philippines. The Church must take advantage of the unprecedented opportunities for evangelism offered there today.[59]

The Atlantic Division was responsible for the church's work in the Caribbean, Latin America and on the shores of West Africa. It was composed of the missionary districts of Mexico, the Panama Canal Zone (including existing work in Costa Rica, Nicaragua, the northern half of Colombia and the whole of Panama), Southern Brazil, Cuba, Haiti, the Dominican Republic, Puerto Rico, the American Virgin Islands and Liberia.[60]

The Episcopal Church's justification for Latin American mission work in the post-war era was similar to that espoused three decades earlier at the founding of the National Council. Episcopalians believed that disaffected Roman Catholics in Central America would find a home in the reformed catholicism of Anglicanism. Writing in 1952, the Rev. F. W. Dillistone, a British priest who had served as a missionary in India and then as professor of theology at the Episcopal Theological School in Cambridge, Massachusetts, emphasized the importance and opportunity for the Episcopal Church's work in Latin America.

> With the possibility of expansion westward almost ended, with the possibility of the expansion eastward unlikely to be contemplated, in which direction will the Church now look? The obvious answer and the one which seems likely to prove correct is *southward*. The possibilities of expansion in Latin America are taking on a new importance and the Episcopal Church seems to have a field of opportunity in this area without parallel elsewhere....Indeed, we may say that if Protestant missionary activity is to be carried on in Latin America in the future it must, in the main, be done by missionaries from the U.S.A.; and further the general temper and tradition of the people in these areas seems often to dispose them more favorable to the ministrations of a Reformed Catholicism such as is found in the Episcopal Church than to any other body.[61]

The strategy for Latin America, espoused by of the Overseas Department of the National Council in the late 1950s, embraced fully the national church ideal. The Episcopal Church's stated aim was to provide a Christian presence that was catholic, reformed and democratic. In a confidential report of the Overseas Department to the National Council and the 1958 Lambeth Conference, the role of the Episcopal Church in Latin America was clearly articulated:

> After giving consideration to the overall missionary enterprise being carried on within the Anglican Communion, and this Church's place within the enterprise, the Overseas Department felt that if its own program was to be extended beyond its present limits, Central and South America would be appropriate areas for such an effort.
>
> Geographically, historically, economically, and politically, many of the countries of South and Central America are bound closely to the United States.

The Overseas Department believes that this Church, as a representative branch within the Anglican Communion, has a very real contribution to make to Latin America. As a Church which is heir to both Catholic tradition and the Reformation, it holds peculiar and precious treasures. Its Liturgy, its Creeds, its Sacraments, and its ministry are understood immediately in lands long accustomed to such forms and traditions, while its democratic organization and ideals and processes make an appeal to men who desire liberty and freedom within the discipline of Christian fellowship.[62]

The catholic, reformed and democratic emphases were echoed in a 1959 compilation of the strategy and policy of the Overseas Department.

Latin American countries offer a challenge and opportunity to the Episcopal Church as fields for evangelistic work. The Churches of the Anglican Communion, with a heritage which is both Catholic and Reformed, are in a position to make a strong appeal to people who value Catholic form and tradition, but who are eager to find a Church which is democratic in its thoughts and government, and which holds and teaches and practices democratic ideals and principles.... If the Anglican Communion is to be represented [in Latin America] in strength, then the Episcopal Church must supply the leadership and support the program for many years to come.[63]

The new drive southward under Sherrill resulted in four new missionary districts in Latin America and the Caribbean. In 1947 the Virgin Islands were separated from Puerto Rico and made a missionary district, although the islands would not have a bishop until 1963. In the same year the Church of England relinquished its work in Costa Rica, Nicaragua, Panama and the northern half of Colombia to the Episcopal Church. These territories were added to the missionary district of the Panama Canal Zone under Bishop R. Herber Gooden.[64] In 1949 work in Southern Brazil was separated into three geographic areas resulting in the addition of two new missionary districts: Southwestern Brazil and Central Brazil. The rationale for this division was to ensure a sufficient number of dioceses so that the Episcopal Church in Brazil could begin steps toward becoming an autonomous church in the Anglican Communion. The report of the General Church Program to the 1952 General Convention celebrated these advances in Brazil.

In Brazil, the Church's work has grown to such an extent that it now comprises three missionary districts, each with its own bishop. With the growth of this field, the pattern of aid provided by the [Overseas] Department has shifted. Now, instead of the Church in the United States supplying the bulk of support, with assistance from Brazil, it is expected that in increasing measure Brazil will support its own work, with assistance at strategic points from the mother Church. The day is not very far off when Brazil will have an independent Church. Special emphasis is therefore being placed on the training of Brazilian clergy. Two of the three bishops are Brazilians, and in the three missionary districts there are only six American appointees. Brazil soon will be an example of what is hoped all the present missionary fields will become — self-supporting autonomous Churches, themselves carrying on and extending Christianity to the new frontiers. [65]

This vision for Brazil was highly optimistic. It reflected more the desire of the Overseas Department to see the Brazilian mission become autonomous rather than Brazilian desires to become independent of United States support. When the Episcopal Church in Brazil finally became an autonomous church in the Anglican Communion in 1965, many Brazilians felt abandoned by the Episcopal Church in the United States. Suffering financially, the Brazilian church would not consider itself truly self-supporting for another fifteen years.[66]

The final addition to Episcopal mission activities in Latin America during Sherrill's tenure as Presiding Bishop occurred in 1956 when the Episcopal church established the missionary district of Central America. Formal discussions leading to this new missionary district began in 1954 when the National Council adopted the following resolution:

> Resolved, That the National Council approves in principle the proposal of the Overseas Department that this Church establish missions in new areas of Central and South America, and its request of the Director of the Overseas Department that he explore the problems and possibilities of such a program to the end that this project be included in the proposed program for the new triennium.[67]

With the blessing of the National Council, the Director of the Overseas Department, the Right Rev. John Boyd Bentley, previously missionary bishop of Alaska, entered into negotiations with the bishop of British Honduras and the Synod of the Province of the West Indies. Because of the increasing political and economic presence of the United States in Central America, the Church of England and the Anglican Province of the West Indies were convinced by Bishop Bentley that the Episcopal Church was better equipped to continue Anglican mission work in Central America. The British thus agreed to relinquish their jurisdiction in the Central American republics of Guatemala, El Salvador and Honduras to the Episcopal Church. In November 1956 the House of Bishops of the Episcopal Church, meeting at Pocono Manor in Pennsylvania, accepted these jurisdictions and added them to the church's work in Nicaragua and Costa Rica, creating the new missionary district of Central America.[68] A missionary bishop was elected by the House but the bishop-elect did not accept his election. Therefore the bishop of the Panama Canal Zone was placed as bishop-in-charge of the new district. The following year, on June 5, 1957, the formal transfer of jurisdiction took place and in September the Right Rev. David Richards, suffragan bishop of Albany and past missionary in the Panama Canal Zone, was elected by the House of Bishops as the first missionary bishop of the district of Central America.[69]

Thus during Sherrill's tenure as Presiding Bishop the Episcopal Church established its missions in what is now considered Province IX of the Episcopal Church, USA. At the same time the church increased significantly the number of missionaries appointed to the region. For example, in 1939, 39 of 293 missionary appointees (13%) served in Latin America. Twenty years later this number had increased to 83 of 268 missionary appointees, or 31% of the foreign missionary contingent of the Episcopal Church.[70] The closing of the China mission with its loss of more than 100 missionary appointments, followed by the increase of work in Latin America, resulted in the Episcopal Church turning its head from the East to Central and South America for its future foreign mission engagement.

Financial grants to British missions and newly autonomous Anglican churches became an increasingly important part of the foreign mission portfolio of the Episcopal Church under Henry Knox Sherrill. At his last General Convention, Philadelphia 1946, Presiding Bishop Tucker challenged the Episcopal Church to expand its relief and rehabilitation program. The convention responded by agreeing to raise a million dollars a year for three years. These monies were to be administered by the Presiding Bishop's Fund for World Relief.[71] As the new Presiding Bishop,

Sherrill spearheaded the fund drive, raising over one million dollars a year from 1947 to 1949. The campaign in 1948 was especially memorable because Bishop Sherrill appealed directly to the church in a nationwide radio address on Sunday, February 29. This program, entitled "A Million Dollars in One Hour" realized $1,458,042. Sherrill's use of the mass media for fund raising aroused the interest of other American Protestant churches. The following year Sherrill and other church leaders made a united appeal for world relief, called "One Great Hour," over three nationwide radio networks. In this campaign Episcopalians alone contributed $1,000,243.23 to world relief.[72]

The priorities for the Presiding Bishop's Fund for World Relief under Bishop Sherrill were refugee resettlement, disaster relief, and assistance to ecumenical councils and sister Anglican Churches.[73] Contributions to churches beyond the historic missionary districts of the Episcopal Church were coordinated through the program on World Relief and Church Cooperation of the National Council. For example, in 1952, the Episcopal Church gave over $500,000 to the National Council of Churches, the World Council of Churches, Eastern Orthodox churches and other Anglican churches through this program.[74] In addition, the Overseas Department began to make block grants and/or missionary appointments to autonomous Anglican churches or churches in communion with Anglicans. By the end of Bishop Sherrill's tenure, the Episcopal Church was providing assistance to Anglican churches in Gibraltar, Hong Kong, Iran, Japan, Jerusalem, Korea, Melanesia, New Guinea, Northern Rhodesia, Singapore and the West Indies; the church was also assisting English missionary societies in South Africa and Uganda. In addition, the Episcopal Church provided missionary support to the Church of India, Pakistan, Burma, and Ceylon. These grants and missionary assignments reflected the Episcopal Church's increasing role in the emerging Anglican Communion.[75]

The 1955 General Convention meeting at the Iolani School in Honolulu, Hawaii, was important in lifting up the worldwide witness of the Episcopal Church. The 1955 convention originally was to be held in Houston, Texas, but Sherrill, exercising his authority as Presiding Bishop, refused to hold the prime meeting of the Episcopal Church in a racially segregated state. In 1953 Sherrill had visited Honolulu during his tour of the church's missions in the Pacific. He was moved by the zeal of the missionary work in the district and hoped that the wider Episcopal Church might share his experience. Sherrill thus decided to move the 1955 General Convention to Honolulu.[76] This was a very significant decision for it both took a stand against racism and meant that the General Convention, for the first and only time in its history, would be held in a missionary district outside of the continental United States. Although the convention was preoccupied with the regular legislative business of the church, the importance of meeting in a "foreign" missionary district was not lost. The Bishops' Pastoral Letter issued from the convention held up the mission imperative of the church as it never had before. Bishops, scholars and mission enthusiasts alike applauded the bishops for their missionary vision gained from meeting in Honolulu.[77]

Americans and the Emerging Anglican Communion

The Right Rev. Walter H. Gray, bishop of Connecticut, played a central role in the emerging Anglican Communion. As the moving force behind the 1954 Anglican Congress, founder and editor of the journal *Pan-Anglican,* chair of the 1958 Lambeth Conference Committee on Missionary Appeal and Strategy, and chair of the Episcopal Church's Committee of Conference on Overseas Missions, Gray embodied the growing power and influence of the Episcopal Church in the emerging Anglican Communion.

Like Tucker and Addison before him, Gray brought together the two centers of ecclesiastical power in the Episcopal Church, Virginia and the Northeast. He was born in Richmond, Virginia, in 1898 and later attended both the College of William and Mary and the University of Richmond Law School. The year he became a member of the Virginia Bar, 1925, he left the legal profession to attend Virginia Theological Seminary (VTS). At VTS he was nurtured in the liberal evangelical tradition and its commitment to mission exemplified by the school.[78] Ordained deacon by Bishop Henry St. George Tucker of Virginia in 1928, Gray was released to the Diocese of Connecticut and served his curacy as assistant rector of St. John's Church in Hartford, Connecticut, from 1928 to 1931. While in Hartford, Gray was ordained a priest by Bishop Chauncey B. Brewster in 1929. Gray's next two pastorates were as deans of cathedrals. He served as dean and rector of Nativity Pro-Cathedral in Bethlehem, Pennsylvania, from 1932 to 1936 and then returned to Hartford as dean of Christ Church Cathedral from 1937 to 1940. Gray's ascendancy to the cathedra once held by Samuel Seabury, the first bishop in the Episcopal Church, was a step-by-step process. In 1940 he was elected suffragan bishop of Connecticut. Five years later he was elected bishop coadjutor. Upon the retirement of Frederick G. Budlong in 1951, Gray became the diocesan bishop of Connecticut and served in this capacity until 1969. Gray's long tenure as a bishop in the Episcopal Church, twenty-nine years, provided him with ample opportunity to participate in the many governing councils of the church.

As bishop in the post-war years, Gray shared the yearnings of many for a new and better world of international cooperation and unity as exemplified by the United Nations and the nascent World Council of Churches. Gray believed that the Anglican Communion would profit greatly by its own similar international organization.[79] In public speeches and writings, Gray advocated a postwar gathering of worldwide Anglicanism.

> In view of the tremendous needs of the postwar world and the vast opportunities to our Churches in that time, it would seem vitally necessary to begin at once to plan, not only for cooperation between the Church of England and the Protestant Episcopal Church in the U.S.A., but also for unity of action within the whole Anglican Communion. To this end it appears advisable to discuss new plans for a postwar Pan-Anglican Congress.[80]

It had been almost four decades since the previous and only other pan-Anglican congress had been held in London in 1908.[81] Gray believed that the time was right for a second Anglican congress. He communicated his idea to Presiding Bishop Tucker and two succeeding Archbishops of Canterbury, Temple and Fisher. In 1948 the bishops of the Anglican Communion gathered at Lambeth for the first post-war conference of bishops since 1930. Gray served on the Committee on the Anglican Communion and in this capacity was asked by Archbishop Fisher to make an opening statement to the conference. In his address Gray spoke of four themes that would later help to define the relations between churches in the emerging Anglican Communion. These themes were: revival of the Pan-Anglican Congress, enlargement of the permanent Consultative Body of Lambeth, establishment of a permanent secretariat for the Anglican Communion, and establishment of a Central Staff College.[82]

Gray's ideas for greater Anglican unity and a more centralized structure were met with consternation by some bishops. British bishops especially saw Gray's suggestions as a challenge to their traditional view of the Anglican Communion as an extension of the Church of England. Both Sherrill and Gray met this challenge by explaining to the British church hierarchy that both the world and inter-Anglican relations had changed in the post-war world. Gray's diary of the Lambeth Conference recalls fondly how the Americans put the British bishops in their place.

> Sherrill made a fine address on the American position, stressing the fact that we are not a province under the Church of England but are also an international church which must maintain its own overseas missions if we are to keep up interest of our people in missionary work.

and

> English Bishops were desirous of killing the Pan-Anglican Congress idea and of retaining firm control of the Central College, while expecting the Americans to pay most of the cost of the latter. It became necessary to tell [them] the facts of life.[83]

By the end of the conference, those gathered at Lambeth in 1948 had accepted many of Gray's ideas. To better coordinate missionary efforts in the Anglican Communion and to encourage Anglican unity, the bishops authorized the creation of both an Advisory Council on Missionary Strategy and Central College and called for a second Pan-Anglican Congress to be held in June of 1953.[84]

At Gray's prompting the 1949 General Convention in San Francisco initiated formal planning for the Pan-Anglican Congress. The Episcopal Church invited all dioceses and missionary districts in the Anglican Communion to send representatives to a Pan-Anglican Congress to be held in the United States in 1953. In addition, the General Convention established a Joint Committee on Arrangements to plan the details of the congress. It was no surprise that when the Joint Committee met for the first time in 1950, Walter Gray was elected its chair. Gray dedicated the next four years to planning the Anglican Congress. The congress was to be held in the weeks preceding the 1953 meeting of the World Council of Churches in Evanston, Illinois. When the WCC changed its date to 1954, the Anglican Congress did the same.[85] The burden for paying for the international gathering of Anglicans was to be borne almost entirely by the Episcopal Church in the United States. The General Convention thus made $50,000 available for congress planning and authorized the solicitation of an additional $100,000 for the costs of the Anglican Congress. Trinity Church of New York contributed an additional $25,000 for discretionary purposes and the Diocese of Minnesota generously offered to host the Anglican Congress with free hospitality to all its delegates. In total, the 1954 Anglican Congress cost the Episcopal Church over $300,000.

The fact that the second Anglican Congress and the first one to be held outside of England was initiated, planned, paid for and hosted by the Episcopal Church in the United States signaled the new predominance of the American church in the Anglican Communion. This fact was not lost on the British. Max Warren, General Secretary of the British Church Missionary Society, acknowledged the new position of the Episcopal Church in the Anglican Communion. Writing for the Lambeth Conference of 1958, Warren predicted: "It may well be that the Episcopal Church of the U.S.A. will, in terms of missionary outreach, become the senior partner in the Anglican Communion."[86]

When Gray suggested the idea of a second Anglican Congress in 1946, he predicted there would be 650 participants. The planning committee foresaw about 300 registrants but final delegates to the Congress numbered 657, exceeding Gray's original prediction.[87] Bishops, priests and lay people, including women, gathered in Minneapolis on August 4, 1954, to discuss in common the calling of the Anglican Communion. Although the planning committee tried to have as many representatives as possible from the younger churches in the Anglican Communion, the majority of delegates were from the United States (290), England (112), and Canada (87). Despite this unequal representation, the breadth and variety of Anglicanism was manifested triumphantly when the 657 delegates from fourteen Anglican churches processed into the Minneapolis Auditorium for the opening service before over 10,000 onlookers.[88]

For ten days the delegates deliberated four topics related to the common life of the Anglican Communion. Through keynote presentations and small group discussions, the congress considered contemporary Anglicanism under four headings: Our Vocation, Our Worship, Our Message and Our Work. Since the gathering was neither legislative nor consultative, no formal resolutions were either presented or adopted. Instead the delegates spent their time together in common worship, prayer, conversation and fellowship. What resulted was a new understanding of the commonalty and uniqueness of the worldwide Anglican tradition. Archbishop of Canterbury Geoffrey Fisher summarized these accomplishments in his concluding words.

> Out of the papers and discussions came what was almost a new discovery to many, that this Anglican heritage of ours is not at all a dull compromise, not at all a middle position uncertain of itself and to be defended apologetically, but a positive tradition of Christian Truth, strong and honest enough to face diversities as old as the New Testament itself, creative enough to make out of them a richer truth. There was no self-laudation; there was a real humility and a deep sense of weakness to be remedied. But the glory of the Congress was that it made us confident that our tradition had its own distinctive truth and was essential for Christ's purpose in the whole witness of His Church. And with that humble confidence possessing us, the joyful fellowship which embraced us all had its perfect work.[89]

The success of the Anglican Congress thus was measured not by written documents but rather by the fellowship and communion afforded to the many who came together in Minneapolis. Bishop Gray stressed this fact in the introduction to the Congress Report.

> Positive values should accrue from this Anglican Congress in the form of greater knowledge of each other's problems and the discovery of better methods of meeting them; but perhaps the most important and abiding

result of the Congress may be the spirit of Christian understanding and fellowship which has come to us when over six hundred and fifty delegates from the worldwide Church have met together for ten days, seeking the guidance of our Lord and Master in doing His work in our critical times.[90]

A final contribution of the 1954 Anglican Congress was that it created a new emblem for the Anglican Communion. Interestingly, the seal adopted by the congress was designed not by an Englishman but by Canon Edward West of New York, yet another example of the American church's central role in defining the modern Anglican Communion. The new emblem consisted of the cross of St. George, surrounded by the Greek "The truth shall set you free," then the points of a compass radiating outward, all crowned by a bishop's miter.[91] Today the "Compassrose," as the seal is now known, is the official emblem of the Anglican Communion. A tile representation of the Compassrose is set at the crossing of the nave in the Minneapolis Episcopal Cathedral of St. Mark, a commemoration of the 1954 Anglican Congress.

In the Anglican Congress, Walter Gray had accomplished much of what he had set out to do: raise the Anglican Communion's consciousness of itself and its mission in the world. To assist and encourage the ongoing development of Anglican self-understanding, Gray founded and edited a worldwide review of the work of the Anglican Communion called *Pan-Anglican*. From 1950 until 1970, Gray and his assistant editors the Reverends E. R. Hardy and S. H. Cook, both of Berkeley Divinity School, published semi-annual issues of *Pan-Anglican*. Each issue generally focused on one particular Anglican church or province and included articles and photographs of the church under study. From 1950 to 1954 issues were presented on the Anglican churches in Canada, South Africa, Japan, the West Indies, Wales, Australia, India, Pakistan, Burma, and Ceylon and China. News of the plans for the upcoming Anglican Congress were also included; the Epiphany 1954 issue was dedicated completely to the congress.[92] Throughout the twenty years of its publication *Pan-Anglican* helped Anglicans around the world to better understand themselves as one Body of Christ. Bishops gathered at the 1958 Lambeth Conference recognized the value of *Pan-Anglican* and passed a resolution commending the review (Resolution 70). Perhaps the greatest tribute to Gray, however, was the calling of another Anglican Congress to be held in 1963 (Resolution 68).[93]

Anglican bishops gathered at Lambeth in 1958 were thus energized by the new-found unity of the Anglican Communion discovered at the 1954 Anglican Congress. The confidential study paper, "Our Overseas Mission," prepared by the Episcopal Church for members of the Lambeth Conference, acknowledged the emerging global nature of the Anglican Communion and reaffirmed the work initiated in Minneapolis.

> The Anglican Congress, meeting in Minneapolis in the summer of 1954, drew attention to the growth of the Anglican Churches around the world, the vastness and complexity of their total programs, and the need of a closer fellowship and cooperation within the family of the Anglican Communion. In Minneapolis, for the first time, the Archbishop's Advisory Council on Missionary Strategy met to consider the over-all missionary enterprise of the Anglican Churches.[94]

It was clear that Lambeth 1958 had to wrestle with the need for increased communication and organization among the churches of the Anglican Communion. The issue was assigned to the Committee on Missionary Appeal and Strategy chaired by Walter Gray.

The report of the Committee on Missionary Appeal and Strategy began with the theological affirmation that the mission of the church was to bring the whole Gospel to the whole world. It noted that there were five threats to the church's mission in the contemporary world: nationalism, distrust, industrialism, the resurgence of some non-Christian religions and "Christian deviations." It emphasized that if the Anglican Communion were to play its appropriate role in the worldwide mission of the church, Anglicans needed to become more unified in their common witness.

> If the responsibilities of a worldwide Communion are to be grasped and its resources mobilized, fuller expression must be given to four vital principles of corporate life — co-ordination, co-operation, consolidation, and cohesion.[95]

How to best achieve this coordination in the Anglican Communion was the question before the committee. Bishop John B. Bentley, Director of the Overseas Department of the National

Council of the Episcopal Church and also a member of the Committee on Missionary Appeal and Strategy, favored an enlargement of the portfolio of the Advisory Council on Missionary Strategy with the addition of a full-time staff. The Advisory Council on Missionary Strategy was set up by Lambeth 1948 as a consultative body on Anglican missionary concerns. Bentley believed that:

> If [the Advisory Council on Missionary Strategy] could meet more often, perhaps annually, and if it had a full time secretariat, even a single executive officer, with a small secretarial staff, it might gain a more complete picture of the total missionary enterprise being carried on...within the Anglican Communion, could formulate a common strategy for the allocation of areas of responsibility, and could encourage and guide the unification, development and prosecution of the missionary task of the churches which form the Anglican Communion, both as that task is related to sister churches within the Anglican Communion, and as it is related to those Christian bodies which are not in communion with Canterbury.[96]

The final report of the Committee on Missionary Appeal and Strategy followed Bentley's suggestions and recommended that a full-time secretary of the Advisory Council on Missionary Strategy be appointed.

The bishops accepted the recommendations of the Committee on Missionary Appeal and Strategy (Resolution 60) and added that the secretary of the Advisory Council on Missionary Strategy should also serve as the secretary of the Lambeth Consultative Body, if endorsed by the Archbishop of Canterbury (Resolution 61).[97] The Lambeth Consultative Body had been in existence since the beginning of the century and served as the continuation committee between Lambeth Conferences. By empowering both the Consultative Body and the Advisory Council on Missionary Strategy to appoint a full time secretary with staff, Lambeth 1958 created, in effect, a central office for the Anglican Communion.

The scope and limits of the secretariat for the Anglican Communion would be defined by its first incumbent. In January 1960, the Right Rev. Stephen Bayne, bishop of Olympia, in the Episcopal Church USA, was appointed the first executive officer of the Anglican Communion. His genius and vision would do much to shape how Anglicans perceived themselves as one body in the modern Anglican Communion.

Two months after returning from England, the bishops of the American Episcopal Church gathered again in October 1958 at the General Convention in Miami Beach, Florida. Both the previous General Convention in Honolulu and the recent Lambeth Conference had impressed upon the bishops the changing nature of the Anglican Communion. It was clear that a reevaluation of the mission work of the Episcopal Church was necessary. On the first day of the convention, the House of Bishops called for a review of the overseas work of the church. The resolution articulated both the rationale and the process for the review:

> Whereas, The call to the missionary outreach of the Church confronts today a revolutionary and changing world — one in which resurgent non-Christian religions are offering new challenges to the Gospel, in which the emergence of autonomous younger Churches demands a recasting of many of our traditional policies and methods, and in which our Church, in particular, is entering a new era of enlarged responsibilities as partner and sister Churches of the Anglican Communion; and

> Whereas, There is needed throughout the Church a greater vision of the missionary need with much greater support and understanding; therefore be it

> Resolved, that the National Council be instructed to appoint a committee representative of the whole Church to confer with the Overseas Department and others, and to make recommendations to the National Council for leading this Church into greater understanding, support and service in its world-wide mission.[98]

Soon after the General Convention a Committee of Conference on Overseas Missions was established to fulfill the convention's mandate. The committee was composed of sixteen men and women, lay people, priests and bishops, and was chaired by the one Episcopalian most familiar with the workings of the wider Anglican Communion, Walter H. Gray.

The report of the Committee of Conference on Overseas Missions, known as the "Gray Report," was the most far-reaching review of the foreign mission work of the Episcopal Church to date. The recommendations of the committee stressed two conclusions: the overseas work of the Episcopal Church needed to cooperate more closely with other Anglican churches, and the

Episcopal Church must increase its overseas mission commitments to counter the growing forces of evil in the world.

The Gray report echoed many of the theological affirmations found in Lesslie Newbigin's influential book on mission: *One Body, One Gospel, One World*. It emphasized that the church's calling was to be an agent of the continuation of the mission of Christ himself. All Christians, therefore, were called to participate in this same mission and are thus rightly considered missionaries.[99] The Committee of Conference on Overseas Missions emphasized the continuity of this position with the 1835 position that all Episcopalians were members of its Missionary Society.

The Gray Report also acknowledged the importance of the increase in new national churches in what were previously Anglican mission fields. The committee stressed that the Episcopal Church needed to do a better job in helping its foreign missionary districts to grow into autonomous Anglican churches. The committee made specific suggestions to assist in this process including upgrading missionary districts to missionary dioceses and encouraging the development of new Anglican provinces in Brazil and South America. Recognizing that the Episcopal Church in the emerging Anglican Communion was called to new levels of cooperation with other Anglican churches, the committee sought canonical legislation that would allow for overseas Episcopal jurisdictions to participate more fully in the life of adjacent Anglican provinces. An outgrowth of this position was the recommendation that the missionary district of Liberia should join the Anglican Province of West Africa. Finally the Committee on the Conference of Overseas Missions recommended that a Permanent Advisory Council of Evaluation and Strategy be established, similar to the Lambeth body, to oversee the development of autonomous churches in Episcopal mission fields and encourage collegiality and cooperation with other Anglican churches.[100]

The report of the Committee of the Conference of Overseas Missions made many sound recommendations for the mission policy of the Episcopal Church. It was, however, a product of the Cold War Era and thus saw the rise in Communism and secularism as a major threat to the church throughout the world.

The Christian churches are threatened today as they have not been for a thousand years. Communism and Secularism are realities in the world. Other religions — Islam, Buddhism, and Hinduism — are resurgent and aggressively missionary. As vast groups of people in Asia and Africa climb to higher economic and educational levels, there are mass movements toward a new way of spiritual and intellectual life. Sometimes the Christian Mission had seized such opportunities, but where Christian witness is absent Communism or another religion is ready and eager to come in.[101]

The Committee of Conference on Overseas Missions believed that the Episcopal Church's global mission was to counter these non-Christian forces. Missionaries were seen as the church's Cold War infantry prepared to do battle with Communism and secularism around the world while protecting the church at home. This position was consistent with the national church ideal.

The most urgent task of the Episcopal Church today is the strengthening of its missionary activity. The Church's mission is one. The eventual success of its efforts at home, our rightful part in the Christianizing of America, depends in large measure on the health and strength of Christian witness and activity in all parts of the world. It is one world, and what affects any remote corner of it will in time come home to us.[102]

Implicit in these assertions was the unchallenged assumption that the future of church at home and around the world rested on the shoulders of Western Christianity.

The Gray Report thus proposed that the Episcopal Church send out more, and better equipped, missionaries to the far corners of the world. It argued for a strengthening of all aspects of the missionary endeavor of the Episcopal Church. More missionaries should be dispatched to existing and new mission fields. The missionaries should be better prepared by a comprehensive training including special course work in the seminaries. The administration of the Overseas Department should be strengthened by assigning new regional secretaries to oversee specific geographic mission fields. The appointment of new officers to supervise training and preparation of the missionaries would ensure the deployment of a strong missionary force. All of these policies should be supported by new programs that would increase awareness of and prayer for missionary zeal throughout the Episcopal Church.

Most of the report's recommendations emphasizing cooperation with other Anglican churches and the drive for an increased
missionary program were accepted by the Overseas Department
of the National Council. Only modest adjustments, however, were
made in the structure and policies of the Overseas Department.[103]
Within two years the work of the Committee of the Conference
of Overseas Missions would be superseded by a more ambitious
reorientation of mission priorities in the Anglican Communion:
Mutual Responsibility and Interdependence in the Body of Christ.

Mutual Responsibility and Interdependence in the Body of Christ

Church leaders and scholars alike agree that the Anglican
Congress of 1963 and its manifesto, "Mutual Responsibility and
Interdependence in the Body of Christ" (MRI), was a watershed in
the life of the Anglican Communion.[104] MRI represented a radical
re-visioning of how Anglicans were to get along in the modern
Anglican Communion.

The specific responsibilities of the executive officer of the
Anglican Communion were not articulated by the 1958 meeting of
the Lambeth Conference. Determining the scope and limits of the
new office were thus left to the Right Rev. Stephen Bayne and he
had to create his job *ex nihilo.* Officially Bayne had three responsibilities. He was to be executive secretary for the Advisory Council
on Missionary Strategy overseeing mission work throughout the
Anglican Communion; as secretary for the Lambeth Consultative
Body he was to pursue issues germane to the Bishops' Conference
between its meetings; finally the Episcopal Church in the United
States appointed Bayne bishop-in-charge of the Convocation of
Episcopal Churches in Europe.[105] Balancing these three jobs was a
considerable task, but Bayne proved he could meet the challenge.
The success of the new office of executive officer of the Anglican
Communion was due almost entirely to the talents and vision that
Stephen Bayne brought to the position.

Bayne's broad experience in the church as scholar, parish
priest, university chaplain and bishop prepared him for his many

and various responsibilities as the first executive officer of the Anglican Communion. Stephen F. Bayne, Jr. was born in New York City in 1908. He was educated at Trinity School in New York and then attended Amherst College, graduating in 1928. Bayne returned to New York City to prepare for ordination at the General Theological Seminary. After receiving a bachelor of sacred theology in 1933 Bayne remained at General as a fellow and tutor, earning a master of sacred theology in 1934. While at General he was ordained a deacon (1932) and priest (1934) by the Right Rev. William T. Manning, bishop of New York. In 1934 Bayne left the seminary for the parish. He served as rector of Trinity Church, St. Louis (1934-1939) and then rector of St. John's, Northhampton, Massachusetts (1939-1942). In 1942 Bayne returned to academia and New York City, this time as chaplain of Columbia University and chair of its Department of Religion. His stay at Columbia lasted five years although it was interrupted by two years as a Navy chaplain (1944-1945). In 1947 Bayne was consecrated bishop of Olympia in the western part of the state of Washington.[106] Bayne's stay in Washington would prove to be his longest cure. During his twelve years as bishop, Bayne attended both the 1948 and 1958 Lambeth Conferences. At the latter conference he chaired the controversial Committee on the Family in Contemporary Society. His skill and diplomacy exercised as chair of this committee and primary author of its report brought Bayne into the limelight at the gathering of Anglican bishops.

As the new executive officer of the Anglican Communion, Bayne had to be an adept diplomat, communicator and administrator. He had to prove to the Anglican Communion that he was neither a watchdog for the Archbishop of Canterbury nor an agent of the Episcopal Church USA. Addressing the Anglican Congress of 1963, Bayne emphasized his role as servant to the whole Anglican Communion.

> The Executive Officer is not a master of the churches, he is their servant. It is the churches who support him, who direct him in working out their common will. I do not speak of myself personally in this; I shall not hold this office forever; I speak of any such officer. He is not an "assistant to Lambeth Palace" or to the Archbishop of Canterbury. He is an assistant to

every archbishop equally, and to every church. He is obedient to no other person or body than ourselves, collectively, in our separate churches. His work is simply and solely that of making the mutual interdependence of the Anglican Communion a little more real — as much as one man can.[107]

Demonstrating his commitment to the wider Anglican Communion, Bayne traveled constantly. During his tenure as executive officer he visited nearly every province of the Anglican Communion.[108] He was also a prolific writer and reported widely on his work and travels.[109] In person and in print, Bayne proved that he was a servant to all.

Bayne was responsible for most of the planning and organization of the next Anglican Congress. At Lambeth 1958 the Anglican Church of Canada offered to host the congress. Although the bishops preferred a location where English was not the primary language to emphasize the growing diversity of the Anglican Communion, no other site proved practicable or affordable. So it was agreed that the next meeting of worldwide Anglicans would be in Toronto in 1963. Delegations to the next congress would be like those at the meeting in Minneapolis with the bishops, one presbyter and one lay person representing each diocese. In preparing for the Anglican Congress, the Church in Canada called for a year of study and prayer in each church in the Anglican Communion. Many accepted this call and there ensued a proliferation of books, articles, pamphlets and study series on the various churches in the Anglican Communion.[110]

Various pre-meetings were planned before the opening of the congress itself. The document "Mutual Responsibility and Interdependence in the Body of Christ" had its genesis in two of these meetings, both held at Huron College in London, Ontario. Stephen Bayne played a central role in these pre-congress gatherings. The first to arrive at Huron College were mission executives from around the Anglican Communion. This collection of mission administrators, secretaries of missionary societies, national church staff and bishops came together to consider changing missionary strategies and methods in the modern Anglican Communion. Max Warren posed the question: How do mission agencies and churches go about supporting newly autonomous churches who both cherish their independence but plead for assistance?[111] For two weeks the mission administrators wrestled with possible solutions to the dilemma. What emerged was a consensus opinion that all churches were called to share equally in the mission work of the Anglican Communion. Their draft paper "Mutual Responsibility for Mission" stressed:

> Our churches in many parts of the world are carrying the load of our common mission with wholly inadequate resources....They need to be freed from the penury which keeps them from carrying out their mission and ours to the world in Christ's name, and to seize opportunities of evangelism which lie before them.[112]

To help the poorer churches accomplish their goals the mission executives called for a $15 million capital fund drive. This was communicated to the Advisory Council on Missionary Strategy, which was next to meet at Huron College.

The Advisory Council on Missionary Strategy was composed of thirty-one bishops and archbishops; every province was represented at the meeting, which was presided over by the new Archbishop of Canterbury, Michael Ramsey, with the assistance of Stephen Bayne as the Advisory Council's secretary. Bayne presented to the bishops the draft paper "Mutual Responsibility for Mission" prepared by the mission executives. He described how the paper represented an attempt to do mission in a more equal and interdependent manner in the Anglican Communion. Moved by the theme of mutual responsibility, the bishops considered the specific proposals of cooperative planning and shared implementation of mission ventures. A position paper was written and reworked by a drafting committee under the leadership of Stephen Bayne. By the end of the meeting, the focus of the draft paper had changed from that of a capital funds drive, first proposed by the mission executives, to a more substantive manifesto signaling a new era for the Anglican Communion.

> What was first conceived of as a capital funds campaign was, after two drafts, something quite different. "Capital Funds had, in effect, disappeared; and the principal emphasis now lay on the element of mutuality." Twice more it had to be redone. "Mission had now been deleted; and what was proposed was nothing less than a new form of the Anglican Communion."[113]

The draft document was then presented to the Lambeth Consultative Body, which followed the Advisory Council on Missionary Strategy with many of the same representatives. A fifth and final revision of the manifesto was prepared.[114] "Mutual Responsibility and Interdependence in the Body of Christ" was now ready to be presented to the Anglican Congress of 1963.

The Anglican Congress opened in the late afternoon on August 13 in the Canadian Room of the Royal York Hotel in Toronto. That evening, congress delegates and visitors, totaling over 16,000, assembled for the opening eucharist in Maple Leaf Gardens. A stately procession of delegates from seventeen Anglican churches testified to the worldwide character of the Anglican Communion. As in Minneapolis, the church with the greatest number of representatives was the Episcopal Church USA, followed by the Church of England and the Anglican Church of Canada. For the next nine days these delegates gathered in the Canadian Room for keynote presentations and small group discussions on the six themes of the congress. The first three themes concentrated on the religious, political and cultural frontiers of "The Church's Mission to the World." The remaining three themes were more pragmatic in nature with specific reference to the contemporary realities of the Anglican Communion. The topics included: "The Challenge of the Frontiers: Training for Action," "The Challenge of the Frontiers: Organizing for Action," and a final summary, "The Vocation of the Anglican Communion." Sandwiched in between the opening talks on the mission of the church and the later organizational conversations of the congress was the presentation and discussion of "Mutual Responsibility."

"Mutual Responsibility and Interdependence in the Body of Christ" was presented by the Archbishop of York as a statement from the primates and metropolitans of the Anglican Communion. It was divided into four sections. The first section was a bold statement of the unified mission of the Anglican Communion. It stressed the new realities before the communion in the post-colonial era:

It is a platitude to say that in our time areas of the world which have been thought of as dependent and secondary are suddenly striding to the centre of the stage, in a new and breath-taking independence and self-reliance. Equally has this happened to the Church. In our time the Anglican Communion has come of age. Our professed nature as a world-wide fellowship of national and regional churches has suddenly become a reality — all but ten of the 350 Anglican dioceses are now included in self-governing churches, of one blood with their own self-governing regions and peoples. The full communion in Christ which has been our traditional tie has suddenly taken on a totally new dimension. It is now irrelevant to talk of "giving" and "receiving" churches. The keynotes of our time are equality, interdependence, mutual responsibility.[115]

The second section stated contemporary concerns before the Anglican Communion. This section called for: a communion-wide study of needs and resources, the $15-million fund drive, projects related to clergy and lay training, construction of new churches, support for diocesan and provincial infra-structures, increased missionary deployment, continued inter-Anglican consultation, and a process of self-study for each Anglican church to determine its own mission needs and resources. The section concluded with a reiteration of the theological assumptions behind mutual interdependence.

> We must face maturely and without sentimentality the nature of the Anglican Communion, and the implications for us all of the one Lord whose single mission holds us together in one Body. To use the words "older" or "younger" or "sending" or "receiving" with respect to churches is unreal and untrue in the world and in our Communion. Mission is not kindness of the lucky to the unlucky; it is mutual, united obedience to the one God whose mission it is. The form of the Church must reflect that.[116]

The third section of MRI outlined an ambitions process by which the Churches of the Anglican Communion could begin to give and receive from each other. This was followed by a summary statement emphasizing that MRI represented a "radical change" resulting in "the rebirth of the Anglican Communion."

MRI and the 1963 Congress were hailed as a breakthrough that would transcend the paternalism and dominance of Western patterns of mission. For the first time the younger churches in the Anglican Communion saw themselves as equal to the older, "richer" churches of the West. In his response to MRI the bishop of Tokyo, the Right Rev. David M. Goto, illustrated this vision:

> In a word, this plan inaugurates a new era in our common life...Formerly we had before us only the sterile and dreary goal of autonomy and self-sup-

port, often forgetting what this self-support was for. Now we can see self-support and independence as worthy intermediate objectives, useful only as they arm us to take our part as we plan together in interdependence and mutual responsibility for a common task...Formerly a giver and receiver faced each other, each preoccupied with the reactions of each to the other, each ashamed, both with anxious eyes fastened on the gift. Now we are released from this, for we stand hand in hand facing one great missionary task. Our whole relationship in giving and receiving will be lifted up to a new dimension. Where, before, some of us felt we had no gifts because we were confronting those we thought had everything, now we shall discover that all have gifts that are needed and in giving we shall receive.[117]

"Mutual Responsibility and Interdependence" thus stood as a challenge to the American preeminence in the post-war Anglican Communion. And in this challenge Stephen Bayne and Walter Gray parted company. Although both were American bishops, they had profoundly different understandings of the Anglican Communion and the place of the American Episcopal Church in it. Although Gray would not admit it, he saw the Anglican Communion as an extension of the Episcopal Church. In this he was not wholly dissimilar to the British view of the Anglican Communion, except that the Episcopal Church, USA, was now the "mother church." Bayne, on the other hand, was a genuine internationalist. He sought an Anglican Communion made up of true equals where no single church had power over the others. He raised the question: Would the Episcopal Church, and other sending churches in the Anglican Communion change their attitudes and theologies of mission to accommodate the realties of the modern Anglican Communion? Could the Episcopal Church, in particular, move beyond the missiological imperatives of its national church ideal? Recalling his diocese in the United States, Bayne reflected on the changes in mission thinking that needed to occur if Episcopalians were to live the truth of MRI.

They need, as I need, to rethink the whole meaning of mission, and that as this happens, the cost of it in the abandonment of old ways of thinking and old comforts and old priorities is going to be very great. Many people in the Diocese of Olympia between 1947 and 1960 had the feeling that the Church was an association of people, a kind of memorial association for a deceased clergyman named Christ, whose ideals were important and who was an early supporter of the "American Way of Life." To such people mission was something you did for somebody else. Mission was a way of keeping God in business.[118]

What would the mission of the Episcopal Church be if the drive to spread the "American Way of Life" was no longer appropriate?

The Overseas Mission Society

In 1953 a group of Episcopalians came together to organize the Society for the Promotion of the Overseas Mission of the Episcopal Church, later known as the Overseas Mission Society (OMS).[119] As a voluntary association of lay people, presbyters and bishops, the OMS both promoted the foreign mission agenda of the Episcopal Church and demonstrated shortcomings of the official policy and procedures of the national church. The advent of a new voluntary movement in the Episcopal Church signaled a rising critique of the national church ideal.

The Rev. Charles Long, who was personnel secretary of the Overseas Department at the time of the founding of the OMS, credits the post-war missionary thrust of the Episcopal Church as instrumental in the founding of the society. The idealism that brought hundreds of veterans to the seminary, the dream of building a lasting peace through international understanding, the task of rebuilding a war-shattered world and taking up the burden that missionary societies in England could no longer sustain, contributed to a new missionary opportunity for the Episcopal Church.[120] In 1952 a handful of laity and clergy in the vicinity of Washington, D.C., many of whom were associated with the Virginia Theological Seminary and its missionary tradition, began a series of conversations about the missionary nature of the Body of Christ with specific attention to the overseas work of the Episcopal Church.[121] A few of these individuals had participated in an overseas summer training program for seminarians and their professors sponsored by Long's office in the Overseas Department of the national church. The circle of participants in the conversation grew such that within a year they had organized themselves as The Society for the Promotion of the Overseas Mission of the Episcopal Church. This new voluntary association was not a missionary sending society but rather a collection of individuals dedicated to the advancement of the international outreach of the

Episcopal Church through greater education and communication. The society's "Statement of Purpose" emphasized its calling.

> The Society is an association of Church People, clergy and lay, who out of zeal for the mission of the church want to share with one another and with the Church at large knowledge of the present state of missions, and suggestions for new methods of promoting missionary enthusiasm and information throughout the parishes of the land.

> Our hope is that constructive suggestions and assistance, better missionary news, more aggressive strategies and more devoted missionary giving can increase support of the National Council's Overseas Department and lend new force to the missionary life of the Church.[122]

Through the 1950s and 1960s the Overseas Mission Society sponsored many programs to foster mission awareness in the Episcopal Church. Each year the OMS brought outstanding leaders in mission thought to the United States. British missiologists and missions administrators such as Max Warren, Douglas Webster, John V. Taylor and Alfred Stanway were all introduced to the Episcopal Church through this program. At the same time, the Rev. A. Theodore Eastman, Executive Secretary of the OMS from 1956 to 1968, traveled widely throughout the Anglican Communion reporting back to the membership of the society. The experiences of both the visiting missiologists as well as the executive secretary were gathered up in a joint annual meeting and educational mission conference held each year.

The most important contribution of the OMS was its role in advancing printed material about the mission work of the Episcopal Church. In 1940 the Episcopal Church's official journal had changed its name and focus from *The Spirit of Missions* to *Forth*, changing its original focus as a publication for and about the domestic and foreign mission work of the Episcopal Church. To fill the void, the OMS published *The Episcopal Overseas Mission Review* (OMR). The OMR came out three times a year at the Feasts of St. Michael and All Angels, Epiphany and Whitsunday (Pentecost); it was published from 1955 until 1968. Substantive original material along with reprinted articles by significant thinkers such as Stephen Bayne, Daisuke Kitagawa, Stephen Neill, Lesslie Newbigin, D. T. Niles, David M. Paton, John V. Taylor and

Max Warren filled the pages of the OMR. Church councils and
missionary meetings were reported on in articles and editorials.
Letters from missionaries and surveys of the overseas work of the
Episcopal Church were included in each issue. Under the editorial leadership of William Clebsch (1955–1959), George Tittmann
(1959–1962) and William MacKaye (1962–1968), *The Episcopal
Overseas Mission Review* served for over a decade as the best
forum for missiological discussion in the Episcopal Church. In
addition to the OMR, the Overseas Mission Society had a hand in
the publication of a variety of books and pamphlets including
titles by Eastman, *Letters from the Rim of East Asia* (1962), and
Christian Responsibility in One World (1965), as well as Max
Warren's *Challenge and Response* (1959), and *Encounter in South
India* (1966) by Charles Ryerson. Working in association with
Forward Movement Publications, the OMS helped to produce a
series of pamphlets introducing Americans to the wider church
throughout the world. This series included *The Directory of
Episcopal Churches Overseas* (1960), "Are You Going Abroad?"
(1960), and "The Family Abroad" (1961).[123]

Although the Overseas Mission Society was organized to support and encourage the official missionary work of the Overseas
Department of the National Council, it sometimes considered its
role as the "loyal opposition" to the national church. The OMS
pointed out that the historic strengths of the missionary work of
the Episcopal Church, the incorporation of all members of the
church into the Missionary Society and the idea of the missionary
bishop had some significant drawbacks. The Overseas Mission
Society emphasized that when all Episcopalians were responsible
for the missionary outreach of the church, as stipulated by the
constitution of the Domestic and Foreign Missionary Society, then
voluntary interest in, and giving to, mission was lost. After a while
dioceses began to consider their support for the National Council
as a tax levied and not a freewill offering.[124] OMS argued that voluntarism as the basis for mission support was jeopardized when
the Episcopal Church and the Missionary Society were merged
into an organic whole. The OMS was thus founded to reconnect
the mission work of the Episcopal Church with its constituency

in the pews.[125] In addition, the Overseas Mission Society was not afraid to point out the drawbacks of the institution of the missionary episcopate. These failings included: the church's narrow support for "our bishops" and "our missionary districts," the lack of restraint on the missionary bishop's autocratic powers, the fact that election of a missionary bishop was often decided by politics in the House of Bishops rather than the needs of the overseas missionary district, and the reality that the missionary bishop who was the best speaker received the most financial support.[126] Finally, and perhaps most significantly, missionary bishops were elected by, and maintained their seat in, the American House of Bishops. As a result, missionary bishops, and by extension missionary districts, were intimately bound to the canons and polity of the Episcopal Church, USA, and not to the culture and conditions of the local people. This constitutional allegiance to the Episcopal Church made autonomy processes in missionary districts difficult at best. These shortcomings of the Missionary Society and the missionary episcopate made the foreign mission work of the Episcopal Church vulnerable to the health and finances of the National Council. If the national church ideal failed to hold the imagination of Episcopalians in the United States, then support for missionary outreach would be in peril. And this is exactly what happened in the next two decades.

NOTES

[1]Sydney E. Ahlstrom, *A Religious History of the American People* (New Haven, Conn. and London: Yale University Press, 1972), 954.

[2]Ibid.

[3]In 1940 there were 2,073,546 baptized Episcopalians, and one in sixty-four Americans professed membership in the Episcopal Church. Twenty years later the number of Episcopalians in the United States had grown to 3,269,325, one in fifty-five Americans. See: "Ratio of Church Members and Communicants," in *The Living Church Annual* (New York: Morehouse Publishing Co., 1962), 12.

[4]James A. Scherer, *Gospel, Church, and Kingdom: Comparative Studies in World Mission Theology* (Minneapolis, Minn.: Augsburg Publishing House, 1987), 94.

[5]Johannes Hoekendijk, in particular, challenged the dominant belief that the church was the sole agent and locus of God's mission (*missio Dei*) in the world. This will be discussed below. See: Johannes C. Hoekendijk, "The Call to Evangelism," *International Review of Missions* 39 (April 1950).

[6]Stephen Neill, *A History of Christian Missions* (New York: Penguin Books, 1964), 572.

[7]William Richey Hogg, *Ecumenical Foundations: A History of the International Missionary Council and Its Nineteenth-Century Background* (New York: Harper and Brothers, 1952), 335.

[8]Feliciano Carino, "Partnership in Obedience," *International Review of Mission* 67 (July 1978): 319-320.

[9]Gerald Anderson, "The Theology of Missions: 1928-1958" (Ph.D. diss., Boston University, 1960), 199.

[10]Hogg, 339.

[11]International Missionary Council, "Christian Witness in a Revolutionary World," in *Renewal and Advance: Christian Witness in a Revolutionary World*, ed. C. W. Ranson (London: Edinburgh House Press, 1947), 215.

[12]Carino, 326.

[13]Anderson notes that the study papers prepared for the 1952 meeting of the IMC in Willingen, Germany, had their genesis in the Whitby mandate to study the theology of Christian mission in a substantive manner. See pages 219-229 in "The Theology of Missions: 1928-1958."

[14]Ibid., 246.

[15]Norman Goodall, ed., *Missions Under the Cross: Addresses Delivered at the Enlarged Meeting of the Committee of the*

International Missionary Council at Willingen, in Germany, 1952; with Statements Issued by the Meeting, (New York: The Friendship Press for the International Missionary Council, 1953), 187.

[16]Ibid., 189-190.

[17]Ibid., 209.

[18]Charles Long, "Christian Vocation and the Missionary Call," *International Review of Missions* 39 (October 1950): 417.

[19]Ibid., 413-414.

[20]Ibid., 417.

[21]Personal correspondence with the author, 8 August 1991.

[22]William R. Hutchison, *Errand to the World: American Protestant Thought and Foreign Missions* (Chicago: The University of Chicago Press, 1987), 183.

[23]Hoekendijk, 163.

[24]Ibid., 170.

[25]Ibid., 171.

[26]Ibid., 168.

[27]Anderson, 327-328.

[28]"The Christian Mission at This Hour" in Ronald K. Orchard, ed., *The Ghana Assembly of the International Missionary Council*, (London: Edinburgh House Press for the International Missionary Council, 1958), 181.

[29]Ibid.

[30]Lesslie Newbigin, *One Body, One Gospel, One World* (London: International Missionary Council, 1958).

[31]Scherer, 104-105.

[32]Joint Committee of the W. C. C. and I. M. C., *A Draft Plan for the Integration of the World Council of Churches and the*

International Missionary Council (London: Joint Committee of the W. C. C. and the I. M. C., n.d.), 3.

[33]Ibid., 9.

[34]Rodger C. Bassham, *Mission Theology, 1948-1975: Years of Worldwide Creative Tensions; Ecumenical, Evangelical, and Roman Catholic* (Pasadena, Calif.: William Carey Library, 1979), 63.

[35]Scherer, 108.

[36]Gerald Anderson, "American Protestants in Pursuit of Mission: 1886-1986," *International Bulletin of Missionary Research* 12 (July 1988): 108. Anderson notes that significantly more American foreign missionaries serving in the 1950s came from conservative-evangelical churches than earlier in the century. This marked the beginning of a trend in which conservative-evangelical foreign missionaries from the United States would come to outnumber the American conciliar-ecumenical missionaries.

[37]Henry Knox Sherrill, *Among Friends* (Boston: Houghton Mifflin Co., 1962), 22.

[38]Ibid., 26.

[39]Ibid., 37.

[40]Ibid., 65.

[41]Province One included all of the dioceses in New England.

[42]Sherrill, 164.

[43]Ibid.

[44]The comparison between the Presiding Bishop and the president of the United States was first made in J. M. B. Gill, *"My Father's Business" World Problems and Personal Responsibility* (New York: The National Council of the Protestant Episcopal Church, 1924), 7.

[45]David E. Sumner, *The Episcopal Church's History: 1945-1985* (Wilton, Conn.: Morehouse-Barlow, 1987), 5.

[46]Ibid.

[47]Ibid.

[48]Roland Foster, *The Role of the Presiding Bishop* (Cincinnati, Ohio: Forward Movement Publications, 1982), 100.

[49]Sherrill, 223.

[50]Ibid., 221-223, 265-266.

[51]Ibid., 233.

[52]The Bushes were neighbors of the Sherrills in Greenwich and close friends. Sherrill stated that one of the saddest memories of his departure as Presiding Bishop was leaving behind close friends like the Bushes in Greenwich. The close association of Episcopal Church leaders with Episcopalians in government is consistent with the national church ideal.

[53]Sherrill, 234

[54]Ibid., 295.

[55]Walter Herbert Stowe, 1930-1940, *An Encouraging Decade for the Episcopal Church*, Church Historical Society Publication Series (Philadelphia: The Church Historical Society, 1944), 33.

[56]For a reflection on the close of the China mission see: Charles H. Long, "The Liberation of the Chinese Church: A Memoir of the Revolution from a Missionary Point of View," *Historical Magazine of the Protestant Episcopal Church* 49 (September 1980).

[57]Robert Prichard reports that one-quarter of the class of 1950 from Virginia Seminary enlisted as foreign missionaries. See: Robert W. Prichard, *A History of the Episcopal Church* (Harrisburg, Va.: Morehouse Publishing, 1991), 238.

[58]Mission work in Okinawa, as well as in American territories gained during World War II including Midway, Wake, Guam, and American Samoa, was overseen by the missionary bishop of Honolulu. See: Protestant Episcopal Church in the United States of America, National Council, Overseas Department, *Our Overseas Missions* (London: SPCK, 1958), 20.

[59]"Appendix 21, The General Church Program as Proposed" in General Convention of the Protestant Episcopal Church, *Journal of the General Convention of the Protestant Episcopal Church: 1952* (New York: The General Convention, 1952), 402.

[60]"Appendix 23, The General Church Program as Proposed" in General Convention of the Protestant Episcopal Church, *Journal of the General Convention of the Protestant Episcopal Church: 1949* (New York: The General Convention, 1949), 461.

[61]F. W. Dillistone, "The Importance of the United States in the Missionary Movement Today," *The Churchman* 66 (March 1952): 41-42.

[62]*Our Overseas Missions*, 22-23.

[63]Protestant Episcopal Church in the United States of America, National Council, Overseas Department, *A Compilation of Current Strategy and Policy Statements Related to the Administration of the Program and Budget of the Overseas Department of the National Council* (New York: The National Council, 1959), 6.

[64]General Convention of the Protestant Episcopal Church, *Journal of the General Convention of the Protestant Episcopal Church: 1949*, 462.

[65]"Appendix 21: The General Church Program as Proposed," in: General Convention of the Protestant Episcopal Church, *Journal of the General Convention of the Protestant Episcopal Church: 1952*, 403.

[66]Charles Henry Long, ed., *Who Are the Anglicans? Profiles and Maps of the Anglican Communion*, (Cincinnati, Ohio: Forward Movement Publications, 1988), 33.

[67]*Our Overseas Missions*, 23-24.

[68]Ibid., 24.

[69]Protestant Episcopal Church in the United States, National Council, Director of the Overseas Department, *Our Overseas*

Missions: Central America (National Council Overseas Department, 1963), 6-8.

[70]Figures from an unpublished memo of the Overseas Department, prepared 16 March 1970.

[71]Samir J. Habiby, ed., "An Analysis of the Evolution of the Fund and its Ministry — Part I" (The Presiding Bishop's Fund for World Relief, New York, June 15, 1986), 10.

[72]"Report of the Presiding Bishop's Fund for World Relief" in General Convention of the Protestant Episcopal Church, *Journal of the General Convention of the Protestant Episcopal Church: 1949*, 675.

[73]Habiby, 16-17.

[74]Protestant Episcopal Church in the United States of America, National Council, *Annual Report of the National Council of the Protestant Episcopal Church in the United States: 1952*, 13.

[75]*Our Overseas Missions*, "Appendix J — Anglican Cooperation," 59-61.

[76]Sherrill, 256-260.

[77]Sherrill reported, "From Hawaii was issued one of the best of the Pastoral Letters of the House of Bishops defining the mission of the church in a rapidly changing world." Sherrill, 263. See also: "The Pastoral Letter" in General Convention of the Protestant Episcopal Church, *Journal of the General Convention of the Protestant Episcopal Church: 1955* (New York: The General Convention, 1955), 41.

William Clebsch and Massey Shepard share Sherrill's evaluation of the 1955 General Convention. See: William A. Clebsch, "The Honolulu Pastoral Letter," *The Episcopal Overseas Mission Review* I (Epiphany 1956): 17; and Massey H. Shepherd, "Honolulu and the Missionary Task," *Anglican Theological Review* 37 (July 1955): 165-166.

[78]Borden W. Painter, "Bishop Walter H. Gray and the Anglican Congress of 1954," *Historical Magazine of the Protestant Episcopal Church* 47 (March 1978): 162.

[79]Gray was not alone in his call for a new international organization of the Anglican Communion. The Right Rev. Ronald Owen Hall, bishop of Hong Kong, had made similar suggestions. See: Ronald Owen Hall, "New Church Order: The Future of the Worldwide Episcopal Church" (Evanston, Ill.: Seabury-Western Theological Seminary, [1941]).

[80]Walter H. Gray, "Pan-Anglican Unity," *The Witness*, April 20, 1944, quoted in Painter, 160.

[81]See: Robert S. Bosher, "The Pan-Anglican Congress of 1908," *Historical Magazine of the Protestant Episcopal Church* 13 (June 1954).

[82]Painter, 161-164.

[83]Ibid., 164-165.

[84]See: Resolutions 80, 86, 87 in: 1948 Lambeth Conference, *The Encyclical Letter from the Bishops; together with Resolutions and Reports* (London: Society for Promoting Christian Knowledge, 1948),47-48.

[85]Painter, 167-169.

[86]Max A. C. Warren, *Missionary Commitments of the Anglican Communion* (London: Society for Promoting Christian Knowledge, 1957), 6.

[87]R. David Cox, "A Vision to Fulfill: 'Mutual Responsibility and Interdependence' in the Anglican Communion" (S.T.M. thesis, Yale Divinity School, 1987), 70.

[88]Powel Mills Dawley, ed., *Report of the Anglican Congress of 1954*, (Greenwich, Conn.: Seabury Press, 1954), 4-5, 252.

[89]Ibid., 215.

[90]Ibid., 3.

[91]Painter, 169.

[92]Ibid., 167-169.

[93]1958 Lambeth Conference, *The Encyclical Letter from the Bishops together with the Resolutions and Reports* (Greenwich, Conn.: Seabury Press, 1958), 146.

[94]"Our Overseas Missions," 59.

[95]1958 Lambeth Conference, 269.

[96]Letter from Bishop Bentley to Bishop Warner K. C. H. Warner, then chair of the Committee on Missionary Appeal and Strategy, dated 30 January 1958, quoted in Cox, 78.

[97]1958 Lambeth Conference, 143-44.

[98]General Convention of the Protestant Episcopal Church, *Journal of the General Convention of the Protestant Episcopal Church: 1958* (New York: The General Convention, 1958), 289-290.

[99]Committee of Conference on Overseas Missions, *Report to the Presiding Bishop and the National Council* (New York: The National Council, 1960), 13.

[100]Ibid., 7-8.

[101]Ibid., 11.

[102]Ibid.

[103]For a summary of the Overseas Department's actions see: National Council, Overseas Department, "A Response by the Overseas Department of the National Council to Certain Recommendations of the Committee of Conference on Overseas Missions" (New York: The National Council, 1961).

[104]The most extensive study of the history and theology of MRI is David's Cox's S.T.M. thesis. See: Cox, "A Vision to Fulfill: 'Mutual Responsibility and Interdependence' in the Anglican Communion."

[105]Ibid., 101.

[106]From a biographical sketch of Stephen Bayne in: Stephen Bayne, *A Bibliography* (n.p.: Lucie C. Bayne, 1978), 89.

[107]E. R. Fairweather, ed., *Anglican Congress 1963: Report of the Proceedings* (Toronto: Editorial Committee of the Anglican Congress, 1963), 186.

[108]Cox, 102.

[109]A collection of Bayne's writings related to his work as the Executive Officer are found in: Stephen Fielding Bayne, ed., *An Anglican Turning Point: Documents and Interpretations*, (Austin, Tex: Church Historical Society, 1964).

[110]Cox, 104-105.

[111]Ibid., 118.

[112]Ibid., 124

[113]Ibid., 129.

[114]Ibid., 130.

[115]Fairweather, ed. *Anglican Congress 1963*, 118. The ten dioceses referred to as not "of one blood with their own self-governing regions and peoples" were the American missionary districts of Central America, Central Brazil, the Dominican Republic, Haiti, Liberia, Mexico, the Panama Canal Zone, the Philippines, Southern Brazil and Southwestern Brazil.

[116]Ibid., 120-121.

[117]Ibid., 125-126

[118]Ibid., 130.

[119]The name was shortened to the Overseas Mission Society in February 1956. Overseas Mission Society, *OMS Milestones: 1953-1966* (Washington, D.C.: The Overseas Mission Society, 1966), 1.

[120]Charles Long, "The Story of the Overseas Mission Society: 1953-1977" (keynote address to the Annual Meeting of the Episcopal Council for Global Mission, Ambridge, Penn. May 22, 1991) [4].

[121]William A. Clebsch, George F. Tittmann, and Theodore O. Wedel, "Introducing the Overseas Mission Review," *The Episcopal Overseas Mission Review* 1 (St. Michael and All Angels 1955): 1

[122]From "The Statement of Purpose" found on the inside back cover of each issue of *The Episcopal Overseas Mission Review*.

[123]*OMS Milestones: 1953-1966*, 2-6.

[124]Allen Green argues that the method of supporting mission through the budget of the National Council was a progressive failure. See: Allen J. Green, "Episcopal Missionary Giving, 1920-1955," *Overseas Mission Review* 1 (Whitsunday 1956): 6-11.

[125]Clebsch, Tittman, and Wedel, 2.

[126]Charles Long, "The Story of the Overseas Mission Society: 1953-1977," [3].

CHAPTER FIVE

CRISIS AND REDEFINITION
The Ideal in a New World
1963 to 1985

The 1960s and 1970s were decades of rebellion, reevaluation and revolt in the United States. The struggle for civil rights, urban violence and upheaval on college campuses threatened the status quo of American society. A rising anti-establishment ethic challenged the prevailing norms of entrenched institutions. The government, the church and the family were all suspect.

Outside the United States the world was changing radically. The colonial era was waning. Newly independent nations in the southern hemisphere cried out for political autonomy while at the same time they were being swept up in the bi-polar conflict of the Cold War. Many Americans, angry and embarrassed about the United States involvement in Southeast Asia, believed the nation should be concerned primarily with its own domestic problems. Efforts to address injustice at home combined with guilt over the sins of Western colonialism resulted in a self-imposed psychological withdrawal from the wider world for Americans.

Turmoil at home and changes abroad had a profound effect on the foreign mission activities of American Protestantism. The decline of mainline churches, both in membership and societal stature, juxtaposed with the increase of newly independent churches in Asia, Africa and Latin America, made old ways of thinking about and doing mission bankrupt. At the same time a new theology of mission emerged in conciliar Protestant thought. The church, especially the church of the Western industrialized nations, was no longer the locus of authority for mission. In the new era, the world was to set the agenda for the missionary outreach of the church. The new missionary calling of the church was to participate with God in the struggle for justice and liberation of all people.

This new understanding of mission became paramount at the Fourth Assembly of the World Council of Churches in Uppsala (Sweden) 1968. This meeting, sometimes referred to as the "Social Justice Assembly," marked a new era in the mission policy of the World Council of Churches. The Uppsala document "Renewal in Mission" stressed that the goal of mission was to produce a new humanity, and the sign of the new humanity was the social engagement of the church in the fight against racism, colonialism and injustice throughout the world. Following Uppsala, Western churches became increasingly involved in international development efforts as an outgrowth of their participation in God's wider mission.

The Episcopal Church was not immune to the social and political turmoil in the United States or the theological upheavals in conciliar missiology. In the 1960s and 1970s the national church ideal, as the impetus for and defining tenet of Episcopal foreign mission work, was challenged both at home and overseas. The civil rights movement, urban unrest and the social upheaval of the 1960s resulted in a questioning of the Episcopal Church's calling in the United States. In addition, the Anglican Congress of 1963 and "Mutual Responsibility and Interdependence in the Body of Christ" had held up a different vision for mission. The Episcopal Church could no longer be lady bountiful dispensing good schools, good hospitals and right-ordered worship to dependent missionary districts around the world. The ferment at home and around the world resulted in a crisis for the national church ideal that could only be resolved by redefining the mission of the Episcopal Church in the new world.

CONCILIAR PROTESTANTS, GOD'S MISSION AND INTERNATIONAL DEVELOPMENT

From 1963 to 1983 the World Council of Churches and its subdivision, the Commission on World Mission and Evangelism, each met three times. During these two decades, conciliar Protestants embraced a new theology of mission. Increasingly the *missio ecclesia* of the Willingen IMC meeting gave way to the *missio Dei* theology promoted by such thinkers as Johannes Hoekendijk. "The Missionary Obligation of the Church" had maintained that God was revealed to the world through the church. Bringing all people to God through Jesus Christ was the church's mission. In the new theological formulation, God was acknowledged as being present outside the church in the wider world. Whereas the old missiological equation read God-church-world, the new formulation was God-world-church.[1] A debate between the old and new vision of Christian mission resulted in a split between liberal and evangelical Protestants that would prove difficult to heal.

The first meeting of the newly constituted Commission on World Mission and Evangelism (CWME) of the World Council of Churches took place from December 8–19, 1963, in Mexico City. Over 200 delegates gathered to consider "God's Mission and Our Task." The chosen theme emphasized that conciliar missiologists had embraced fully the centrality of God's mission. As a result, Mexico 1963 signaled a shift away from the preoccupation with the church that had dominated ecumenical mission theology since Madras 1938 to the idea that mission must take place within the world.[2] With the whole world as the locus for God's mission, the CWME reaffirmed the position that distinctions between old and young churches, Christians in the north and those in the south, are no longer appropriate in the new world. The responsibility to participate in God's mission was one and the same for all Christians in all corners of the globe. The Mexico meeting is best remembered for the missiological affirmation: "Mission in six continents." This new motto of conciliar mission theology illustrated both the worldly context of God's mission as well as the commonalty of all Christians who participate in it. Bishop

Anastasios Yannoulatos of Androussa, one of the early Greek Orthodox participants in the CWME, remembered the Mexico meeting as shifting the ground of mission from a theocentric to an anthroprocentric model. He believed, however, that Mexico 1963 went too far in its embrace of the world as the locus for God's mission.

> The increased sensitivity to social duties and concerns with the agenda of the world, which marked the Mexico talks, ultimately contributed to a quiet shift in the anthropocentric direction. Significantly, the meeting began with "God's mission and our task," where the emphasis was on mission being God's and went down in history with the slogan *Mission in six continents* (no mention here of "God's mission"), where the emphasis is on the broadness of the geographical horizon rather than on the depth and height of the initial theological vision. Thus the vertical dimension of theological sensitivity was finally overshadowed by the strongly highlighted horizontal aspect, and the Cross, that authentic symbol of Christianity which appears when both dimensions receive an equal amount of light, failed to be made visible. (Parenthesis in original)[3]

Finally the Mexico City meeting of the CWME opened up the question of Christian witness to people of other faiths. In its document "The Witness of Christians to Men of Other Faiths" Mexico sought to understand how Christians could relate to people of other faiths through genuine dialogue that avoided relativism and syncretism.[4]

Between the Mexico meeting of the CWME and the Fourth Assembly of the World Council of Churches in Uppsala, 1968, the WCC published two reports (one each from an American and European working group) on the "Missionary Structure of the Congregation." Both of the reports continued the ecumenical movement away from the church to the world as the locus for God's mission. Johannes Hoekendijk was involved in the preparation of both reports and through them his earlier protestations against "churchification" as the end of mission became widely accepted.

> The reports of the working groups that prepared for the Uppsala meeting, and those that emanated from it, nearly all displayed the same forthright insistence on relocating the church within the structures presented by the secular order. At some points challenging the most hallowed assumptions of traditional evangelism, these reports raised serious questions about bringing converts into existing churches...The European and American working groups of which the Dutch theologian [Hoekendijk] was involved, agreed with him to the extent of denouncing denominational differences

as dysfunctional and irrelevant in the modern world; and denouncing proselytism as a one-sided conception of conversion. It was one-sided because
the more important kind of "conversion" arises "on the corporate level in
the form of social change," and also because the church must go to the
world, not simply wait and invite outsiders in.[5]

"The Missionary Structure of the Congregation" set the stage for
the new emphasis on social action as mission, over against evangelization, for which Uppsala 1968 is best remembered.

The Fourth Assembly of the World Council of Churches took
place at Uppsala, Sweden, from July 4–19, 1968. At the meeting, 704
delegates from 235 WCC churches gathered to consider the theme
"Behold, I make all things new." The meeting was not isolated
from the changes in world Christianity in the post-colonial era
nor from the revolutionary tumult of the late 1960s. "At Uppsala
the sense of crisis in world affairs and its shattering impact upon
Christian institutions and on what is generally assumed to be
meant by 'the Christian tradition' broke in again and again with
the effect of a thunder-clap and lightning-flash."[6] At Uppsala the
world set the agenda for the meeting.

The major missiological statement of Uppsala was found in
Section Two, "Renewal in Mission." The report itself was much
less radical than the earlier studies on the "The Missionary
Structure of the Congregation." It began with the affirmation that
the mission of God was "the gift of a new creation which is a radical renewal of the old and the invitation to men to grow up into
their full humanity in the new man, Jesus Christ."[7] The report
affirmed that in Jesus' life, death and resurrection a new creation
was born. The mission of God was to bring all people into this
new creation. All who work for justice and peace in the world participated in this new creation. Uppsala thus went on record as
stating that the new creation was not coterminous with the
church. The church participated in the new creation but it was
not the sole purveyor of God's renewing presence in the world.

> We must see achievements of greater justice, freedom and dignity as a part
> of the restoration of true manhood in Christ. This calls for a more open and
> humble partnership with all who work for these goals even when they do
> not share the same assumptions as ourselves.[8]

The radical worldliness of the Uppsala report on "Renewal in Mission" was found in many of its strategic proposals.[9] These proposals called on churches to reexamine their structures in order to be more open to God's new creation as it was being manifested in the wider world, including people of other faiths.

The final endorsement of the *missio Dei* by the WCC was not shared by all delegates to the Assembly. Evangelicals, in particular, felt that Uppsala's embrace of the world neglected the missiological imperative to proclaim Jesus Christ as Lord and Savior to the whole world. The attack from the conservative side of Protestant mission thought was led by Donald McGavran of Fuller Seminary. In his article "Will Uppsala Betray the Two Billion?," first published in the *Church Growth Bulletin*, McGavran chastised the liberals for turning their backs on evangelization as the central aim of Christian mission.

> ["Renewal in Mission"] intends to divert the whole missionary movement into the movement toward Christian unity on the one hand and Christian behavior toward one's closest neighbor on the other...Christian unity and Christian neighborliness are good ends, to be sure, but they are not mission and should not masquerade as such.

> The attempt on theological grounds to direct the missionary enterprise of the Church into channels not even remotely connected with bringing the nations to faith and obedience or reconciling men to God in the Church of Jesus Christ must excite the suspicion and earn the rejection of Christians everywhere.

> Do [the authors of the report] intend to direct the whole complex [missionary] enterprise away from discipling the nations, away from preaching the gospel, away from the multiplication of churches of baptized believers, and into various forms of revivifying the Church?[10]

In McGavran's opinion, Uppsala had betrayed the two billion people who had not yet heard the Gospel of Jesus Christ. What resulted was a split between liberal conciliar Protestants who embraced *missio Dei* theology and conservative evangelicals who, following McGavran and John Stott, dissented from the WCC line. The conciliar-evangelical debate over mission would define Protestant missiological thought for the next two decades.

The next conference of the Commission on World Mission and Evangelism took place in Bangkok, Thailand, in 1973. Of the

330 participants from sixty-nine countries that came together in Bangkok, 55% of them came from churches in the two-thirds world. The fact that Christians from the "Southern hemisphere" outnumbered Christians from the "industrialized West" (the first time ever at an IMC or CWME gathering) significantly altered the conversations and power dynamics of the conference.[11]

The theme chosen for the conference was "Salvation Today." In considering the meaning of salvation as it pertains to mission, the CWME was attempting to formulate a comprehensive missiology that would hold together mission as social action and mission as evangelization. Although evangelicals declared that salvation and the church were inseparable, the strongest emphasis at Bangkok was the social dimensions of salvation.[12] Salvation was understood as liberation from oppressive structures both in the world as well as in the churches. Bangkok stated that

> the churches must be liberated from their captivity to interests of class, race, and nation in order to initiate action for liberation in the world, "Mission under these conditions should be conceived of particularly in terms of what is required in obedience to Christ the Liberator."[13]

The appropriation of Jesus as Liberator meant that the good news of the Gospel was best heard among the poor, oppressed and disadvantaged of the world. Mission thus meant identification with such persons and participation with them in the struggles against injustice and oppression.

The 1973 meeting of the CWME did not break significant new theological ground but instead advanced the *missio Dei* along liberationist lines. The conference signaled, however, that the ground for missiological discussion in the WCC had changed. The anger and resentment of churches in the two-thirds world against Western dominance was heard loud and clear at Bangkok. Christians from Asia, Africa and Latin America claimed their full stature as equal participants in God's mission. Thus the real significance of the Bangkok meeting of the Commission on World Mission and Evangelism was the coming to the forefront of liberation concerns in conciliar ecumenical mission thought and the transition from Western dominance to two-thirds world leadership in the CWME.[14]

Whereas the Uppsala meeting of the WCC resulted in a split between the social action and evangelism camps in ecumenical mission thought, the Fifth Assembly of the World Council of Churches meeting in Nairobi, Kenya, in November of 1975 sought to reconcile these two poles. The chosen theme for the Assembly was "Jesus Christ Frees and Unites." Evangelism figured prominently in the meeting's deliberations. The time and the place contributed to this renewed interest in evangelism as African churches were adding converts in record numbers in the early 1970s.[15] Nairobi can thus be seen as a consolidating Assembly.

> The thrust of Uppsala — to put Christians, the Church and the ecumenical movement in the world rather than over against it — was certainly sustained at Nairobi. Yet the strong interest in evangelism, and the definite attempt to give a theological rationale for the work of the church in the world were efforts to make clear that such an involvement was in response to the call of God, and a sign of the church's obedience to its divine vocation.[16]

Nairobi sought to rehabilitate the church as playing an important role in God's mission. In his address to the WCC as Moderator, M. M. Thomas of India emphasized that conciliar and evangelical Protestants as well as Roman Catholics were beginning to find a new commonality of opinion with regard to mission. He pointed out that all three streams of thought now sought a holistic understanding of mission that included both evangelism and social action.[17] Nairobi's mission statement "Confessing Christ Today" thus emphasized the church's role in declaring, and participating in, God's mission.

> The world is not only God's creation; it is also the arena of God's mission. Because God loved the whole world, the Church cannot neglect any part of it — neither those who have heard the saving Name nor the vast majority who have not yet heard it. Our obedience to God and our solidarity with the human family demand that we obey Christ's command to proclaim and demonstrate God's love to every person, of every class and race, on every continent, in every culture, in every setting and historical context.[18]

Although the church was rehabilitated as an appropriate agent for God's mission, the Nairobi Assembly did not shy away from its commitment to the poor and the struggle for liberation.

> In the witness of our whole life and our confessing community we *work* with passionate love for the total liberation of the people and *anticipate*

> God's Kingdom to come. We *pray* in the freedom of the Spirit and *groan* with
> our suffering fellow human beings and the whole groaning creation until the
> glory of the Triune God is revealed and will be all in all. (Italics in original)[19]

Nairobi provided a trinitarian statement on mission that sought to bring together evangelism and social action. It also marked "the beginning of a new phase in the development of ecumenical mission theology, as seen in the attempt to reconcile 'churchly' and 'worldly' approaches to mission."[20]

> Nairobi pointed to a convergence of theological viewpoints; it confirmed
> the emphasis on the world as the locus for mission and highlighted the
> concern for evangelism expressed at the [evangelical] International
> Congress on World Evangelization in Lausanne [1974], the Synod of Bishops
> meeting on evangelism [Rome 1975], and the Orthodox contribution on
> "Confessing Jesus Christ Today." In drawing together these strands, it strove
> to present a comprehensive understanding of salvation and of the mission
> of God's people in the world.[21]

The new reconciled approach to mission with its ongoing commitment to the poor was stressed at the 1980 Commission on World Mission and Evangelism meeting held in Melbourne, Australia. This meeting was considered to be one of the most important missionary conferences since the integration of the International Missionary Council into the WCC.[22] At the Melbourne meeting "Kingdom centered" missiology became dominant in ecumenical mission thought. The conference's theme, "Your Kingdom Come," implied a call both to pray and to work for God's kingdom in the world. The report from Melbourne stated at the outset that "the kingdom of God which was inaugurated in Jesus Christ brings justice, love, peace and joy and freedom from the grasp of principalities and powers."[23] The evangelistic task of the church was to "preach good news to the poor" by becoming churches in solidarity with the struggles of the poor, joining the struggle against powers of exploitation and impoverishment, establishing a new relationship with the poor inside the churches, and praying and working for the kingdom of God.[24]

James Scherer summarized the main contributions of the Melbourne conference to ecumenical mission thought. First, the kingdom of God, both as a gift and as a task, was appropriated as the most comprehensive biblical expression of the *missio Dei.*

Second, there emerged a new christological emphasis on mission and evangelism where the ministry of Jesus Christ as liberator replaced Paul and the apostles as the missionary *par excellence*. Third, Melbourne declared that the church had a "preferential option" for the poor. Any and all missionary initiatives needed to be measured by their solidarity with the poor and their commitment to fighting sources of oppression and injustice in the world. In addition Melbourne finally rehabilitated the church as having an important role to play in God's mission as it struggled to both proclaim and work for the "good news to the poor."[25]

The missiological affirmations of both the Nairobi Assembly and the Melbourne Conference came together in the significant document *Mission and Evangelism: An Ecumenical Affirmation*, published by the Central Committee of the WCC in 1982. The contribution of *Mission and Evangelism* was not that it broke any new theological ground but that it represented a new consensus of thought on mission in conciliar ecumenical circles. The polarities between evangelism and social action had given way to a common ground. The church was redeemed as an agent in God's mission and the poor had claimed their place in God's kingdom. The fact that no major plenary session was devoted to the theme of world mission and evangelism at the Sixth Assembly of the World Council of Churches in Vancouver, Canada, (1983) signaled that the maelstrom over mission and the church in the new world had subsided.

American Missionaries, Development, and the United States Government

In the decades following World War II, international aid and development became a major American response to economic and political realities throughout the world. Beginning with the Marshall Plan under President Truman, continuing in the International Cooperation Administration and the Development Loan Fund under Eisenhower, and resulting in the Agency for International Development (USAID) instituted by the Kennedy administration, the United States government played a new and active role in international aid and development. Although the level and type of international aid provided has fluctuated since the 1950s, the United States has remained the single largest aid and development donor in the world. Today the United States provides over $5 billion annually in food and development aid through bilateral and multilateral development programs.

American churches have become increasingly involved with the United States government as partners in development programs. Many conciliar Protestant churches are now registered with the government as Private Voluntary Organizations (PVOs). Church agencies such as Church World Service, Lutheran World Relief, the Adventist Relief and Development Agency, and the Overseas Development Office of the Episcopal Church have served as conduits for USAID assistance overseas. This cooperation between the United States government and the churches in international aid and development is a new phenomenon unique to the 1970s and 1980s.

WCC pronouncements made at Uppsala in 1968 strengthened Protestant commitment to development as an appropriate mission response in the new world.[26] The report on "World Economic and Social Development" adopted by the Assembly stated that God's mission to bring about a new human and social order was intimately connected to the struggle for social justice and world development. To participate in world development was to participate in the liberating mission of God.

> Our hope is in him who makes all things new. He judges our structures of thought and action and renders them obsolete. If our false security in the old and our fear of revolutionary change tempt us to defend the *status quo* or to patch it up with half-hearted measures, we may all perish. The death of the old may cause pain to some, but failure to build up a new world community may bring death to all. In their faith in the coming Kingdom of God and in their search for his righteousness, Christians are urged to participate in the struggle of millions of people for greater social justice and world development.[27]

The report recommended that mission projects oriented toward social transformation be incorporated into the new development agenda of the churches.

> The churches are already engaged in mission and service projects for economic and social development and some of these resources could be used

strategically on a priority basis for pioneer or demonstration projects as an important response to the most acute needs of specific peoples and areas...The churches should use their resources for God's purpose of abundant life for all men.[28]

To foster communication and coordination in development activities between the churches of the World Council, the Uppsala meeting established the Commission on the Churches' Participation in Development (CCPD).

The Uppsala Assembly thus gave both a theological rationale and a programmatic process for churches to redirect their international work from mission projects to development projects. In many cases this change was simply semantic since missionaries had been working "to give life more abundantly" for generations.[29] In many ways the development rubric was not wholly dissimilar to earlier efforts in civilization practiced by Western missionaries.

By the Fifth Assembly of the WCC, held in Nairobi in 1975, debates over churches' participation in development had become a primary agenda item of the World Council of Churches. The Assembly reaffirmed the Uppsala position that its constituent members continue to be involved in the struggle for liberation and development throughout the world. The official report on human development of the Nairobi Assembly noted in part:

The churches' involvement in struggles for liberation and development will vary in nature according to the local context. In some cases, the churches' role will be one of leadership. In others, it may involve joining hands in cooperation with secular forces. In yet other situations the churches may not have a struggling but a serving role to play. But in no cases should they retreat into the comfort of socially uninvolved "other-worldliness."[30]

Consonant with the rising emphasis on development as mission was a belief that the presence of Western missionaries thwarted the raising up of indigenous leadership in the younger churches. Church councils in the southern hemisphere, especially the All Africa Council of Churches led by Canon Burgess Carr, called for a moratorium on the sending of missionaries.[31] Responding to the missionary moratorium, leadership in mainline Protestant churches in the United States increasingly questioned the role of missionaries in the post-colonial era. What resulted from these discussions was both a change in the nature of missionary work as well as a decline in the number of missionaries sent overseas by American conciliar Protestant churches. No longer were missionaries sent to an overseas post for thirty or forty years in the same ministry. Instead missionaries, sometimes referred to as mission partners, were posted to a specific position for a short time (two to three years). Over time the role of the missionary changed from that of a lifetime evangelist to a short-term development specialist with specific skills requested by the indigenous church.

The numbers of missionaries supported by American conciliar Protestant churches reflect the changing nature of missionary appointments following Uppsala and Nairobi. In the two decades after World War II, the number of foreign missionaries sent by the twenty-six churches belonging to the National Council of Churches of Christ in the United States (NCC) averaged about 10,000.[32] In 1969, however, the NCC agencies began to show a decrease in the number of overseas missionaries. By 1985, the number of conciliar Protestant missionaries had dropped to 4,349, a 43.3% decrease. If the two largest missionary agencies in the NCC (the Seventh-Day Adventists and the Mennonite Central Committee) are not considered, the percentage of missionary decrease was 58.8%.

It is important to note, however, that the changing definition of mission and missionaries presented above pertains to the conciliar or mainline Protestant churches in the United States. The more conservative and evangelical Protestant mission agencies, those not related to either the NCC or the WCC, were not affected significantly by the questions over modern mission. Generally the churches that stressed mission as development were the more liberal Protestant churches while the conservative evangelical and fundamentalist churches continued to emphasize primary evangelism and church planting. Thus, while the number of missionaries decreased in conciliar Protestant churches during the last three decades, the number conservative evangelical missionaries grew significantly. In 1953 missionaries supported by unaffiliated, conservative evangelical mission boards numbered 3,565. Fifteen years later in 1968, that number had increased to 11,601, and, by 1985, they numbered 19,905; they were the largest group of

American Protestant missionaries, far surpassing their more liberal counterparts.[33]

Beginning in the early 1970s the focus of United States government assistance overseas also began to change. By the end of the second development decade, it became increasingly evident that the large-scale economic aid and national development projects of the 1960s had not been as successful as hoped. Under the "big push" and "trickle down" theories of development, the poor of the world seemed to be as bad off or, in some cases, worse off in terms of underemployment, income levels, infant mortality and nutrition.[34] It had become clear that the United States government needed a new policy or "new direction" in international development assistance.

In 1973, the United States Congress voted into law legislation in support of a basic human needs approach to development. By amendment to the U.S. Foreign Assistance Act, Congress outlined "New Directions" for the United States Agency for International Development, in which more help was to be directed to the poorest people in the poorest countries.[35] The "New Directions" amendment of 1973, followed by additional legislation in 1975, forced USAID to reexamine and reevaluate its methods of operation. A shift from large-scale economic development to a more grass-roots approach was stressed. Under the "New Directions" program, USAID began to emphasize income distribution as well as national economic growth, the selection of labor-intensive "appropriate technologies" and other means of employment generation, the participation of low-income intended beneficiaries in decision making, and the need to adapt programs to the local ecological, social, and cultural conditions.[36]

As USAID targeted more programs to meet the needs of rural villagers and the "poorest of the poor," the agency increased collaboration with other grass-roots-oriented organizations. In 1978, joint directives from the heads of both USAID and the U.S. Peace Corps acknowledged a common interest and concern in responding to basic human needs in such areas as rural development and health and education, and called for a more systematic effort at collaboration. By 1985, USAID and the Peace Corps were working together in thirty countries, involving some 110 projects and 995 "volunteer years."[37]

The collaboration of USAID with colleague agencies begun under the New Directions Act was not limited to the Peace Corps. In the late 1970s, legislation was enacted to require USAID to channel no less than 12%, and preferably 16%, of its development resources through Private Voluntary Organizations (PVOs) working in development. It was estimated that in 1983 over 900 Private Voluntary Organizations were involved in international development with reported receipts of over $1 billion in private contributions. Of these 900 PVOs, approximately 170 were registered with USAID. The Office of Private and Voluntary Cooperation (PVC) in USAID's Bureau for Food for Peace and Voluntary Assistance coordinated the agency's work with PVOs. From 1972 until 1984, USAID's cash financial support for PVO programs expanded from $35 million to over $250 million annually. In addition, in 1983, USAID-administered Food for Peace commodities and ocean freight reimbursement represented an additional $340 million in support for PVO programs. This expansion in support of PVO initiatives reflected USAID's increasing cooperation with Private Voluntary Organizations.[38]

Religiously based agencies constituted approximately one quarter of the 170 United States Private Voluntary Organizations registered with the Office of Private and Voluntary Cooperation of USAID. Increasingly USAID realized that churches represented a wide network of private individuals living and working abroad in development. As conciliar mission methods changed to embrace development, the possibility for cooperation between churches and USAID increased. Addressing a conference on the role of the Episcopal Church in global development, Thomas A. McKay, Director of the Office of Private and Voluntary Cooperation of USAID, emphasized the opportunities presented by religiously based institutions working in international development.

> The Episcopal Church is among a small group of organizations who can successfully work both sides of the development issue. Your network extends throughout the developed nations, where we need to increase understanding of development issues, and throughout the developing nations, where

manpower is needed to undertake the development projects. It is an extremely vast but underutilized resource. The personal one-on-one relationship established between individuals of different nations, working together to improve the quality of life in a developing country and reflecting the genuine compassion of people for people, is a tremendously powerful tool in working to address development needs of the Third World.[39]

Cooperation in development projects between churches and the United States government and a concomitant decrease in the numbers of missionaries characterized the post-Uppsala response of American conciliar Protestants to the new world.

EPISCOPAL FOREIGN MISSION IN THE POST-COLONIAL ERA

In the post-colonial world of the 1960s to the 1980s, the national church ideal was challenged at home and overseas. Unrest in the inner cities and on college campuses across the United States caused a reevaluation of the domestic mission of the Episcopal Church. "Mutual Responsibility and Interdependence" challenged the Episcopal Church to rethink its foreign mission agenda. The watchword "good schools, good hospitals and right-ordered worship" seemed to be anachronistic to the changing times. The turmoil at home and around the world caused a crisis for the national church ideal and a redefinition of the mission of the Episcopal Church in the new world.

MRI: New Wine in Old Wine Skins

Stephen Bayne and MRI had posed a new vision of mission for the Anglican Communion. Ingrained habits and century-old missionary methods, however, were not easy to change. The new wine of mutual responsibility and interdependence was put in the old wine skins of traditional missionary methods where the richer, older churches continued to support the financially strapped, younger churches in one-way transfers of personnel and money. The Episcopal Church, especially, was unwilling to change its missionary methods as long as the national church ideal remained intact.

At first many American Episcopalians applauded the commitment to mutuality envisioned by MRI. The Toronto Anglican Congress was recognized as charting a new course for the foreign mission work of the Episcopal Church and MRI was seen as an important mission manifesto for the post-colonial era.[40] After returning from Toronto, Presiding Bishop Arthur Lichtenberger called together a select committee of bishops, priests and lay people to consider how the Episcopal Church USA could respond to MRI. Well known, highly visible Episcopalians such as Supreme Court Justice Thurgood Marshall and "Father Knows Best" actor Robert Young were appointed to the new Presiding Bishop's Committee on Mutual Responsibility. In addition, Stephen Bayne, who had recently left his position as executive officer of the Anglican Communion to replace Bishop Bentley as director of the Overseas Department of the national church as well as vice-president of the Executive Council, was a member of the "MRI Committee" and played a significant leadership role.[41]

The MRI Committee began its work during a time of organizational transition at the national church. In 1962 the staff of the National Council moved into a new multi-million-dollar church center located at 815 Second Avenue in mid-town Manhattan. The old Church Missions House at 281 Park Avenue South could no longer house the increased staff of the National Council. It was decided in 1960 that a new modern national church center was needed.[42] Two years later "815" replaced "281" as the icon of the national church. Increasingly the leadership of Presiding Bishop Arthur Lichtenberger was hampered by his failing health. Lichtenberger had been elected by the 1958 General Convention to follow Henry Knox Sherrill. Presiding Bishop Lichtenberger was known for his quiet, prayerful and reflective style. As a leader, however, he was more prophetic than any of his predecessors. Lichtenberger was profoundly concerned with relating the Gospel to the issues of justice and freedom that were beginning to emerge in the United States.[43] Parkinson's disease, however, forced Lichtenberger to step down from his office following the 1964 General Convention.

In addition to these changes in location and leadership, the National Council itself was experiencing transition. In 1963 there was a movement to change the name of the National Council to the Executive Council. Ostensibly the reason for the change was to differentiate the name of the governing body of the Episcopal Church from that of the National Council of Churches of Christ in the United States (NCC/USA). Another rationale for the change, however, was that the work of the National Council was becoming more administrative than programmatic. The name Executive Council, and other suggestions such as Administrative Council, seemed to better represent the modern reality of the national leadership.[44] Thus at the 1964 General Convention in St. Louis, the name was changed to Executive Council and a new Presiding Bishop was elected, the Right Rev. John E. Hines.

At the same convention the MRI Committee made its first report. The report began by affirming the principles of the Toronto document. It called on the Episcopal Church to begin a self-study as to the church's participation in mutual responsibility and interdependence. To coordinate this study the MRI Committee proposed that a Mutual Responsibility Commission be established, replacing the Strategic Advisory Committee that had been set up following the Gray Report. The bulk of the report of the MRI Committee, however, focused on financial matters. For American Episcopalians interpreted their role in MRI as that of donor to financially strapped mission projects around the world.

> Mutual Responsibility is, in part, a call for money from the members of this Church, for a very simple reason; because we have money — more money, perhaps than is good for us, while others are in desperate need; and because God requires us to be stewards of the resources he has given us.[45]

The Committee report thus called for a graduated schedule of contributions to MRI-inspired projects totaling $6 million in the years 1965 to 1967. Dioceses were encouraged to give directly to mission projects.

> The goal is the establishment of truly Church to Church, person to person relationships across the world. We feel that the best way to achieve this kind of responsible relationship is by encouraging, to the maximum possible

degree, the adoption of specific projects by Provinces, Dioceses, and Parishes [of the Episcopal Church].[46]

The newly established Mutual Responsibility Commission was asked to disseminate information on project requests as well as to develop new possibilities for exchange between American Episcopalians and Anglicans around the world. The commission published many pamphlets and promotional materials to excite dioceses, parishes and individuals to become involved in MRI.[47]

Unfortunately many of the Episcopal Church's efforts at mutual responsibility and interdependence fell far short of the manifesto's hopes and dreams. The Right Rev. William Frey, Episcopal missionary in Central America and missionary bishop of Guatemala from 1967 to 1972, recalled the irony of one project. As an overseas missionary working in Guatemala, Frey and two other missionary appointees in Central America were sent to Hispanic congregations in New York and Florida to help them develop outreach programs to Puerto Ricans and Cubans living in the United States. Everyone failed to realize that this bold experiment in receiving from the "overseas church" was in fact a continuation of the one-way relationship where the "gringos" were the purveyors of the "goods."[48]

The one-way relationship where the richer churches in the West gave to the poorer churches in the Anglican Communion was unabashedly presented in a directory of projects published by the MRI Commission with the assistance of the Overseas Department of the Executive Council. The directory emphasized that by the fall of 1966 only $1 million of the $6 million proposed by the 1964 General Convention had been raised by the Episcopal Church for MRI initiatives. To encourage increased donations, the directory listed thirty-five projects to which Episcopalians could contribute. Every project was located in an Anglican church found in Africa, the Middle East, Asia or the South Pacific.[49] The directory's title, *Our Immediate Responsibility*, reflected the Episcopal Church's presumption that its role in MRI was to provide funds to struggling churches in the Anglican Communion. The directory became little more than a shopping list by which the younger Anglican churches petitioned the Episcopal Church in the United States for financial assistance. It did little to break down the stereotypes of givers and receivers. Instead, the directory contributed to the divisions between the "haves" and the "have-nots" in the Anglican Communion. Thus the warning that MRI would be interpreted as simply a new process for the exchange of personnel and money from rich to poor Anglican churches, as cautioned in Douglas Webster's publication *Mutual Irresponsibility: A Danger to be Avoided*, had come to pass.[50]

In addition to maintaining a one-way exchange of resources from the United States to poorer Anglican churches, MRI resulted in an unprecedented increase in the number of American Episcopal missionaries sent to the historic mission fields of the Church of England. Under the MRI rubrics of mutuality and open sharing, the sending of American missionaries was no longer restricted to the historic missionary districts of the Episcopal Church. For example, in 1959 the Episcopal Church supported 230 missionary appointees in twenty-two jurisdictions, seventeen of which were American missionary districts. By 1967 the number of appointees had increased to 259 spread over forty jurisdictions, only eighteen of which were attached to the Episcopal Church. In the five years following MRI, Episcopal missionaries were sent, for the first time ever, to the dioceses or Church of England missionary districts of Argentina, Central Africa, Damaraland, Dar-es-Salaam, Ecuador, Iran, Jesselton, Korea, Malawi, Masasi, Maseno, Nairobi, Natal, New Guinea, Niger Delta, Polynesia, Portugal, Zambia and Zululand.[51] The dramatic increase of missionary appointments in overseas jurisdictions that were not historic missionary districts of the Episcopal Church demonstrated the growing presence of Americans in what were mission fields of the Church of England. It can be argued that with regard to the overseas mission work of the Episcopal Church "Mutual Responsibility and Interdependence in the Body of Christ" had backfired. Rather than encouraging mutuality, MRI had resulted in an increase of American Episcopal missionaries and money throughout the Anglican Communion.

Crisis for the National Church Ideal

While the foreign mission work of the Episcopal Church saw an increase immediately following the Anglican Congress of 1963 these gains were to be short lived. By the mid-1960s the Episcopal Church, like all mainline churches in the United States, could no longer continue with a "business as usual" mentality. The racial strife in our country, especially the violence and destruction of the summer of 1967, needed to be addressed.

At the 1967 General Convention in Seattle, Presiding Bishop John Hines called on the Episcopal Church to reorient its priorities in order to address the turmoil in the United States. Hines's election as Presiding Bishop three years earlier was seen as an affirmation of the socially prophetic stance of his predecessor Lichtenberger. For nineteen years Hines had served as both coadjutor and diocesan bishop of the diocese of Texas. In Texas he had taken on segregation and racism with courageous and often controversial stands.[52] Hines carried his commitment to the social engagement of the church to his position as Presiding Bishop; in the wake of the urban riots of 1967, Hines toured the inner city in Brooklyn and Detroit.[53] He believed strongly that the Episcopal Church needed to respond to the crisis in America. In his opening address to the 1967 General Convention, Hines charted a new course for the program of the national church.

> As at least the beginning of this Church's response to the deep human need dramatized by the conflict in the cities I am recommending the development of a program, to be extended over the next triennium, by which this Church can take its place, humbly and boldly, alongside of, and in support of, the dispossessed and oppressed peoples of this country for the healing of our national life. Among its aims will be the bringing of peoples in the ghettos into areas of decision-making by which their destiny is influenced. It will encourage the use of political and economic power to support justice and self-determination for all men. It will make available skilled personnel assistance, and request the appropriation of substantial sums of money to community organizations involved in the betterment of depressed urban areas, and under the control of those who are largely black and poor, that their power for self-determination may be increased and their dignity restored. It is suggested that these efforts be administered through coalitions with other Churches and agencies such as the Inter-Religious Foundation for Community Organization, that we may be joined with and by other groups in similar efforts directed toward the same goals.

> I am requesting the funding of such a program in the amount of approximately $3 million annually; such funds to be secured from various sources, principally from the General Church Program.
>
> Finally, a reordering of primary emphases and priority-ratings in the proposed General Church Program will be required, in order to support the programmatic response outlined here.[54]

The General Convention responded by initiating the General Convention Special Program (GCSP) giving it top priority for the church's use of personnel, time and money for the years 1968 to 1970. The women of the church, who had gathered in Seattle for their triennial meeting and had heard the Presiding Bishop's call, were the first to respond by granting 46% ($2,265,917) of their United Thank Offering to GCSP.[55]

Support for the new program proposed by Hines, however, was not unanimous. J. L. Caldwell McFadden, a deputy from Hines's old diocese of Texas and a member of the Program and Budget Committee of the General Convention, objected to the new initiative in a minority report.[56] He saw the GCSP as subverting the established program of the national church.

> The suggested program, for the first time that we know of, requests this Convention to approve large grants to non-Church-related agencies for the expressed purpose of enabling Black People, under their sole control, with no strings attached, to achieve economic and political power. This we cannot endorse; because first, we consider it a wrongful use of our funds; and second, it seriously endangers the remainder of our whole missionary program.
>
> To this we cannot agree. Our offerings, made on the altars to God, should not be diverted to achieve economic and political power for any group, White or Black. This is a most divisive proposal and most dangerous. It will alienate thousands of members of our Church, and we fear, seriously endanger our [national church] program.[57]

McFadden's words, although dissenting from the opinion and program proposed by Hines, were also prophetic. He correctly foresaw that the General Convention Special Program was in conflict with and threatened the national church ideal.

In practice the General Convention Special Program attempted to reorient the national church program and budget in support of the poor and oppressed in the United States. The underlying philosophy that guided the work of the General Convention

Special Program was: sizable sums of money would be given directly to the people's own local community organizations, and the money would be given for them to spend on plans and priorities that they, themselves, had set. In its commitment to providing large sums of money to financially strapped organizations GCSP was not wholly dissimilar to what MRI and the directory of projects had advocated for Anglican churches overseas[58]

The implementation of the General Convention Special Program represented a break with the established program of the national church. Instead of the National Council purveying "good schools, good hospitals and right-ordered worship" in a top-down model, the GCSP sought to enable development from the grassroots up. New administrators were brought into the Episcopal Church Center to oversee the granting procedures of the GCSP. Older church officials, who had been nurtured by the national church ideal, found their work unsupported by the new regime.

> Not only were major staff personalities edged, pushed, and shunted aside; their secretaries and minor staff people were also fired or forced to resign for fear that they would have some lingering loyalty to their former bosses. Within a very short time the church headquarters had no collective memory of what had gone on before. A desperate siege mentality affected the entire building and an unarticulated fear of the GCSP infected the working relationships of the church.[59]

Under the GCSP all previous funding commitments, especially the overseas work of the Episcopal Church, were called into question. In the 1967 annual report of the Executive Council, Bishop Hines conceded that the new program did put pressure on some of the long-standing programs of the national church.

> Such a special program for the urban crisis as adopted by the General Convention, while not discounting the thrust of other missionary and educational programs, did place them under some restraint dollar-wise.[60]

The effect of GCSP on the national church and its programs did not go unnoticed. Two years into GCSP, the Episcopal Church called for a Special General Convention to consider the future direction of the General Convention Special Program.

The Special General Convention was held at the University of Notre Dame in South Bend, Indiana, from August 31 to September

5, 1969. In its report to the convention, the Executive Council noted that exactly half a century earlier the National Council had been created. It cautioned, however, that the national church structure put in place in 1919 might have lost its efficacy in the new world.

> A word must then be spoken, of sober appraisal of the very great and unprecedented pressures now bearing on the Executive Council, as on every national voluntary agency. The pressures are born in the nature of the social and political crisis through which the nation is passing. Whether any fragile, voluntary, national structure, ecclesiastical or otherwise, can bear such weight is yet to be proved. Certainly, no report of the Executive Council could be written which does not begin by thoughtfully recognizing the possibility that the Church, in this representative national embodiment of its life cannot carry the strains our history puts on us.[61]

Whereas the Executive Council alluded to the fact that the Episcopal Church's national church ideal was in jeopardy, the reality that this was so became clearly evident when two African-American Episcopalians from Pennsylvania, the Rev. Paul Washington and Muhammed Kenyatta, seized the microphone in the House of Deputies at the Special General Convention. After a heated exchange between Presiding Bishop Hines and Kenyatta, the black leader demanded that the Episcopal Church contribute $200,000 to the Black Economic Development Conference as a response to the "Black Manifesto" drawn up by African-American church leaders.[62] The General Convention eventually acceded to Kenyatta's demands.

GCSP and the South Bend decision to support the Black Economic Development Conference were seen by many as a misappropriation of the national church's calling and money. Increasingly dioceses and individuals criticized the programs and decisions of the Executive Council and its staff. Upset by GCSP's grants to groups that had supported or practiced violence, dioceses began to hold back their money from the national church. Hines tried to address this loss of confidence and revenue in his 1969 Annual Report of the Executive Council. He noted that dramatic changes were occurring in the Episcopal Church. Groups that had previously been excluded from the decision making processes in the Episcopal Church were now finding their voice.

The year 1969 marked the end of one decade and the beginning of another. It was a year of transition in which the Episcopal Church began moving out of old ways into ways more in keeping with the needs of the 70's.

South Bend saw the test of an official church meeting in which minorities, young people and women were given a voice in setting program priorities. It sought to respond to the cries of our own black churchmen for trust and help, and it voted assistance for our Indian brothers. It asked for a strengthening of the General Convention Special Program and endorsed broader representation of the church's membership for the 1970 General Convention at Houston, including particularly minorities and young people.

It also was a year of conflict and controversy, much of it directed toward the General Convention Special Program and reflecting some of the reaction expected when the church embarks on new bold ventures on the frontier of Christian mission.[63]

The annual report, however, could not hide the fact that these changes had taken a toll on the program and budget of the Executive Council. Hines wrote of the dwindling support from the dioceses for the national church.

It was a year of financial difficulties, in which conflict and controversy was one factor. Another direct influence on declining revenue has been inflation, and another has been the pressure of local needs in the dioceses and parishes where financial pressures have been critical.

The outlook for 1970 is even more sobering. Forty-seven dioceses are pledging less than their quotas. The 1970 budget will come to $13,065,032, nearly 8 percent less than the 1969 total of $14,171,000 and more than 17 percent under the level approved by General Convention. To balance the budget, the Executive Council has taken an unprecedented step in committing itself to try and raise $500,000 in extra support for 1970 to offset dipping into reserves.

These cutbacks mean a time of retrenchment for the Episcopal Church, a re-examination of priorities and reductions in staff and program. The staff at the Episcopal Church Center has been cut by 20 percent. Hardest hit have been programs for lay education, campus ministries, and ministries to the deaf and blind. Overseas work has been cut, as well as support to the World Council of Churches and the National Council of Churches.[64]

Long gone were the triumphant annual reports of the National Council written during the height of the national church ideal. The National/Executive Council was now on shaky ground and its foundation, the national church ideal, was crumbling.

The program and budget of the national church continued to lose support as more and more individuals and dioceses became increasingly disgruntled with GCSP. Dr. Clifford Morehouse, president of the House of Deputies, spoke forcefully about the controversial grants of GCSP at the 1970 General Convention.

First, they have antagonized thousands of church people, many of whom have retaliated in the only way they know — by cutting pledges to the national church. Second they have escalated a sizable credibility gap between the Presiding Bishop and the Executive Council, on the one hand, and the dioceses, parishes, and individual church members on the other hand. Third, they have placed the future of GCSP itself in serious jeopardy, because if the funds for support of the church's program are further reduced, neither GCSP nor other important aspects of [the national church] program can long survive.[65]

Funding continued to decline as conservatives and progressives alike became increasingly disillusioned with the national church and the GCSP program. From 1969 to 1971 the budget for the support of the Executive Council program dropped by more than $2.25 million from $14,015,769 to $11,745,559. Faced with a severe shortage of funds, the Episcopal Church Center abruptly cut its staff from 204 persons to 110 in December 1970. The days of glory for the national church and its program were over forever.

The seizing of power by previously disenfranchised groups in the Episcopal Church and in the United States at large, especially African-Americans and women, had resulted in a crisis for the national church ideal.

The civil rights movement of the 1950's and 1960's, the political organization of minority and special interest groups, the development of sub-cultures that repudiated the standards and values of the dominant white Anglo-Saxon culture caused strain and fractures in American Society and placed in jeopardy the Episcopal Church's establishmentarian program.[66]

The self-perceived role of the Episcopal Church as a corporate body responsible for social regeneration through Christian moral truths and American democracy at home and abroad could no longer be maintained. Criticized from within and without, the national church ideal was lost as the motivating and unifying force in the Episcopal Church's mission in the United States and overseas. The national church ideal died at the hands of the political and social revolutionaries in the United States and around the world.

Missionary Losses

The financial crisis for the national church brought on by the General Convention Special Program had a profound effect on the mission work of the Episcopal Church. Offices and programs at the Episcopal Church Center were reorganized when staff was cut by 50% overnight. The Overseas Division responsible for the care and nurture of missionaries was subsumed under the new Office for Jurisdictional Relations. The General Division of Women's Work was closed, marking the end of the missionary legacy of the Woman's Auxiliary. The number of missionaries appointed by the Executive Council dropped precipitously as budgets were slashed. After 1970 the Executive Council no longer published an annual report celebrating the work of the national church.[67]

The overseas work of the Episcopal Church was hardest hit during the budget crisis of 1970 to 1971. Of the $2,270,210 decrease from the 1969 to the 1971 Executive Council Budgets, $1,074,648, or 47%, came out of what had been known as the Overseas Department.[68] The line item that was most vulnerable in the Overseas Department was support for appointed missionaries. Missionaries were in a precarious position for a variety of reasons. First, missionaries were expensive. The increase in salaries, pensions and field costs continually added pressure on the resources of the National/Executive Council. Related to this was the fact that missionaries did not have a natural constituency in the United States who were willing to fight for their appropriations. Since the advent of the National Council in 1919, all support for missionaries of the Episcopal Church came out of the budget of the national church. A large gulf had developed between the person in the pew who contributed a weekly pledge and the foreign missionary who was supported by a portion of that contribution. As a result, the missionary, who as an appointee of the National Council was everyone's responsibility, had become the subject of no one's interest.[69] Finally the missionary moratorium movement allowed church administrators to cut back on missionary appointments with the justification that they were responding to the wishes of overseas church leaders. The cumulative effect of these pressures on missionary appointments resulted in a 54% reduction in the number of Episcopal foreign missionaries from 263 in 1968 to 121 in 1971.[70] The number of appointed missionaries continued to drop even after 1971. Missionaries who were nearing retirement age were offered early retirement and support for missionaries who remained in the field was increasingly shared by their host churches. This downward spiral continued until the mid-1970s when the number of foreign missionaries supported by the Executive Council leveled out at approximately seventy. Thus, in five years, the number of foreign missionaries had been slashed by 70% from over 250 to under seventy. The number of individuals supported by the Episcopal Church as full missionary appointees would never again exceed 100.[71]

The budget cuts of 1970 and 1971 also affected the Volunteers for Mission program. In 1962 the Rev. Donald Bitsberger, a member of the Overseas Personnel Office at the National Council, began Volunteers for Mission as a church counterpart to the new Peace Corps begun under President Kennedy. The program provided for the appointment of volunteers to specific short-term assignments in overseas mission fields. By 1967 this program had grown to include twenty-one volunteers serving overseas as missionary personnel of the Episcopal Church. Like the other missionary programs of the Episcopal Church, the financial crisis of 1970 forced the suspension of the Volunteers for Mission program. The volunteer program had made a significant contribution in a short time and its loss was noted in a survey of the church's overseas mission work.

> Everywhere our visitors went they heard the same question: What happened to our Volunteers for Mission? This modified peace-corps type program has made a deep impression on many mission areas. It has caused some overseas leaders to wonder whether it might not be the best possible kind of missionary endeavor. It is tragic that our financial situation ended this program. Exploration of its possible expansion should be one of the continuing responsibilities of the Review Committee.[72]

Six years later, when the Executive Council was flush with resources from the Venture in Mission fund raising campaign initiated by Presiding Bishop John Allin and the 1976 General Convention, the Volunteers for Mission program was reinstated.[73]

Paul A. Tate, Deputy for Jurisdiction at the Episcopal Church Center in the early 1970s, apologetically summed up the missionary losses in a letter of February 1, 1972 to George W. Carpenter, Chairman of the Planning Committee of the Overseas Study Center:

> There are two notable reasons for the decrease [in missionaries]: 1) the budget crisis experienced by most churches; 2) the increase in the numbers of nationals who are able to take on the leadership roles formerly provided by missionaries.[74]

What Tate's communication did not mention, however, was that women missionaries had been cut at a higher level than their male counterparts. From 1940 to 1970 the number of women missionaries appointed by the Episcopal Church dropped from 137 to only 14. This decline was partly concealed by the inclusion of wives, for the first time, in the rosters of foreign missionaries during the 1960s. The position of missionary wife, however, was considered a second class appointment since "her status was derived from and dependent on that of her husband."[75]

The assumption that "nationals" were taking on leadership roles formerly filled by missionaries, alluded to by Tate, contributed to the loss of women missionaries. In the post-colonial era, the younger churches of the Anglican Communion began to assume responsibility for the work in schools and hospitals previously run, in good part, by women missionaries. This new self-reliance coupled with the nationalization of mission schools and hospitals by post-colonial governments resulted in a dramatic decline in the need for missionary educators and medical workers. For example, in 1935, 247 out of a total of 452 Episcopal foreign missionaries were serving as teachers, physicians, nurses, and administrators in church institutions.[76] Three decades later, in 1965 the total number of Episcopal foreign missionaries had dropped to 278 of which there were only 44 working directly in education and health care.[77] Since women had served overseas primarily as educators and medical workers, the decreased demand for teachers, nurses and doctors in the post-colonial era resulted in fewer women missionaries appointed by the Episcopal Church. The Rev. Leslie Fairfield, one of the last missionaries to serve in the China Mission of the Episcopal Church, recalls that the single greatest factor that led to the decline of women missionaries in China was the increasing responsibility for educational and medical work assumed by the Chinese. He says: "the more the Chinese took control of the schools and hospitals the fewer the opportunities were for American women."[78]

A second factor contributing to the loss of women missionaries in the post-colonial era was the increasing clericalization of missionary appointments. In keeping with partnership principles initiated by MRI, the sending of missionaries was no longer a one-way process controlled by church offices in New York and London. Missionaries were to be sent, instead, at the request of indigenous bishops from the emerging autonomous churches in the Anglican Communion. With few exceptions, bishops asked first for expatriate priests who could minister sacramentally in their severely understaffed dioceses. The priority on priestly ministries unwittingly resulted in a clericalization of the missionary appointments, thus adding to the decline in women missionaries, who were excluded from the ordained ministry at that time. Thus while overall missionary numbers dropped from 452 in 1935 to 278 in 1965 the number of clergy missionaries increased from 140 to 209 in the same time period.[79] In other words the percentage of foreign missionaries sponsored by the Episcopal Church who were male priests had risen from 31% in 1935 to 75% in 1965, all but eliminating the appointment of women missionaries, who were shut out from ordination.

A final factor that contributed to the decline of women Episcopal foreign missionaries was the incorporation of the Woman's Auxiliary into the National Council and its ultimate dissolution in 1970. As Episcopal churchwomen became increasingly integrated into the structures of the National Council the portfolio and *raison d'être* of the Woman's Auxiliary slowly slipped away. In the 1940s two important programs of the Auxiliary, the Supply Box Program and the United Thank Offering Missionary Worker, were abandoned. The demise of these two forms of outreach limited the connection between women in the United States and the church's work overseas.

The Supply Box, or Supply Work, program was one of the oldest projects of the Woman's Auxiliary. The goal of this program was to provide missionaries and mission stations with materials (especially clothing) that were unavailable in the foreign field. At the initial organization of the Woman's Auxiliary in 1871, earlier missionary supply efforts were centralized in the Office of the General Secretary. This "Box Work" was carried forward by the Auxiliary for over forty years and became a very valuable supplement to missionary support offered by the Board of Missions. When the Auxiliary was reorganized in 1919, the work was enlarged and a full-time supply secretary was added to the staff.[80] By the late 1930s, however, there was some question as to the best way to advance the Supply Box program. At the Triennial Meeting of 1940 the program was decentralized with local diocesan Woman's Auxiliaries becoming responsible for sending supplies to missionaries going out from their own dioceses. Three years later the Triennial Meeting of 1943 voted to eliminate the gift of personal clothing to active missionaries, believing that salary increases for overseas church workers, voted by the 1943 General Convention, eliminated the need for a clothing supplement.[81] As Episcopal mission work embraced large-scale ecumenical relief efforts in the post-war years, the efficacy of the Supply Box Program began to disappear. The material support to struggling missions and missionaries provided by the Supply Box Program was superseded in the 1940s by the Presiding Bishop's Fund for World Relief and the Reconstruction and Advance Fund. In 1962 the Home and Overseas Departments agreed that mission needs should be cared for strictly from within the National Council's budget and not by supplemental means. Five years later, at the 1967 Triennial meeting, the women of the Episcopal Church decided to terminate what was left of the Supply Box program.[82]

Just as the supply work of the Woman's Auxiliary became the responsibility of the departments of the National Council, financial support for women missionaries increasingly was assumed by the general budget of the national church. During the first three decades of the twentieth century, close to half of the women foreign missionaries of the Episcopal Church were supported as

United Thank Offering Workers.[83] In the late 1930s, however, the number of United Thank Offering Workers declined as the Woman's Auxiliary transferred responsibility for the support of active and retired women missionaries to the National Council. In 1940, the Triennial agreed that the income from the United Thank Offering Workers Pension Fund would no longer be reserved for retired UTO workers but would be added to the National Council pension fund for the support of all retired women missionaries.[84] Three years later the Triennial Meeting of 1943 dropped the distinction "UTO Worker" and the majority of the United Thank Offering was given directly to the National Council for support of women workers and missionary projects at home and overseas.[85] For the next two decades the major portion of the United Thank Offering would go directly into the budget of the National Council. While grants to the National Council budget seemed to represent the participation of Episcopal churchwomen in the total program of the national church, it separated women from the particularity of supporting women missionaries and their direct participation in mission projects. As a result, the distinct women's voice in mission work of the Episcopal Church was increasingly lost in the larger bureaucratic machine of the National Council.

The loss of women's mission activities like the Supply Box and United Thank Offering Worker raised the old question of the need for a separate women's mission organization in the Episcopal Church. At the 1955 Triennial Meeting a resolution was presented proposing that the name "Woman's Auxiliary to the National Council," be replaced with "the Women of the Protestant Episcopal Church."[86] The proposed name change was not simply semantic for it implied the dissolution of the Woman's Auxiliary as a semi-autonomous organization within the Episcopal Church. The resolution was not adopted, but the Triennial authorized the Executive Board of the Auxiliary to look into the relationship between the women of the Episcopal Church and the National Council.

Six months before the next Triennial, the National Council, meeting in April 1958, reorganized the Executive Board of the Auxiliary as the new General Division of Women's Work and transferred the majority of the portfolios of the Woman's Auxiliary staff to the related departments of the National Council.[87] The General Division of Woman's Work would continue to facilitate the ministries of Episcopal churchwomen, although at a much smaller level than that of the Woman's Auxiliary, until 1970 when the financial crisis brought about the restructuring of the Executive Council. Under this new structure, the General Division of Woman's Work was eliminated. There was no longer an organization or department at the national level representing and coordinating the educational, social service and mission work of Episcopal churchwomen. The unique and direct involvement of women in the missionary outreach of the Episcopal Church that was embodied in the Woman's Auxiliary had become history.

Redefinition of the Ideal: Partnership in Mission

The cutbacks in missionary support in the 1970s were supported by, or justified by, a redefinition of mission priorities for the Episcopal Church. Whereas under the national church ideal the watchword for Episcopal mission work was "good schools, good hospitals and right-ordered worship," the latest watchword for the new world became "partnership in mission."

The new emphasis on partnership grew out of ongoing conversations in the wider Anglican Communion. The 1968 Lambeth Conference was a forum to review and evaluate MRI initiatives undertaken during the five years since Toronto. The conference acknowledged that many of the hopes and dreams of MRI had been unfulfilled. The bishops recognized that "the time has come for a reappraisal of the policies, methods, and areas of responsibility of the Anglican Communion in discharging its share of the mission of Christ."[88] They thus called for a new, more integrated strategy for coordinating the common mission of the Anglican Communion.

> The growing together of Christians has brought the Churches of the Anglican Communion to a new stage in their relations with one another and with other Churches and organizations. We appreciate the work hitherto done by the Lambeth Consultative Body, by the Advisory Council on Missionary Strategy,

and, more recently, by the office of the Anglican Executive Officer and his advisory committee; but we believe that a more integrated pattern is now necessary, in which, as "members severally one of another," Anglicans may fulfill
their common inter-Anglican and ecumenical responsibilities in promoting
the unity, renewal, and mission of Christ's Church.[89]

In response to this concern, Lambeth 1968 proposed that the
Lambeth Consultative Body and the Advisory Council on Missionary
Strategy be brought together into one unified body. This new body
would be called: The Anglican Consultative Council (ACC). The
functions of the ACC were clearly stated in the Lambeth Report.

1. To share information about developments in one or more
Provinces with the other parts of the Communion and to
serve as needed as an instrument of common action.

2. To advise on inter-Anglican, Provincial and diocesan relationships, including the division of Provinces, the formation
of new Provinces and of regional councils, and the problems
of extra-Provincial dioceses.

3. To develop as far as possible agreed Anglican policies in the
world mission of the church and to encourage national and
regional churches to engage together in developing and implementing such policies by sharing their resources of manpower, money, and experience to the best advantage of all.

4. To keep before national and regional churches the importance of the fullest possible Anglican collaboration with
other Christian churches.

5. To encourage and guide Anglican participation in the
Ecumenical Movement and the ecumenical organizations; to
co-operate with the World Council of Churches and the
world confessional bodies on behalf of the Anglican
Communion; and to make arrangements for the conduct of
pan-Anglican conversations with the Roman Catholic Church,
the Orthodox churches, and other churches.

6. To advise on matters arising out of national or regional
church union negotiations or conversations and on subsequent
relations with united churches.

7. To advise on problems of inter-Anglican communication and to help in the dissemination of Anglican and ecumenical information.

8. To keep in review the needs that may arise for further study and, where necessary, to promote inquiry and research.[90]

Lambeth 1968 thus designed a set of programmatic policies and procedures that would serve the Anglican Council to the present day. Lay people, presbyters and bishops from each of the churches in the Anglican Communion would meet as the Council every two years in different churches throughout the Anglican Communion. The number of representatives from each church would vary depending on the size of the church, but no church would have more than three representatives. The Archbishop of Canterbury would serve as the president of the ACC. In addition the ACC would elect its own chair and vice chair and appoint a secretary general to oversee its ongoing operations.

At the first meeting of the ACC the post of executive officer of the Anglican Communion, begun by Stephen Bayne and followed by the Right Rev. Ralph Dean of Canada and Right Rev. John Howe, bishop of St. Andrews, Dunkeld and Dunbane, was terminated. Howe was then reappointed by the Anglican Consultative Council as its first secretary general. He served in this position until 1982 when the Rev. Canon Samuel Van Culin, Director of the Overseas Department for the Executive Council in the Episcopal Church USA, assumed the position. The ACC was thus the only body in the Anglican Communion with a permanent secretariat continuously in existence with an income derived from all the churches in the Anglican Communion.[91] The Anglican Consultative Council has stood as a symbol of the continuity and interrelatedness of the Anglican Communion for the last two decades.

The first Anglican Consultative Council meeting (ACC 1) was held in Limuru, Kenya, from February 23 to March 5, 1971. Fifty-one church people from around the Anglican Communion, composed almost equally of lay people, priests and bishops, came together to discuss common issues as one body. "Throughout the meeting the Council lived together as a community at Limuru.

Not in London or New York, but in the Kenya countryside. Neither North nor South, but virtually on the equator. Not as senders or receivers, but as representatives of equal partner Churches in the Body of Christ."[92] The agenda for the meeting was compiled from 1968 Lambeth Conference Resolutions. The bulk of the items focused on unity and ecumenical affairs, church and society issues, renewal and organization in the Anglican Communion, and mission and evangelism. The historic importance of ACC 1 was not so much the resolutions passed, but rather the fact that Christians from all corners of the Anglican Communion had come together in a new consultative body as equal partners to pray together, to talk together, to work together, to worship together and to live together in a mature family of churches.

The second meeting of the Anglican Consultative Council (ACC 2) was held in Dublin, Ireland, from July 17–27, 1973. Whereas the Limuru meeting of the ACC was occupied with the niceties of a new consultative body meeting for the first time, the second meeting was much more substantive. At ACC 2 the council spent a significant amount of time reviewing the progress and problems of "Mutual Responsibility and Interdependence in the Body of Christ." It had been ten years since the original MRI document was adopted in Toronto; during the decade four new provinces had been created in the Anglican Communion. In 1965 the Episcopal Church of Brazil became autonomous from the Episcopal Church in the United States and in 1970 the three provinces of Kenya, Tanzania and Burma became independent Anglican churches. Other missionary districts were on their way to autonomy and within four years Anglican churches would be formed in the Indian Ocean (1973), Melanesia (1975), Sudan (1976), Jerusalem and the Middle East (1976) and Papua New Guinea (1977).[93]

ACC 2 emphasized the unity in mission that was the foundation of the original "Mutual Responsibility and Interdependence in the Body of Christ." The Anglican Consultative Council recognized, however, that true mutuality and interdependence had not yet been realized and that efforts such as the directory of projects, although well-intended, had not fostered equality in the Anglican

Communion. As a result, a new approach to sharing of mission had to be embraced. The council proposed to the Anglican Communion a new implementation of MRI entitled "Partners In Mission" (PIM). "Partners In Mission" reiterated the universality of God's mission throughout the world but emphasized that the primary responsibility for mission in any one place belongs to the local, indigenous church. In a now famous quote ACC 2 stated that:

> the emergence everywhere of autonomous churches in independent nations has challenged our inherited idea of mission as a movement from "Christendom" in the West to the "non-Christian" world. In its place has come the conviction that there is but one mission in the world, and that this one mission is shared by the world-wide Christian community. The responsibility for mission in any place belongs primarily to the church in that place. However, the universality of the gospel and the oneness of God's mission mean also that this mission must be shared in each and every place with fellow-Christians from each and every part of the world with their distinctive insights and contributions. If we once acted as though there were givers who had nothing to receive and receivers who had nothing to give, the oneness of the missionary task must make us all givers and receivers.[94]

Partners In Mission was proposed as a new planning and consultation process that would foster mutuality and interdependence in the Anglican Communion. The "PIM Process" was designed to involve three stages. First, each diocese in the Anglican Communion had to establish its own priorities and objectives for mission. Second, the diocesan priorities were gathered together into one national or provincial plan. Third, this plan was shared with partner churches in the Anglican Communion in a larger "PIM Consultation." ACC 2 emphasized that the PIM consultation must embrace the partnership ethic. It

> should at all times preserve the proper freedom of choice of these partners in mission and also maintain the integrity of the church in each place. The partnership of giving and receiving must also help and not hinder the process by which each church secures its own identity and integrity.[95]

It was hoped that this new consultation and planning process would avoid the money- and project-centered approach of the earlier MRI. The focus of Partners In Mission was to be on the person-to-person interactions between all churches in the Anglican

Communion. The mutuality involved in the joint consultation was to enable churches better to appreciate one another's needs and opportunities as well as one another's responsibilities in relation to the resources entrusted to them. Partners In Mission was thus designed to break down bilateral relations between two churches that resulted in a giving and receiving mentality. In its place would be a consultation of peers working together in a mutual planning process that would foster new opportunities for open sharing and interdependence among the churches in the Anglican Communion.

In the decade following the Dublin meeting of the ACC, PIM consultations were held in the majority of churches in the Anglican Communion. In 1977 the Episcopal Church in the United States hosted its own Partners In Mission consultation. By that time sixteen other churches in the Anglican Communion had held PIM consultations.[96] Desiring to show their new-found commitment to mutuality in mission planning, American Episcopalians took seriously the planning of their own PIM consultation. Priority was given to person-to-person exchanges between Americans and other members of the Anglican Communion. The planners hoped that such interpersonal contact would break down barriers and contribute to new levels of partnership. The planning team emphasized:

> Many assumptions and presuppositions surrounding "giving and receiving" churches, traditional missionary loyalties, autonomy, and other factors present formidable hazards which must be dealt with if the consultation is to be mutually productive for our partners and for the participants of the Episcopal Church. Hence, we have tried to think of events and processes which would have a high potential of interpersonal contact and exchange.[97]

To facilitate these exchanges "mini-PIM consultations" were planned for each of the nine provinces of the Episcopal Church. The learnings from these provincial meetings would then be brought together in one large national PIM consultation.

The "mini-PIMs" held in each of the nine provinces of the Episcopal Church took place from April 19–23, 1977. Six to eight partners from Anglican churches around the world met with diocesan representatives in each province. Following the format established by the Anglican Consultative Council in Dublin, the provincial consultations drew up reports that summarized the resources and needs for mission engagement. These reports were passed on to the national PIM consultation held in Louisville, Kentucky, from April 27–30. Here the provincial representatives and the forty-five Anglican partners met with Presiding Bishop John Allin (who had succeeded Hines in June 1975) and the Executive Council. Common issues raised in each of the nine provincial meetings were passed on to the Executive Council for its consideration. These included a recognition that urban problems were a concern for the whole church, the need to emphasize and support the universality of ministry of all baptized persons, the need for increased ecumenical cooperation at all levels of church life, the need for increased stewardship including the stewardship of environmental and energy resources, the need to break down pervasive attitudes of parochialism and the need for a new commitment to evangelism.[98] The partners, in particular, stressed that the Episcopal Church must rededicate itself to mission and evangelism both at home and around the world.

In hindsight, the American Partners In Mission consultation was a great event for all who participated, but one could argue that it had little effect on the day-to-day life of most Episcopalians in the United States. Many of the conclusions and recommendations of the PIM Consultation were subsumed under the Episcopal Church's Venture in Mission (VIM) campaign. Venture in Mission, the brainchild of Presiding Bishop Allin, was enacted by the 1976 General Convention as a church-wide renewal program; "a challenging opportunity for every Episcopalian to gain new insights and to make a new commitment to the mission of this church, within the context of the Great Commission, 'Go ye.'"[99] Some, however, criticized Venture in Mission as nothing more than a fund-raising effort planned to divert attention from the issues of a new prayer book and the ordination of women that were tearing at the heart of the church at the time. The fact that the American Partners In Mission consultation took place at the same time as the initial stage of the Venture in Mission Program was considered coincidental. The common goals of both initiatives were affirmed.

The Agreed Statement [of the PIM Consultation] recognized the "need to relate *Venture* in Mission with the priorities identified during the *Partners* in Mission consultations," and the Executive Council agreed that "the planning and program activities of Partners In Mission and Venture in Mission be coordinated so as to emphasize the common renewal goals of these programs." (Italics in original)[100]

In the late 1970s and early 1980s Venture in Mission became a major initiative of the Presiding Bishop and Executive Council and by 1983 over $150 million had been raised for mission projects in the United States and overseas. Venture in Mission thus served as a kind of last-gasp effort to prop up the ailing national church. With the growth of VIM, however, PIM faded into memory.

The Anglican Consultative Council continued to meet regularly in Trinidad (1976), London, Ontario, Canada (1979), Newcastle upon Tyne, England (1981), and Badagry, Nigeria (1984). These meetings resembled other international gatherings of Christians with large agendas including: unity and ecumenical affairs, church and society issues, and mission and evangelism concerns. The particularity of the ACC meetings was that they were limited to Anglicans seeking to clarify their relationship to each other as well as to the wider world.

At the 1978 Lambeth Conference, the bishops of the Anglican Communion asked the Anglican Consultative Council to evaluate Partners In Mission.[101] A year later an initial study was presented to the fourth meeting of the ACC in London, Ontario. The report recognized that the variety of mission activities in the Anglican Communion were more complex and diverse than the PIM process could manage. The council thus requested the secretary general of the ACC to initiate a serious study and review of what mission means in the Anglican Communion.[102] To effect this study the next meeting of the Anglican Consultative Council in Newcastle upon Tyne established the Mission Issues and Strategy Advisory Group (MISAG). MISAG's task was to:

a. review mission issues and strategy;

b. identify exceptional needs and opportunities for mission and development which call for a Communion-wide response, and

c. find ways and means for collaboration with other Christian bodies in mission and evangelism.[103]

MISAG comprised an international group of Anglican church leaders and mission administrators. Meeting three times between 1982 and 1984, MISAG prepared an interim report in time for the sixth meeting of the ACC in Badagry, Nigeria, 1984. The report, entitled *Giving Mission Its Proper Place*, emphasized the missionary calling of the Anglican Communion. Theologically the MISAG report broke little new ground. It affirmed that the mission of the church is first and foremost God's mission. Borrowing a line from the catechism found in the new American prayer book, the MISAG report stated that God's mission is one of reconciliation.

> The mission of the Church is always God's mission and God's mission is to reconcile all people to Himself and to unite one another in and through Christ. It is God's purpose to unite all people in love for him and one another.[104]

The MISAG report recommended a recommitment to Partners In Mission and provided guidelines for the PIM process and PIM consultations. The MISAG report also acknowledged the need for greater ecumenical cooperation throughout the Anglican Communion. And finally, *Giving Mission Its Proper Place* raised questions about the relationship between mission and development. MISAG was not condemning the emergence of the churches' involvement in international development but rather sought to initiate a discussion about the theological assumptions that lay behind this work. ACC 6 thanked MISAG for its report and asked the group to continue its work.

In addition to the Lambeth Conference, the Anglican Consultative Council and its working group (MISAG), one additional forum had developed to foster partnership in the Anglican Communion — the Primates Meeting or Archbishop's Meeting. Although antecedent to the ACC, the Lambeth Consultative Body included a meeting of Anglican primates (archepiscopal representatives from each church in the Anglican Communion), the more formal meeting of archbishops grew out of the 1978 Lambeth Conference. At Lambeth 1978 the prime bishops from each Anglican church were called together as a council of advice for the Archbishop of Canterbury. The conference felt that this "Primates' Committee" should continue to meet on a biennial basis between Lambeth gatherings. The exact purpose of such meetings was not clear except to serve as another opportunity for inter-Anglican conversation and sharing and to continue as an advisory group for the Archbishop of Canterbury.[105] Some believe, however, that the real rationale for the Primates' Meeting was to serve as a foil for the ACC and its increasingly supportive stance on the ordination of women.[106] From 1978 through 1985 three meetings of the Primates were held in Ely, England (1979), Washington, D.C., USA (1981), and Nairobi, Kenya (1983).[107]

With the collapse of the national church ideal, the Episcopal Church in the United States was open to embrace Anglican partnership as its new missiological imperative. At the Special General Convention in South Bend, Indiana, in September 1969, the House of Bishops acknowledged that recent changes in both the United States and the world had had an important effect on the overall mission work of the Episcopal Church. They realized that the General Convention Special Program had raised serious theological and financial questions about the overseas work of the Episcopal Church. These questions were forced into the limelight when Ecuador petitioned the General Convention for a missionary bishop. To respond to these questions, the bishop of Massachusetts, the Right Rev. Anson Stokes, on behalf of the convention's Committee on Overseas Missions, moved the following resolution:

Whereas, the overseas mission of the Church is deeply influenced by new attitudes and by social, religious, and political movements, both at home and abroad, which influence the ways in which the injunction to preach the Gospel must be expressed today; and

Whereas, There has been a great emphasis on the re-examining of our mission and ministry, and the best use of our resources, at home; and much less emphasis on re-examining such matters in respect of our overseas responsibility; and

Whereas, The request for the election of a Bishop of Ecuador at this time not only confronts us with the need to rethink our whole overseas mission strategy, but more particularly offers us the opportunity to consider our responsibility to that particular country and our people there, so as to build rightly on the devoted work already done; now, therefore, be it

> *Resolved,* That a process of rethinking the overseas mission and ministry of the Church be instituted now by the Executive Council, and that such a report on its conclusions up to that time be submitted for consideration at Houston, 1970; and be it further
>
> *Resolved,* That the decision on the election of a Bishop for Ecuador be postponed at this time; and be it further
>
> *Resolved,* That the Presiding Bishop be requested to provide episcopal oversight for the members of this Church in Ecuador and for such other services as the Church can render to that country.[108]

Shortly after the Special General Convention, twenty-four people were asked by the deputy for Overseas Relations to serve as a planning committee to launch this investigation. The Overseas Review Committee, established by the planning group, would carry forward the process of rethinking the foreign mission work of the Episcopal Church.

The Overseas Review Committee was made up of twelve individuals from the United States and from elsewhere in the Anglican Communion. Men and women, lay people, priests and bishops were all represented. Included on the committee were academics Marion Kelleran, Joseph Kitagawa and Massey H. Shepherd, bishops John Burgess, Lyman Ogilby and Antonio Ramos as well as future bishop John Spong. The Overseas Review Committee was chaired by Marion Kelleran, Professor of Pastoral Theology and Christian Education at Virginia Theological Seminary. (Kelleran would later go on to chair the Anglican Consultative Council from 1976 to 1979.) The Overseas Review Committee was charged with reviewing and reinterpreting the missionary work of the Episcopal Church. The stated objective of the committee was to answer the single question: "How does this Church do Mission Overseas in a post-colonial age?"[109] The task before these individuals was truly overwhelming.

To begin with, the Overseas Review Committee established two working groups: the Task Group and the Strategy Group. The first group was made up of "non-North American [Episcopalians] who had themselves grown up in missionary Churches and understood the *ethos* of these Churches."[110] The task of this group was to interview lay people, clergy and bishops in the "overseas jurisdictions" of the Episcopal Church and thus provide primary data for the committee's review. The Strategy Group then took these reports and wove them into an extensive interim report presented to the House of Bishops at the Houston General Convention in September, 1970.

The "Interim Report to the Church, Made Through the House of Bishops" was radical in both its observations and recommendations. It began by lifting up Henry Venn's century old formula of "self-government, self-support, and self-extension" as the marks of a mature church. The report noted, however, that the structures and policies of the Episcopal Church mitigated against the development of self-government, or autonomy, of its overseas jurisdictions. The Review Committee emphasized that autonomy for missionary districts is impossible when the bishop is a U.S. citizen elected by the U.S. House of Bishops; when the bishop must take an Oath of Conformity to the Protestant Episcopal Church in the USA; when the leadership, both episcopal and clerical, is so related to the USA salary and pension standards that they find themselves in the top 3%, or even, the top 1% income bracket of their country; when the diocese's finances and policies are administered by an arrangement with authorities 2,000 miles away; and when it is not free to determine its own liturgy and develop its own worship.[111] The Overseas Review Committee applauded the decision of the 1969 General Convention permitting the election of an overseas bishop by the people of the jurisdiction he will serve rather than by the House of Bishops. This was seen as an important first step in the handing over of ecclesiastical power, ultimately leading to church autonomy. To further facilitate self-government in overseas jurisdictions of the Episcopal Church, the Review Committee recommended significant changes to the constitution and canons of the Episcopal Church. The changes were designed to assist overseas missionary districts to become missionary dioceses with all of the rights and privileges of domestic dioceses in the United States. These changes and others recommended by the Overseas Review Committee addressed, for the first time, steps the Episcopal Church would have to take if its overseas missionary districts were to develop into genuinely autonomous Anglican churches. It set the stage for autonomy discussions that would dominate Episcopal mission conversations in the 1980s and 1990s.

While the Overseas Review Committee made specific recommendations regarding self-government of the new missionary dioceses, the matter of self-support was more problematic. The committee acknowledged that the historic missionary procedures of the Episcopal Church had held up a model of the church that was both expensive to maintain and mitigated against true self-support. It thus criticized many of the missiological presuppositions of the national church ideal.

> Another factor that had worked against independence is our transfer of many ideas about buildings, institutions, and programs which were the model of Church life we knew, and seemed a good one for people overseas, too... In many places we have imported with us structures that are expensive to begin with and equally expensive to maintain. So we have been willing to continue support long after a more restrained policy would have suggested moving toward "self-support."[112]

To prove this point, the committee's report emphasized that in 1968, eight overseas jurisdictions of the Episcopal Church received between 90% and 97% of their annual support from the church in the United States, three between 86% and 89% and one received 77%.[113] The committee recognized that as the newly constituted missionary dioceses moved toward autonomy, financial support from the church in the United States could not be cut off abruptly. Instead the Episcopal Church should do all in its power to help newer churches develop their own resources. Emphasizing the unity of Christ's mission in the world, the Overseas Review Committee cautioned that self-support should not lead to isolation of either the newer Anglican churches or the Episcopal Church in the United States.

Finally, the Overseas Review Committee urged greater assistance for the national church administrative offices involved with the overseas work of the Episcopal Church. It applauded the increased communication between the American Episcopal Church and other Anglican churches resulting from the area desks for Latin America, Asia and the Pacific, and Africa and the Middle

East, instituted following the Gray Report of 1960. The committee suggested that the area desk offices as well as the Presiding Bishop's Deputy for Overseas Relations would profit from an ongoing advisory committee.

The final report of the Overseas Review Committee was made to the 1973 General Convention of the Episcopal Church held in Louisville, Kentucky. This report began with a recapitulation of the interim report presented in 1970. It then continued with an investigation into the three basic types of relationships between the Episcopal Church and other jurisdictions or churches. Overseas missionary dioceses, independent churches of the Anglican Communion, and inter-Anglican responsibilities were noted. In all of these relationships, autonomy and self-support were held up as realistic goals to which all churches must commit themselves. Specific proposals were made to assist in the autonomy processes of overseas missionary dioceses, especially in Latin America. The report closed with an extensive review of emerging trends and patterns for mission throughout the Anglican Communion and emphasized the ongoing contributions of "Mutual Responsibility and Interdependence in the Body of Christ."

The final report noted that many of the Overseas Review Committee's resolutions to the 1970 General Convention regarding the self-determination of overseas missionary dioceses had been crowded off the convention's agenda by the pressures of time. The report of 1973 thus presented a series of seventeen resolutions that would grant even greater autonomy to missionary dioceses.[114] The majority of these resolutions were adopted by the Louisville General Convention. In addition the General Convention, following the recommendations of both the interim and final reports of the Overseas Review Committee, established a Joint Commission on World Mission. The Joint Commission on World Mission was to provide continued oversight of the Episcopal Church's participation in what was now known as "world mission."[115]

The Joint Commission on World Mission was made up of three bishops, three presbyters and nine lay persons with at least a majority of the total membership coming from outside the United States. For two trienniums the Joint Commission fulfilled its mandate "to review, evaluate, plan, and propose policy on world mission to the General Convention and Council."[116] A primary responsibility of the Joint Commission was to cooperate with the Executive Council staff in implementing Partners In Mission programs and policies. During the triennium 1973-1976, the Joint Commission began an exploration of the Episcopal Church's work in Liberia with an eye to transferring jurisdiction for the Liberian mission to the Anglican Church of the Province of West Africa. The commission also recommended to the 1976 General Convention the resumption of the voluntary missionary program that had been dropped because of the budget cuts in 1970. The Volunteers for Mission Program, endorsed by the 1976 General Convention in Minneapolis and funded in part by funds provided by the Venture in Mission program, was seen as a positive step forward in missionary outreach of the Episcopal Church. By the mid-1980s this missionary program, consisting of short-term volunteers, would rival the longer term "appointed missionaries" in numbers with approximately sixty individuals working outside the United States.[117]

In its report to the 1979 General Convention, the Joint Commission established four goals for the next triennium, specifically: 1) to assist in the follow-up and seek proper coordination to the response of the PIM process and 1977 American consultation; 2) to assist the Executive Council in developing covenant planning before and after autonomy in the overseas dioceses of the Episcopal Church; 3) to study the relationship and propose new policy between companion relationships and PIM processes; and 4) to undertake a thorough and comprehensive review of world mission policies and priorities of the Episcopal Church.[118] The Joint Commission's concern for autonomy for overseas dioceses of the Episcopal Church resulted in a specific plan leading to the transfer of the Episcopal Church's work in Liberia to the Anglican Church of the Province of West Africa.[119] In addition, the 1979 General Convention upgraded the Joint Commission to a Standing Commission of the General Convention, thereby instituting an ongoing body in the Episcopal Church's legislative structure to oversee the world mission concerns of the church.

The majority of the efforts of the Standing Commission on World Mission have been centered on partnership issues and autonomy processes. In response to the Joint Commission's call for a "thorough and comprehensive review of world mission policies and priorities of the Episcopal Church," the Standing Commission produced a draft statement in 1982 on the theology of mission espoused by the Episcopal Church. The statement entitled "Mission in Global Perspective" was drafted with the assistance of significant Episcopal scholars including the Rev. Frank E. Sugeno, Professor of the History and Mission of the Church at the Episcopal Seminary of the Southwest; the Rev. Philip Turner, Professor of Christian Ethics at the General Theological Seminary; the Rev. A. Theodore Eastman, then rector of St. Alban's Parish in Washington, D.C.; and Edward A. Bayne, a member of the Standing Commission and brother of Stephen Bayne.[120]

"Mission in Global Perspective" represented a significant attempt to wrestle with the meaning of Christian mission for the Episcopal Church in the 1980s and beyond. It began with a historical review of Episcopal mission from nineteenth century Western expansionism through the new emphasis on autonomy and partnership in the post-colonial era. Theological affirmations then followed that lifted up the sovereignty of God and the uniqueness of Christ. The statement emphasized that the Episcopal Church must move beyond its parochial mentality and recognize its common calling to participate in God's mission with other Christians from around the world.

> There are several points that must be made. The first is certainly that *the Episcopal Church itself exists in a missionary situation.* Just as Christians in Uganda or Shanghai are called to proclaim what God has made known in Christ, so are Episcopalians. It will be difficult for this shift in consciousness to come about but come about it must. The Episcopal Church has long thought of itself as "established." Its origins in England hardly make such a view surprising and it is probably because of this historical heritage that the Episcopal Church has for so many years thought of itself as in some way appointed or destined to be *the* "national church." (Italics in original)[121]

"Mission in Global Perspective" closed with a review of contemporary church policies and programs related to world mission. Future directions were suggested, all of which were in keeping with the vision and priorities of MRI and PIM. The statement emphasized:

> In a time when relationships between the developed and developing parts of the world are shifting markedly:
>
> –each local, national and regional church needs to take primary responsibility for mission in its own setting;
>
> –the more established churches need to move into a new level of mutuality in mission, as previously dependent churches attain and consolidate ecclesial autonomy; and
>
> –those who have seen themselves as givers and senders need to discover what they need to receive and how to receive it, even as those who have traditionally thought of themselves as receivers need to learn what they have to give and how to give it.[122]

The document "Mission in Global Perspective" and the ongoing work of the Standing Commission for World Mission demonstrated that "partnership in mission" had become the new ideal for the foreign mission of the Episcopal Church.

Redefinition of the Ideal: Development

In the post-colonial Partners In Mission era, the Episcopal Church could not leave behind its historic commitment to education and social service. Beginning in the mid-1970s the Episcopal Church uncritically embraced international development activities as the next generation of the church's involvement with schools and hospitals around the world. As the Episcopal Church pursued these development programs and projects, its cooperation and collaboration with United States government agencies, especially the United States Agency for International Development (USAID), increased. From 1976 to 1985 the Episcopal Church received over $13 million in U.S. government funds to support its work in international development.

The emergence of the Episcopal Church's participation in international relief and development began in 1940 with the establishment of the Presiding Bishop's Fund for World Relief (PBFWR). At first the fund's stated goal was specific and limited to dealing with relief of human needs created by World War II. A primary focus of this work was assistance to and resettlement of refugees displaced by the war in Europe. Refugee relief and resettlement thus became a cornerstone of the work of the PBFWR. With the cooperation of the U.S. government and the United Nations High Commissioner for Refugees, the fund came to the aid of thousands of refugees and displaced persons since 1940.

As the nature of American international assistance matured from relief to development in the post–World War II era, the scope of the fund's work also grew. Increasingly the PBFWR began to underwrite development projects in cooperation with ecumenical, interfaith and other nonprofit humanitarian relief groups. Acknowledging this expanded ministry, the charter of the fund was changed in 1977 to address the totality of human needs, both spiritual and physical. The new charter emphasized that the "specific task of the Presiding Bishop's Fund for World Relief is to respond to the Christian imperative to minister to the hungry and thirsty, the sick and those in prison, to cloth the naked and welcome the stranger." (Matthew 25)[123] Following the new charter, the fund embraced a four-fold ministry of relief, rehabilitation, development and education. The Presiding Bishop's Fund for World Relief provided millions of dollars of church and government funds for relief, education and development projects throughout the world. For example, in 1983 the fund's disbursements totaled $4,891,761. Of this total, $2,611,690 (53.39%) was derived from Episcopal Church contributions and $2,280,071 (46.61%) was provided by the Bureau of Refugee Programs of the U.S. Department of State and the Office of Refugee Resettlement of the U.S. Department of Health and Human Services.[124]

In 1976 two events occurred that significantly added to the role of the Episcopal Church in international development. The first was the establishment of the Venture in Mission Program. The second was a $4.1 million five-year grant awarded by the United States Agency for International Development to the Executive Council of the Episcopal Church for its work at Cuttington University College (CUC) in Liberia. This first operational grant by USAID signaled the registration of the Domestic and Foreign Missionary Society (the incorporated name of the Executive Council and the Episcopal Church) with the U.S. government as an authorized Private Voluntary Organization.

As noted above, the Venture in Mission Program (VIM) was the initiative of Presiding Bishop John Allin. Venture in Mission was conceived as a campaign: 1) to restate and revitalize the mission and ministry of the Episcopal Church and 2) to create funding to achieve its purpose of working "in full cooperation with each overseas jurisdiction, for self-government, self-support and self-propagation."[125] Venture in Mission funds contributed by American Episcopalians were thus used to further the outreach of the Episcopal Church in the United States and overseas by training clergy, translating the Bible, providing medical services, teaching agriculture, generating new efforts in development, training indigenous leaders abroad, expanding the human services of the church, transforming community life, assisting the poor and the oppressed, funding church building and supporting educational activities. It was emphasized that each VIM project had to clearly state the way by which the funding of a project was expected to transform rather than simply maintain the status quo. In its commitment to assisting with the transformation of individuals at the "grass-roots," Venture in Mission resembled the "New Directions" approach to international development undertaken by the United States Agency for International Development.

In 1976 the Episcopal Church entered into two major capital improvement programs for Cuttington University College in Liberia with the assistance of USAID funding. Cuttington was founded in 1889 by the Episcopal Church as an all-male school with programs in liberal arts, agriculture and theology to meet the training and educational needs of the Liberian people. In 1948 CUC was relocated to Suacoco, in central Liberia, one hundred miles from the capital of Monrovia.[126] Since its founding Cuttington had struggled to meet both its capital and operating financial needs. In the late 1970s, under the direction of Dr. Edward A. Holmes, an American educator and dean of Cuttington, the Episcopal Church and the United States Agency for International Development began a cooperative venture in support of the school. With the assistance of USAID's American Schools and Hospitals Abroad Program (ASHA), Cuttington significantly improved its physical plant in the late 1970s and early 1980s. By 1983, over $3.2 million had been granted to Cuttington by ASHA. These funds were used to build a new science and technology building as well as water, electric and sewer system development.[127] In 1984 and 1985, an additional $1.25 million was granted by ASHA to Cuttington, through the Executive Council and its staff, to supplement faculty and administrative services as well as to rehabilitate existing campus facilities. This brought the total of U. S. government funding for Cuttington to $4.35 million.[128]

In addition, from 1978 to 1983 the Episcopal Church received over $4.1 million from USAID in support of the Rural Development Institute (RDI) at Cuttington University College. Proposed, built and supervised by Holmes, RDI was set up as a two-year agricultural training program for mid-level managers and extension agents in Liberia. From 1978 until 1982, the Rural Development Institute graduated more than 200 students.[129] The Rural Development Institute was in keeping with the integrated rural development goals of the USAID "New Directions" initiative. It thus became a prototype for the cooperation of the Episcopal Church and the United States government in the support of a well-trained agricultural infrastructure in sub–Saharan Africa.

By the late 1970s the administration of Venture in Mission projects and USAID grants overburdened the existing bureaucratic structure at the Episcopal Church Center. At the initiative of both the Executive for World Mission, the Rev. Samuel Van Culin, and Presiding Bishop John Allin, the World Mission Overseas Development Planning Office was established in 1980. (The name of the office was later changed to simply the Overseas Development Office, or ODO.) The stated objective of the Overseas Development Planning Office was:

> to assist the Overseas Dioceses of the Church to plan, finance and administer programs for development of human and material resources for the alleviation of problems underlying hunger, disease, and ignorance in their communities.[130]

Dr. Edward Holmes was hired as the first director of the new Overseas Development Planning Office at the Episcopal Church Center and moved to the Episcopal Church Center from Liberia in 1980. The establishment of this office coincided with the generation of funds through Venture in Mission to overseas dioceses for development projects, and with a decision on the part of the Board of the Presiding Bishop's Fund to become more pro-active in providing funds for development projects in Anglican dioceses overseas. As a result of this convergence of Venture in Mission and the Presiding Bishop's Fund for World Relief, augmented by U.S. government grants, involvement in overseas development projects by the Episcopal Church expanded significantly.[131]

The first large cooperative venture of the Overseas Development Office, the Presiding Bishop's Fund for World Relief and the United States government was the Southern Sudan Refugee Assistance Project (SSRAP) begun in 1982. The SSRAP represented a coming together of the Episcopal Church of the Sudan's request for aid for refugees from Uganda and the Bureau of Refugee Programs of the U.S. Department of State desire to provide refugee assistance in East Africa. The SSRAP began when the World Mission Executive directed the Overseas Development Office to work with the PBFWR in creating and administering a refugee development assistance program in the southern Sudan.[132] From 1983 through 1985 the Overseas Development Office, in association with the Episcopal Church of the Sudan, coordinated an $8 million refugee assistance and development project with a staff of fifty-three including six expatriate personnel. Funding for the SSRAP was provided through the Presiding Bishop's Fund and other agencies, including: $5 million from the Bureau of Refugee Programs of the U.S. Department of State, $2 million from the United Nations High Commissioner for Refugees and $1 million from private donors including the Ford Foundation and Catholic Relief Services.[133]

The relationship between the U.S. government and the Episcopal Church expanded in 1984 when the Overseas Development Office entered into a new three-year, $501,000 matching grant program with the United States Agency for International Development. The purpose of the matching grant program was to assist four over-seas partner churches in Haiti, Kenya, Liberia and the Philippines to establish development offices and build up their own develop-ment capabilities. The stated objectives of the matching grant program were:

1. Help select and train development officers for dioceses and provinces;

2. Provide training in how to plan and manage community based development programs in overseas dioceses;

3. Provide technical assistance for long range planning for development programs in overseas dioceses;

4. Set up and test curriculum at the UCLA Development Institute to train both U.S. and overseas development officers.[134]

Within two years development offices were established in each of the four countries and development training had taken place in all four.[135] The fact that each of these offices was established in countries where the United States propped up "anti-communist" totalitarian regimes, (Haiti under Jean Claude Duvalier, Kenya under Daniel Arap Moi, Liberia under Samuel Doe, and the Philippines under Ferdinand Marcos) was lost on church officials. The United States government, however, was pleased with its growing partnership with the Episcopal Church and renewed the matching grant for an additional $175,000 in 1987.

The focus on development training in the matching grant pro-gram represented a significant change of strategy in the Episcopal Church's development work. In 1983 the Overseas Development Office began to critically reexamine its process and methods of international development. In January, Jane Watkins of the New Transcentury Foundation in Washington, D.C., facilitated a work-shop for Episcopal Church leadership concerned with the church's role in development. What resulted from this workshop was a commitment by the Episcopal Church to become increas-ingly active in development training and planning rather than funding of overseas development projects.

This new emphasis on development training instead of fund-ing development projects was reaffirmed in 1985 when the

Overseas Development Office experienced a change of leadership. When Presiding Bishop John Allin retired at the end of 1985, Dr. Edward Holmes resigned his position as the director of the ODO to head the new, independent Foundation for Assistance of Church Institutions Overseas (FACIO), located in Sewanee, Tennessee. Jane Watkins was hired to replace Dr. Holmes as the primary Overseas Development Officer of the Episcopal Church. Under Watkins's leadership and with funds provided by the matching grant, the Overseas Development Office increased its staff from two to four officers and planned new development training and management workshops specifically designed for women in East Africa.

The development work of the Episcopal Church in the 1970s and 1980s was not unified under one strategy or one approach but was subject to the vicissitudes of government funding and changes in leadership personnel. From the Rural Development Institute in Liberia to the Southern Sudan Refugee Assistance Project, from the matching grant program to development planning and management workshops for women, the Episcopal Church experimented with different development initiatives. The primary impetus for all of these programs came not from the General Convention or the Executive Council but from administrators and "development professionals," many of whom were not members of the Episcopal Church. As a result, the fact that the Episcopal Church had cooperated extensively with the United States government in overseas ventures was little known in the church.[136]

The involvement of the Episcopal Church in development activities supposedly represented a new mission paradigm, one that was more open and responsive to the needs and aspirations of indigenous church leaders around the world. The question needs to be raised, however, as to how different the development efforts were from the older mission strategy of constructing schools, hospitals and churches in dependent missionary districts. In its efforts to build up Cuttington University College and provide assistance to refugees in the Sudan, the Episcopal Church had not varied significantly from its earlier motives under the national church ideal. The only new wrinkle was the Episcopal

Church's cooperation with the United States government and its new role as a conduit for United States government funds around the world. The ethical question as to whether the Episcopal Church should have been a tool of the foreign policy of the United States government was never addressed in the wider church.

Voluntarism after the Ideal

The upheaval in the established structures and policies related to the foreign mission work of the Episcopal Church in the 1960s and 1970s deeply affected those Episcopalians who were interested in and committed to the church's work outside the United States. The tensions caused by General Convention Special Program and the loss of the national church ideal had repercussions in the Overseas Mission Society, eventually leading to its demise. At the same time some Episcopalians, believing that the national church had abandoned its responsibilities overseas, organized new voluntary missionary societies to pick up the mantle thrown off by the Executive Council. Many of these new voluntary societies did not stand in the theological tradition of the national church ideal but rather embraced a more conservative and evangelical missiology that put them at odds with the legacy of the national church.

Although independent from the national church, the Overseas Mission Society was caught in many of the painful changes of the new world. The debate over the role of the church in society and the related General Convention Special Program was played out in the various constituencies of the society. Some OMS members supported the vision of GCSP. Others, however, were upset that the changes in program priorities of the national church resulted in the abandonment of foreign mission commitments. All seemed to be frustrated with the apparent competition between the church's domestic agenda and foreign mission work. As a result, the energy and enthusiasm for promoting the foreign mission of the Episcopal Church, the reason why the Overseas Mission Society was founded, waned. From 1967 to 1968 the OMS suffered a sharp loss in membership and income. Emergency meetings of the society's leaders revealed disagreement as to the goals of the society. These disagreements were not resolved in a fuller debate at the 1968 OMS Annual Meeting. Shortly thereafter George Tittmann resigned his position as editor of *The Overseas Mission Review* and A. Theodore Eastman left his post as executive secretary of the society.[137] The Whitsunday 1968 issue of *The Overseas Mission Review* was the last issue published. The OMS was officially "moth-balled" in April, 1969. Although a few attempts were made to revive the society, they all failed; the remaining assets and charter of the OMS were transferred to a new organization known as the Companions in World Mission in 1977. Companions in World Mission was a group of twenty-four parishes in the Washington, D.C., area that supported various projects and theological schools around the world, especially in East Africa.[138]

Having been involved closely with the life and workings of the Overseas Mission Society, the Rev. Charles Long speculated as to the reasons why the OMS came to an end. He believes that the disagreement over mission theology, from personal evangelism to support of liberation movements, in the OMS leadership was a cause of tension and division in the organization. These tensions were exacerbated by the need to address crises in the United States and the growing sense that neither Americans nor missionaries were welcome in other parts of the world. In addition, Long maintains that the OMS had failed to provide a real channel of communication to the American church for missionaries and for church leaders in newly autonomous churches other than overseas bishops. Finally, Long concludes that the Overseas Mission Society failed to develop a core constituency and a vision of itself as a voluntary missionary sending society along the lines of the British Church Missionary Society. Thus, by the early 1970s, the original coalition of causes and persons that had supported the OMS had fallen apart. The time had come to pass the torch to others.[139]

As the OMS and one generation of voluntarism faded away, a new wave of Episcopalians committed to world mission swept over the Episcopal Church. Seeing that large numbers of American missionaries were being brought home by the national church, a handful of Episcopalians rededicated themselves to overseas mission work by starting voluntary societies independent of the control and authority of the National/Executive Council. Whereas the OMS had been the "loyal opposition" to the national church, these new voluntary societies stood in direct opposition to the national church ideal. In 1974, returning from a long career in the missionary diocese of Alaska, the Rev. Walter W. and Louise Hannum founded the Episcopal Church Missionary Community (ECMC). ECMC was not organized as a missionary sending society but as an educational resource and missionary support agency. ECMC was dedicated to developing an informed, active and effective concern for mission at all levels of the Episcopal Church through parish and diocesan workshops and the training of missionary personnel. To facilitate their educational and training ministry, the Hannums located ECMC in Pasadena, California, next to Fuller Theological Seminary and the conservative-evangelical United States Center for World Mission.[140] In 1976, two years after the Hannums had begun ECMC, the South American Missionary Society of the Episcopal Church (SAMS/USA) was founded. SAMS/USA was the first independent missionary sending society organized in the Episcopal Church since the American Church Missionary Society in the nineteenth century. Modeled after, and in association with, the South American Missionary Society of the Church of England, SAMS/USA committed itself to sending missionaries to Latin America. By 1984 SAMS/USA had twenty-seven missionaries working in Latin America from Peru to Honduras.[141]

The transplant of a British voluntary society into American soil proved to be successful and soon three additional societies related to historic Church of England institutions had been founded. In 1982, A Christian Ministry among Jewish People (CMJ/USA) opened its doors with a specific calling to evangelize Jews. In November of the following year, the Society for Promoting Christian Knowledge/USA (SPCK/USA) was established. SPCK/USA was founded as the American arm of the oldest Protestant mission society in the world, the British Society for Promoting Christian Knowledge. By creating, preparing and distributing Christian printed resources around the world SPCK/USA hoped to augment the work of the British SPCK. In 1985, Sharing of Ministries Abroad (SOMA/USA) was organized as a Christian parachurch ministry dedicated to fostering worldwide renewal in the Holy Spirit through conferences and short-term missions. One additional missionary sending society, Episcopal World Mission, Incorporated, was started in 1982.[142]

Almost without exception, each of these voluntary societies was organized as a reaction to the perception that "the national church was getting out of the missionary business." Like their predecessor, the American Church Missionary Society, these new voluntary societies subscribed to a more conservative, evangelical theology of mission than that of the national church. The advent of independent voluntary societies with their dissenting theological viewpoint emphasized the fact that a single national church ideal was no longer operative as the overriding missiological imperative for the Episcopal Church.

Perhaps the best illustration of the loss of the national church ideal was found in a renewed interest throughout the Episcopal Church in the work and life of Roland Allen. Roland Allen was a little-known English missionary who served in north China under the auspices of the Society for the Propagation of the Gospel (SPG), from 1895 through 1903. As a missionary Allen argued that established missionary methods did not encourage the development of an indigenous church. He believed that the preoccupation with mission schools and hospitals coupled with the reliance on professional clergy alienated the people at the grass-roots. Allen instead emphasized that the missionary should emulate the methods of St. Paul by raising up local leadership and turning over control of the church to new believers at the outset. Above all, Allen relied on the work of the Holy Spirit and not mission administrators in New York and London to guide his missionary outreach. Allen thus

> became severely critical of the reluctance of Western missionaries to allow Chinese Christians to take over Church leadership. In an era when the English and the Americans were so proud of their expanding religious, educational, and medical missions in China, Allen offended his contemporaries by predicting that Western missionaries would someday be driven out.[143]

Returning to England in 1903 because of ill health, Allen produced significant works outlining his radical mission theory. His books *Missionary Methods; St. Paul's or Ours* (1912), *Voluntary Clergy* (1923) and *The Spontaneous Expansion of the Church and the Causes which Hinder It* (1927) were not well received for they sharply criticized accepted mission thought of the time.

It is no surprise that Allen's critique of established missionary methods found a sympathetic audience in the antiestablishmentarian ethos of the 1970s. Allen's thoughts, although half a century old, seemed to address directly the ills of Episcopal mission policies under the national church ideal. By the mid-1980s, Roland Allen had a significant popular following throughout the Episcopal Church. His emphasis on the Holy Spirit, on lay leadership and local empowerment for ministry seemed to be the perfect antidote for the top-down approach to mission espoused by the centralization and bureaucracy of the National/Executive Council.

The crowning event for the Roland Allen movement in the Episcopal Church was the Pacific Basin/Roland Allen Conference at Hawaii Loa College near Honolulu in June, 1983. The impetus for such a meeting came from American bishops who had begun to wrestle with Allen's missionary strategies in their own dioceses. Bishops Wesley Frensdorff (Nevada), George Harris (Alaska), Shannon Mallory (El Camino Real) and Edmond Browning (Hawaii) were instrumental in the planning of the conference. For a week, 150 lay people, deacons, priests and bishops from fifty-one Anglican dioceses bordering the Pacific came together to consider Allen's theology and what it might be saying to the contemporary church. Major papers were presented by scholars such as Kosuke Koyama, Bernard Cooke, Hone Kaa, Patricia Page and Ross Kinsler. Each day, Archbishop Paul Reeves of New Zealand gave a brief summary and reflection on the proceedings.[144] In plenary sessions and small group conversations, the Allen Conference emphasized forcefully that the old way of doing mission under the national church ideal had to pass.

England, the United States, and Canada can no longer send a procession of dedicated men and women across the Pacific, not only paying their salaries but also building and maintaining the churches, hospitals, schools and convents for them to work in. Even if the Western English speaking churches could do this, such efforts would be unwelcome in many areas today. The conference expressed and to some extent implemented the conviction that indigenous leaders must be allowed to speak, even if they cannot, in some cases, do so in the academic patois familiar in the ecclesiastics of the West.[145]

And so this group of 150 Anglicans from around the Pacific rim, who had gathered outside the auspices of any official church structure to consider the thoughts of Roland Allen, were in keeping with the missiological imperatives of the new world. It is no coincidence that the host bishop of the Roland Allen Conference, the Right Rev. Edmond L. Browning, bishop of Hawaii, was at the same time chair of the Standing Commission on World Mission. Many of the conclusions of the Standing Commission's study document "Mission in Global Perspective" were echoed in the findings of the Allen conference. None at the time knew that within two years Browning would become Presiding Bishop of the Episcopal Church. Under Browning's leadership the Episcopal Church would be challenged to discover its new calling in God's mission while abandoning the vestiges of its national church ideal.

As the twentieth century draws to a close, the question before all Episcopalians is: Can the Episcopal Church participate in God's mission without the national church ideal? It will not be easy, but Episcopalians are a resurrection people who believe that in the death of old ways we are always given new possibilities and opportunities to engage in God's global mission of reconciliation and redemption.

NOTES

[1]James A. Scherer, *Gospel, Church, and Kingdom: Comparative Studies in World Mission Theology* (Minneapolis, Minn.: Augsburg Publishing House, 1987), 113.

[2]Rodger C. Bassham, *Mission Theology, 1948-1975: Years of Worldwide Creative Tensions; Ecumenical, Evangelical, and Roman Catholic* (Pasadena, Calif.: William Carey Library, 1979), 65.

[3]Bishop Anastasios Yannoulatos of Androussa, "Mexico City 1963: Old Wine into Fresh Wineskins," *International Review of Mission* 67 (July 1978): 364. The image of the vertical and horizontal aspects of mission is borrowed without citation from a plenary address to the Fourth Assembly of the World Council of Churches, Uppsala 1968, by W. A. Visser t'Hooft.

[4]Bassham, 66.

[5]William R. Hutchison, *Errand to the World: American Protestant Thought and Foreign Missions* (Chicago: The University of Chicago Press, 1987), 186.

[6]Norman Goodall, ed., *The Uppsala Report 1968: Official Report of the Fourth Assembly of the World Council of Churches*, (Geneva: World Council of Churches, 1968), xvii.

[7]Ibid., 28.

[8]Ibid., 29.

[9]Scherer, 119.

[10]Donald McGavran, "Will Uppsala Betray the Two Billion?" in Donald McGavran, ed., *Eye of the Storm: The Great Debate in Mission*, (Waco, Tex.: Word Books, 1972), 238-239.

[11]John V. Taylor, "Bangkok 1972-1973," *International Review of Mission* 67 (July 1978): 365.

[12]Bassham, 95-97.

[13]Scherer, 122.

[14]Ibid., 123-124.

[15]James A. Scherer and Stephen B. Bevans, eds., *New Directions in Mission and Evangelism 1: Basic Statements 1974-1991*, (Maryknoll, N.Y.: Orbis Books, 1992), 3.

[16]Bassham, 99.

[17]Scherer, 127.

[18]David M. Paton, ed., *Breaking Barriers: Nairobi 1975, The Official Report of the Fifth Assembly of the World Council of Churches*, (London: Society for Promoting Christian Knowledge, 1976) 53.

[19]Ibid., 45.

[20]Scherer, 126.

[21]Bassham, 106.

[22]Scherer makes this point both in *Gospel, Church, and Kingdom,* 130-131 as well as in Scherer and Bevans, eds., *New Directions in Mission and Evangelism 1,* 27.

[23]Scherer and Bevans, eds., *New Directions in Mission and Evangelism 1,* 27.

[24]Ibid., 29-31,

[25]Scherer, *Gospel, Church, and Kingdom,* 141-145.

[26]Development as mission was not limited to Protestants. The 1967 Encyclical on the Development of Peoples (*Populorum Progressio*) by Pope Paul VI stressed the connection between mission and development in the Roman Catholic Church. See: Philip Land, "Populorum Progressio, Mission and Development," *International Review of Mission* 58 (October 1969).

[27]Goodall, ed., *The Uppsala Report 1968,* 45.

[28]Ibid.

[29]"To give life more abundantly" echoed the missiology of the National Council of the Episcopal Church articulated by W. C. Sturgis. See Chapter III above.

[30]Paton, 136.

[31]See: All Africa Council of Churches, *Drumbeats from Kampala: Report of the First AACC* (London: United Society for Christian Literature, 1963) and James Scherer, *Missionary, Go Home! A Reappraisal of the Christian World Mission* (Englewood Cliffs, N.J.: Prentice-Hall, Inc., 1964). In an interesting turn of the tables, Canon Carr later became African Partnership Officer for the Episcopal Church, USA, in the late 1980s. One of his responsibilities in this position was to assist with the appointment of Episcopalian missionaries to Anglican churches in sub-Saharan Africa.

[32]For example, in 1953 the National Council of Churches reported that its member churches were responsible for 9,844 overseas missionaries. In 1968, the reported number was 10,042. See: Robert T. Coote, "Taking Aim on 2000 A.D.," in *Mission Handbook*, 13th Edition, ed. Samuel Wilson and John Siewert (Monrovia, Calif.: Missions Advanced Research and Communications Center, 1986), 38-40.

[33]Ibid.

[34]Allen Hoben, "Anthropologists and Development", *Annual Review of Anthropology* 11 (1982): 359.

[35]A. F. Robertson, *People and the State* (Cambridge: Cambridge University Press, 1984), 73.

[36]Allen Hoben, "Agricultural Decision Making in Foreign Assistance," in *Agricultural Decision Making: Anthropological Contributions to Rural Development*, ed. P. Bartlett (New York: Academic Press, 1980), 356.

[37]Agency for International Development, *A Guide to AID, Peace Corps, PVO Collaborative Programming* (Washington, D.C.: United States Agency for International Development, 1984), 1.

[38]Thomas A. McKay, "Development Today: The State of the Art," in *In Development: Giving People Hope; Extracts from Presentations Given at the Fifth Episcopal World Mission Conference, The Church in Global Development*, (New York: Episcopal Church Center, Overseas Development Office, 1984), 75-76.

[39]Ibid.

[40]One of the best discussions of MRI is found in a series of articles published in the Epiphany 1964 issue of *The Episcopal Overseas Mission Review*.

[41]With the failing health of Lichtenberger, Bayne returned to the United States to advance his chances of being elected the next Presiding Bishop.

[42]Protestant Episcopal Church in the United States of America, National Council, *Annual Report of the National Council of the Protestant Episcopal Church in the United States: 1960* (New York: National Council of the Protestant Episcopal Church, 1960), 4.

[43]Roland Foster, *The Role of the Presiding Bishop* (Cincinnati, Ohio: Forward Movement Publications, 1982), 104.

[44]General Convention of the Protestant Episcopal Church, *Journal of the General Convention of the Protestant Episcopal Church: 1964* (New York: The General Convention, 1964), 220-222.

[45]"Report of the Presiding Bishop's Committee on Mutual Responsibility to the General Convention" in *Journal of the General Convention of the Protestant Episcopal Church: 1964*, 722-723.

[46]Ibid., 729.

[47]R. David Cox, "A Vision to Fulfill: 'Mutual Responsibility and Interdependence' in the Anglican Communion" (S.T.M. thesis, Yale Divinity School, 1987), 156-157.

[48]Interview with Bishop Frey, at Trinity Episcopal School for Ministry, Ambridge, Penn., May 22, 1991.

[49]Mutual Responsibility Commission, *Our Immediate Responsibility: Projects for Partnership* (New York: Mutual Responsibility Commission, 1966).

[50]Webster also criticized, appropriately, the loss of ecumenical engagement following MRI. See: Douglas Webster, *Mutual Irresponsibility: A Danger to be Avoided* (London: Society for Promoting Christian Knowledge, 1965).

[51]Data on missionary appointments from an unpublished memorandum to the Presiding Bishop from Warren H. Turner, Jr. of the Executive Council Staff, New York, 7 June, 1967 .

[52]Foster, 108.

[53]Ibid., 114-115.

[54]General Convention of the Protestant Episcopal Church, *Journal of the General Convention of the Protestant Episcopal Church: 1967* (New York: The General Convention, 1967), 2.

[55]Executive Council, *Showdown at Seattle* (New York: The Seabury Press, 1968), 49.

[56]David E. Sumner, *The Episcopal Church's History: 1945-1985* (Wilton, Conn.: Morehouse-Barlow, 1987), 47.

[57]*Journal of the General Convention of the Protestant Episcopal Church: 1967*, 240-241.

[58]See: The Executive Council, *Report to the Church on the General Convention Special Program* (New York: The Executive Council, 1968), 2.

[59]Vine Deloria, "G.C.S.P.: The Demons at Work," *Historical Magazine of the Protestant Episcopal Church* 48 (March 1979): 87.

[60]Protestant Episcopal Church in the United States of America, Executive Council, *Annual Report of the Executive Council of the Protestant Episcopal Church: 1967* (New York: Executive Council, 1967), 2.

[61]General Convention of the Protestant Episcopal Church, *Journal of the Special General Convention, 1970* (New York: The General Convention, 1970) 258.

[62]Sumner, 52-53.

[63]Protestant Episcopal Church in the United States of America, Executive Council, *Annual Report of the Executive Council of the Protestant Episcopal Church: 1969* (New York: Executive Council, 1969), 2.

[64]Ibid.

[65]Clifford P. Morehouse, "The General Convention Special Program: Past and Future," General Convention News Release No. 38 (Houston, 1970). 14 October 1970, quoted in Sumner 53-54.

[66]Frank Sugeno, "The Establishmentarian Ideal and the Mission of the Episcopal Church," *Historical Magazine of the Protestant Episcopal Church* 53 (December 1984): 293.

[67]From 1971 to the present the annual report of the Executive Council has consisted simply of an auditor's report, available on request, although Title I Canon 4, Section 8 of the *Constitution and Canons of the Episcopal Church* states: "The Council, as soon as possible after the close of each fiscal year, shall make and publish a full report of its work to the Church." The lack of clear reporting has further alienated Episcopalians from the Executive Council and its program.

[68]Figures from: Protestant Episcopal Church in the United States of America, Executive Council, *Annual Report of the Executive Council of the Protestant Episcopal Church: 1969*, 4, and Protestant Episcopal Church in the United States of America, Executive Council, "1971 Commitment Budget Summary" (Executive Council, New York, 1971),4-7. It is difficult to discern exactly the "Overseas Department" budget for 1970 since the department had been combined with support for domestic dioceses in the new Office of Jurisdictional Relations.

[69]Neil G. Lebhar, Martyn Minns, "Why Did the Yankees Go Home: A Study of Episcopal Missions, 1953-1977," *Historical Magazine of the Protestant Episcopal Church* 48 (March 1979): 37.

[70]Figures from: Protestant Episcopal Church in the United States of America, Executive Council, Overseas Department, *Statistical Reports of Foreign Missionaries: 1965-1970* (New York: Executive Council, 1965-1970). Also quoted in Lebhar and Minns, 33.

[71]The number of full missionary appointees of the Episcopal Church in 1992 is approximately thirty-five.

[72]Overseas Review Committee, "An Interim Report to the House of Bishops in General Convention of the Protestant Episcopal Church, *Journal of the General Convention of the Protestant Episcopal Church: 1970*, 584.

[73]In 1992 the number of "volunteers" supported by the Executive Council outnumbers the "appointees."

[74]From an unpublished response of 2 February 1972, from Paul Tate of the Executive Council to an information gathering questionnaire sent by the Overseas Ministries Studies Center in Ventnor, N.J., to missionary sending agencies.

[75]From Explanatory Notes, *Statistical Report of the Overseas Department* (New York: Executive Council of the Episcopal Church, September, 1965-1970).

[76]*Annual Report of the National Council of the Protestant Episcopal Church in the United States: 1935* (New York: The Domestic and Foreign Missionary Society, [1936]) Reports from Overseas Bishops.

[77]*Statistical Report of the Overseas Department*, 2.

[78]Interview with Leslie Fairfield, May 14, 1988.

[79]*Annual Report of the National Council of the Protestant Episcopal Church in the United States: 1935* and *Statistical Report of the Overseas Department* 1965.

[80]Avis E. Harvey, *Every Three Years: The Triennial Meetings, 1874-1967* (New York: Executive Council of the Episcopal Church, n.d.), 24.

[81]Ibid., 26.

[82]Ibid.

[83]See Chapter 3 above as well as: Mary Donovan, "Women as Foreign Missionaries in the Episcopal Church, 1830-1920," *Anglican and Episcopal History* 62 (March 1992) and Ian T. Douglas, "A Lost Voice: Women's Participation in the Foreign Mission Work of the Episcopal Church, 1920-1970," *Anglican and Episcopal History* 62 (1 1992).

[84]Francis M. Young, *Thankfulness Unites: The History of the United Thank Offering, 1889-1979* (Cincinnati, Ohio: Forward Movement, 1979), 40

[85]Out of a total UTO of $1,119,878.91, $800,000 was designated for the budget of the National Council. Young, 49.

[86]Harvey, 21.

[87]Ibid., 22-23.

[88]1968 Lambeth Conference, *The Lambeth Conference, 1968: Resolutions and Reports* (London and New York: SPCK and Seabury Press, 1968), 46.

[89]Ibid., 145

[90]Ibid., 46-47.

[91]John Howe, *Highways and Hedges: Anglicanism and the Universal Church* (Toronto: Anglican Book Centre, 1985), 87.

[92]Anglican Consultative Council, *The Time Is Now, First Meeting: Limuru, Kenya, 23 February-5 March 1971* (London: Society for Promoting Christian Knowledge, 1971), vii.

[93]Howe, 220-222.

[94]Anglican Consultative Council, *Partners in Mission, Second Meeting: Dublin, Ireland, 17-27 July 1973* (London: Society for Promoting Christian Knowledge, 1973), 53.

[95]Ibid., 57.

[96]James W. Kennedy, ed., *Partners in Mission, 1977: One Mission — Many Missioners*, (Cincinnati, Ohio: Forward Movement, 1977), 6.

[97]Ibid., 18.

[98]Ibid., 84-85.

[99]Ibid., 101.

[100]Ibid., 103.

[101]Resolution 15 in: 1978 Lambeth Conference, *The Report of the Lambeth Conference 1978* (London: The Secretary General of the Anglican Consultative Council, 1978) 42.

[102]Anglican Consultative Council, *ACC-4, Fourth Meeting: London, Ontario, Canada, 8-18 May 1979* (Cowley, Oxford: Bocado and Church Army Press, 1979), 17-27.

[103]Anglican Consultative Council, *ACC-5, Fifth Meeting: Newcastle upon Tyne, England, 8-18 September 1981* (London: Anglican Consultative Council, 1981), 31.

[104]Anglican Consultative Council, *Giving Mission its Proper Place: Report of the Mission Issues and Strategy Advisory Group,* ACC Mission and Ministry Study Series, 2d ed., Anglican Consultative Council, (London: Anglican Consultative Council, 1985), 13. See also "An Outline of the Faith" in The Episcopal Church, The Book of Common Prayer (New York: The Church Hymnal Corporation, 1979), 855.

[105]Howe, 92.

[106]Personal observation of the Most Rev. Sir Paul Reeves, previous archbishop of the Anglican Church in New Zealand and Anglican observer to the United Nations, made at Episcopal Divinity School, December 5, 1991.

[107]Howe, 221-222.

[108]General Convention of the Protestant Episcopal Church, *Journal of the Special General Convention: 1969* (New York: The General Convention, 1970), 33.

[109]Overseas Review Committee, "Interim Report to the House of Bishops," 566.

[110]Ibid., 566.

[111]Ibid., 569.

[112]bid., 572.

[113]Ibid., 573.

[114]The Overseas Review Committee, "Final Report of the Overseas Review Committee," in *The Blue Book: Reports of the*

Committees, Commissions, Boards and Agencies of the General Convention Prepared for the 64th General Convention of the Episcopal Church, ed. (New York: The General Convention of the Episcopal Church, 1973), 66-71.

[115]General Convention of the Protestant Episcopal Church, *Journal of the General Convention of the Protestant Episcopal Church: 1973* (New York: The General Convention, 1973), 461-462.

[116]Ibid., 461.

[117]In 1984, 64 Volunteers for Mission (VFM's) were posted to Anglican churches around the world. Because the burden for financial support of VFMs rests on individual parishes in the United States, they are less vulnerable to the budget constraints of the national church than the longer-term "appointed missionaries," who receive all of their support from the program budget of the Executive Council.

[118]"Report of the Joint Commission on World Mission" in General Convention of the Protestant Episcopal Church, *Journal of the General Convention of the Protestant Episcopal Church: 1979* (New York: The General Convention, 1979), AA-340.

[119]This plan was completed in 1982 when the Missionary Diocese of Liberia became a member of the Anglican Church of the Province of West Africa.

[120]Standing Commission on World Mission of the General Convention of the Episcopal Church, "Mission in Global Perspective" (Cincinnati, Ohio: Forward Movement, 1985), 5.

[121]Ibid., 23.

[122]Ibid., 36.

[123]Edward A. Holmes, "A History of the Episcopal Church's Involvement in Development" (New York: Overseas Development Office, Episcopal Church Center, 1983), 1.

[124]The Presiding Bishop's Fund for World Relief, *Where Your Dollars Go: 1983 Annual Report* (New York: The Presiding Bishop's Fund for World Relief, 1984), 37

[125]Protestant Episcopal Church in the United States of America, Overseas Development Office, *World Mission — Overseas Development* (New York: Overseas Development Office, Episcopal Church Center, February, 1983), 11.

[126]Bruce Woodcock, "African Development Program Management as Sponsored by The Episcopal Church in the United States" (Unpublished paper submitted to the School for International Training, Brattleboro, Vt., 1984),

[127]Holmes, 7.

[128]Protestant Episcopal Church in the United States of America, Overseas Development Office, *Summary of Active and Pending Government Grants* (New York: Overseas Development Office, Episcopal Church Center, December, 1985).

[129]Woodcock, 9.

[130]Protestant Episcopal Church in the United States of America, Overseas Development Office, *Statement of Purpose for the World Mission Development Planning Office* (New York: Overseas Development Office, Episcopal Church Center, December, 1980), 1.

[131]Samuel Van Culin, "The Episcopal Church's Participation in Development" (Unpublished memorandum to various Committees and Commissions concerned with the world mission activities of the Episcopal Church, February 1983, 1983), 2.

[132]Woodcock, 12.

[133]Jane M. Watkins, *Briefing Paper of the Overseas Development Office for the Right Rev. Edmond L. Browning, Presiding Bishop-Elect* (New York: Overseas Development Office, Episcopal Church Center, November, 1985), 9.

[134]Protestant Episcopal Church in the United States of America, Overseas Development Office, *Report to the Standing Committee for World Mission* (New York: Overseas Development Office, Episcopal Church Center, November, 1986), 5.

[135]In addition personnel from Kenya, the Philippines, and Liberia received development training at the Episcopal Church–sponsored Development Institute located at the University of California, Los Angeles.

[136]Cuttington College closed in the late 1980s because of the civil war in Liberia. Charles Taylor, a leader of a faction in the war, had used Cuttington as his base of operations.

[137]Charles Long, "The Story of the Overseas Mission Society: 1953-1977" (Keynote Address at the Annual Meeting of the Episcopal Council for Global Mission, Ambridge, Penn., May 22, 1991), 11-12.

[138]Ibid., 12-13.

[139]Ibid., 12-14.

[140]In 1991 ECMC moved from Pasadena to Ambridge, Pennsylvania, to become associated with Trinity Episcopal School for Ministry.

[141]From responses to a "Questionnaire for Missionary Sending Organizations within the Episcopal Church" produced under the auspices of the Standing Commission for World Mission, 1984.

[142]It is important to note that many of these voluntary mission societies, styled after those in England, had priests from England as their first executive directors, including Philip Bottomley (CMJ/USA), Derek Hawksbee (SAMS/USA) and Richard Kew (SPCK/USA).

[143]Gerald Charles Davies, Eric Chong, H. Boone Porter, eds., *Setting Free the Ministry of the People of God*, (Cincinnati, Ohio: Forward Movement, 1984), 12.

[144]H. Boone Porter, "Church Order and Missionary Expansion," *Anglican Theological Review* 66 (July 1984): 285.

[145]Ibid., 287.